SHARE YOUR STORY

Author Seeks Stories

I am currently developing a unique series of books of shared experiences called *The Gift of Depression*. I am president of The Fun Foundation, a nonprofit corporation devoted to assisting, educating, and ultimately ending the public stigma associated with mental illness, especially as it concerns the important medical, pharmacological, and social attitudes toward depression. The goal is to present, in an easily readable style, the inner lives of those with mental illness and the lives of those who live with and love us. I am seeking participants willing to share their stories, particularly those dealing with moments prior to diagnosis, the diagnosis itself, treatment, medications, or simply the "inner experience" of living with a serious brain disorder.

Writer Guidelines

Stories for this continuing series will be published by Inspire Hope Publishing. The enclosed outline will give you a good idea of what we are looking for. Stories range in length from 3500-7000 words. Please don't hesitate to call or E-mail if you have any questions.

D1279678

Inspire Hope Publishing

We would like to acknowledge the following publishers and individuals for permission to reprint the following material.

"This Life, This Death" from *Night Falls Fast* by Kay Redfield Jamison, copyright © 1999 by Kay Redfield Jamison. Reprinted by permission of Alfred A. Knopf, a Division of Random House, Inc.

"The Colouring to Events: The Death of Meriwether Lewis" from *Night Falls Fast* by Kay Redfield Jamison, copyright © 1999 by Kay Redfield Jamison. Reprinted by permission of Alfred A. Knopf, a Division of Random House, Inc.

"Stopping the War" from *A Path With Heart* by Jack Kornfield, copyright © 1993 by Jack Kornfield. Reprinted by permission of Bantam Books, a Division of Random House, Inc.

The back cover material reprinted from the National Depressive and Manic-Depressive Association, NDMDA, *A Guide to Depressive and Manic-Depressive Illness.* See resources.

Library of Congress Cataloging-in-Publication Data

The Gift of Depression
Twenty-one inspirational stories sharing experience, strength, and hope. Together we will end the stigma.
Compiled by John F. Brown
Copyright © 2001
ISBN0-9704529-0-X (softcover)

Publisher: Inspire Hope Publishing Corporation
              2721 Poipu Road, Suite 533
              Koloa, HI 96756

Cover design, interior format and production:
Paragon Communications Group, Tulsa, Oklahoma

Contents

Chapter Six

Chapter Seven

INTRODUCTION
By John F. Brown

This book series is intended to enlighten the world about people living with depression. Its main objective is to remove the public stigma keeping tens of millions of sufferers from seeking treatment for this illness. We believe if people read about what actually has happened in the lives of those with a mental illness, it will dispel their fears and ultimately end the stigma. After all, most of our reactions to life are nothing more than learned behaviors and habits. We hope, by reading this book and the series to follow, you will change your attitudes and interactions toward the mentally ill. It's that simple.

In a recent exhaustive review of research on mental disorders, Surgeon General Dr. David Satcher reported that *stigma* keeps two-thirds of the one in five Americans affected by a mental disorder from receiving treatment. Yet eighty to ninety percent of patients with depression who seek treatment demonstrate significant improvement, leading to productive lives. Twenty million Americans were diagnosed with a depressive disorder requiring medication and/or therapy in 1997, and most health care professionals believe that there may be three or four times that number. How are we going to reach out to those individuals? Through these books.

These "one of a kind" books contain stories written by average people with depression living in neighborhoods across the United States and Canada. Readers will easily identify with their honest, sometimes lighthearted approach telling what depression is like for those who are successfully living with it, as well as the tragic and heartbreaking stories of those who could not. No one feels more lost, alone, misunderstood, confused, and hopeless than someone experiencing a depressive episode. This book will not only benefit the patient; it will also aid their family members, who are just as confused and bewildered.

Having had depressive episodes, lasting about six months of the year, for twenty-seven consecutive years out of forty-one years of my life, and spending two difficult periods in psychiatric wards, I firmly understand the spiritual, emotional, and physical bankruptcy one endures during those times. Recovery encompasses treating all three together, but first we must forgive ourselves for having symptoms of a disease that is stigmatized, a disease not of any fault of our own doing.

In her book *A Return to Love*, Marianne Williamson asserts, "Some of the best and brightest that America has to offer are dropping through the cracks because they can't shake their pasts. How sad for America that anyone who has had too much sex or drugs in their past, for instance, is too scared to enter politics for fear of being crucified for their personal histories. The important thing about our past is not what happened, but what we have done with what happened. Anything can contribute to our being a more compassionate person now, if we choose."

As I am writing this, Joseph Lieberman has been nominated to run as Vice President with Al Gore on the Democratic ticket. What strikes me as odd is that most of the attention is focused on the man's religious beliefs — the "first Jew" to be nominated to this level of high office.

I believe it is noteworthy that Joe Lieberman believes in a higher power, but as any good Twelve-Step program will teach, it really doesn't matter what or who you believe to be your Higher Power, just as long as **you are not it.** This point is very important because it has taught me that this force is available to anyone, anywhere, anytime — twenty-four hours a day, seven days a week. It does not matter what color you are, how old you are, what sex you are, what sexual preference you have, what religious background you came from, and the list goes on. Everyone has an equal opportunity to as much or as little as they choose, not as someone else chooses for them. You need not wait for a Second Coming, shave your head and hand out flowers, or go to a particular place on a special day of the week, nor have any rules placed upon your belief. All you are suggested to do is "fake it till you make it." And don't try to make others believe as you. Believe as if there is such a force until you have seen for yourself that it actually exists. Does this really work? Go into any Twelve-Step open meeting and listen for yourself and see the living miracles in each and every seat.

Carl Jung, the eminent psychologist, when asked toward the end of his career if he believed in the existence of a higher power, replied, "No, I do not believe this exists. **I know this exists.**"

Aleksandr Solzhenitsyn, the Russian philosopher, said, "More than half a century ago, while I was still a child, I recall hearing a number of older people offer the following explanation for the great disasters that had befallen Russia: 'Men have forgotten God. That's why all this has happened.' Since then I have spent well nigh fifty years working on the history of the revolution. If I were asked today to formulate as concisely as possible the main cause of the ruinous revolution that swallowed up some sixty million of our people, I could not put it more accurately than to repeat: 'Men have forgotten God. That's why all this has happened.'"

I bring this to your attention because, as you will read in many of the following stories, the faster you believe in some power other than yourself or someone else, the faster your recovery will begin. If you still believe, as I did, that the world revolved around me and I was special, go and stop the sun from coming up or make a flower or stop the wind from blowing. I'm only suggesting something that has worked for so very many. I'm only trying to get you to trust in something other than what this fearful world would have you believe. Trust in something other than yourself, let it be whatever is comfortable to you, and realize that this really does work. Others would have you believe in their fears. Fear is simply a lack of faith.

Most average members of the human race haven't a clue as to the anguish, despair, and physical, emotional, and spiritual pain one endures during a depressive episode. If I could somehow transform the inexperienced and allow them to walk for a week in the shoes of someone in the throes of a depressive episode (complete with the unrelenting torment, fear, anxiety, suicidal thoughts, hopelessness, uselessness, worthlessness, dark oozing emptiness, and the sheer terror of being totally alone), the stigma of having a mental illness would be lifted overnight. We hope that by sharing our personal experiences, we may give you insight into this world so many of us experience yet is so poorly understood. It is our hope that by introducing the graphic details of what our lives have been like as well as the lives of those who could no longer endure the pain, the general public will achieve a better understanding of who we are, why we act the way we do, and how we maintain our recovery in a society that stigmatizes disease.

I decided, about one month after coming out of my last depression, that I desperately wanted to do something that has been burning in my soul for as long as I can remember. I wanted to follow a path that I was sure existed in my heart but never before had the insight, connectiveness, concentration, courage, or energy to follow. I wasn't sure where to begin, so I did what felt comfortable — I prayed for guidance.

In the preface to her book *If Life is a Game, These are the Rules,* Cherie Carter-Scott describes receiving clear guidance as to what direction her life was to take, writing, "After several weeks, I received three clear 'messages' (from what divine source, I was not really sure) that answered my questions."

This is precisely what had occurred to me, only the answers flowed one right after the other in about five minutes:

- Start a book series to stop the stigma of depression and call it *The Gift of Depression.*

- Start a nonprofit foundation to financially aid people starting a medication procedure for depression. The foundation will assist qualified persons during the period of medication adjustment through a grant program. This will allow them to adjust to these medications at home without the pressures of financial instability. Call the nonprofit foundation The Fun Foundation.

Having spent most of my life hiding my illness from people, I was not exactly sure if this path was correct. But in the months that followed, I clearly realized that as long as I stayed out of the way, became still, and listened to the small guiding voice (that exists in all of us), the faster these messages started to manifest. I made a plan; I did not plan the results.

Many have asked why the names for the foundation and the book series were chosen. There is nothing fun about being in a depressive episode, and most don't perceive depression as being a gift. Most would agree that before discovering the proper medication, trusted doctor and therapist, and educating them-selves about this disease, this surely is a "gift" they would have gladly given back. Fun is absent to such an extent that one forgets what life was really like before being depressed. I know now that depression has two sides. I want others to experience the positive side, as I, and many of the other authors, will attest truly does exist. Therefore, I want to help individuals ultimately discover, through recovery therapy (medi-cinal, therapeutic, and physical), that life can be fun again. Depressed individuals need to work on all three to bring back the joy of life.

About three months into my recovery, my wife asked if I was concerned about the potential long-term effects of taking an antidepressant for quite pos-sibly the rest of my life. I explained to her that it real-ly did not matter to me if I grew another head. As long as I could live life with the present stability, I was con-tent. The following winter (1999-2000) was the first one I did not experience a depressive episode in twenty-eight consecutive years. Was this all because of taking an antidepressant? Of course not. But, (and this is a huge **BUT**), if the pharmaceutical industry were not working as successfully and earnestly as they are, I guarantee you many of my fellow recovering partners (myself included) would not be alive today. Many of the uneducated criticize this industry for making a profit at the expense of the ill. This is nonsense. The business of this industry is to help. Any business needs to make a profit to stay in business. It is not a perfect system, but it works, and it is the best we presently have. More progress has been made in this field in the past twenty years than in all the time before it. Your chances of recovery are better today than ever.

There will always be skeptics. I listened to Lance Armstrong, after winning the 1999 Tour de France Championship the first time, talk to an interviewer about his critics. Before his cancer was discovered, he was criticized for being the wrong body type. "He will never win," they said. Once his cancer was discovered, they said he would never recover. "He will never win," they said. After winning the race for the first time, these same critics claimed his performance had been enhanced from the medications he was taking. "We won't allow him to win," they said. Although the circumstances changed, the critics stayed the same. You are my hero, Lance. What a gift and an inspiration you are to all of us.

Since we all received many gifts coming into this life, what one chooses to do with those gifts determines one's path. I choose to embrace my depression rather than work against it. During her twilight years, Helen Keller was asked whether, if given the opportunity to live life again without her afflictions, she would choose the same path. She responded that she would not change anything because she was blessed with gifts that allowed only someone who understands to help others on the same journey. I agree. This depression is a gift we've been given to experience and learn from so we can share our honest experiences and teach others about the journey. After all, isn't that why we are all here? If our purpose on this planet is not to help each other out, then why is it that we get such a wonderful feeling when we do?

As Marianne Williamson aptly describes in *A Return to Love*, "The meaningful question is never what we did yesterday, but what we have learned from it and are doing today. No one can counsel a recovering alcoholic like another recovering person who has been on the road to recovery longer. No one can counsel a person in grief like someone who has grieved. No one can help with anything like someone who has been through the pain themselves."

I needed to trust others with similar problems in order to start my recovery. It was difficult to trust strangers because I was taught at an early age not to talk to strangers. I believe it would be best to empower children with the knowledge of how to escape from someone and allow them to talk with everyone. We have given away our power of communicating and trusting strangers to the few who commit heinous crimes against children. I found it was much easier to trust those who had been through what I was going through. I listened to their experiences and applied them to my life. I learned during my recovery that insanity is doing the same thing over and over and expecting different results. I always feared what other people thought of me and was under the illusion that people would not like me if they found out who I really was inside and how scared and awful my life was. I wanted desperately to be "normal." I realize today that these assumptions are as far from the truth as I could get. I know that there does exist a large part of the population that may be considered "average" in statistical numbers (similar to a bell curve), but there is no such thing as "normal." We all come from some sort of dysfunctional family, and if you don't agree with me, you are denying the truth. And I'm certainly not pointing the finger at being part of a dysfunctional family as the cause of my problems because as I know, whenever I point the finger, the real problem is with me (there are always three pointing back whenever I point one out). My parents did the best job they knew how to do, and I love, respect, and am very proud of my family. I have learned a great deal from all of them, and I am grateful.

I have also learned that I cannot give my power away to other people or things. I am responsible for this life. I am the only one who can have my life experience. Therefore, if I choose to live someone else's fear or beliefs, I am giving my power away. I need to respect others' beliefs, but I must live my own. I recently watched an interview on "60 Minutes" with Eric Clapton. Here is a man who had everything that I thought would make me happy before I became sober — fame, fortune, talent, the whole nine yards. Yet he described the ultimate happiness as experiencing life sober — no drugs, no alcohol, no bizarre behavior. This was his thirteenth year of being sober. I believe that experiencing life sober is really the ultimate high. There exists a true sense of peace, yet I still experience all of life's ups and downs.

And as we hope to show through this continuing series, no one can expel the fears of the unassociated like the mentally ill. You cannot tell a book by its cover. If you could, I don't believe Stephen Hawking would command the respect he deserves. The same is true for those of us who are made to feel ashamed of a disease by a society that doesn't understand. We cannot afford to lose even one more "gifted" individual because of our past and present society's stigmatization of a person suffering from depression. Imagine how different and empty our world would be had we not enjoyed the fruits of the individuals on the front and back cover of this book. Imagine what we may be losing if we don't stop this senseless stigma.

Please reach out and help us by sharing this with someone you know. And remember that life is too short to take seriously.

Chapter One

THIS LIFE, THIS DEATH

By Kay Redfield Jamison, Ph.D.

A lonely impulse of delight
Drove to this tumult in the clouds;
I balanced all, brought all to mind,
The years to come seemed waste of breath,
A waste of breath the years behind
In balance with this life, this death.

—WILLIAM BUTLER YEATS,
"An Irish Airman Foresees His Death"

THERE is a moment as you watch that your heart stops and you wish you could return the videotape to its owners and forget what you have seen. You know the end of the story; you know that what is done is done; and still there is a terrible sadness in it, more even than you had reckoned on. The tape is difficult to watch, impossible not to, and dreadful in its foretelling.

The home video, no doubt like a hundred others taken that same day, scopes across the Rampart mountain range of the Colorado Rockies, which in turn sets the stage for the man-made jags and triangulars of the buildings of the U.S. Air Force Academy. Lurching, the camera continues to record landscape and people and the day's events, settling at last on the parade ground covered with squadrons of marching cadets in their dress blue jackets, white pants, white gloves, and golden sashes. A thousand, or nearly, graduating seniors; all of them, but one, newly commissioned officers.

The marching ends, and one by one the cadets receive their diplomas, salute, and return to their seats. Each name, a moment; each brisk salute, an exercise in pent enthusiasm. Slowly, the camera's field becomes more focused, more personal, and a name is called out. It is clear from the crowd's response — a roar of appreciation goes up from his classmates — that the young man is immensely popular; indeed, a fellow cadet has described him as the most respected senior at the Academy, and his squadron has given him its outstanding leadership award.

The young man takes his diploma, raises gloved hand to hat, and salutes sharply, quickly. He smiles gloriously, graciously, contagiously, and you begin to understand the warmth and extent of his classmates' response.

But it is not at this moment that your heart stops, although a certain melancholy seeps in. Rather, it is later, after all the names have been called, all the salutes given and received. For the moment, the martial measures of the Air Force song pound out across the parade field and stadium, and then, suddenly, a thousand freshly minted second lieutenants snap their heads back and watch six F-16s streak overhead in tight formation, the traditional flyover tribute to the Academy's new officers. Before the jet contrails begin to fade, total pandemonium breaks out and hundreds of white hats are flung high into the air, sailing every which way into the sky, creating a higgledy-piggledy of bobbing specks of white. Cheers and embraces obliterate the remaining shreds of order.

The home video focuses once again on the young man whose slowly spreading smile had so captivated, whose appearance had evoked such spontaneous warmth and cheers from his classmates. He, like them, had watched the jets overhead and flung his hat into the air. But this is the moment that causes your heart to stop — his face displays a subtle but chilling confusion. He seems unmoored, not quite sure of what to do next, slightly glassed off from the swirl around him. It is painful to watch because you know the end of the story, and almost unbearable because you know that this is in some way the beginning of that end.

The young man, Drew Sopirak, did not return to the Air Force Academy the night of his graduation, nor did he receive his officer's commission. Although he had dreamed for years of becoming a pilot and had won a highly competitive slot in flight school, he never received his pilot's wings. That evening, instead, he left the celebrations to return to a place in which no one could have imagined him, the psychiatric ward of a nearby military hospital. There he tried to sort out the most recent hand he had been dealt. Unlike all previous hands, which had been flush with love and luck and ability, this one was a nightmare of all things lost. It was unexpected and, ultimately, unplayable.

Success, it would seem, was not a sufficient teacher. Nor, would it seem, were remarkably caring friends and family. Drew Sopirak had all these in full measure. He was, by every account of his friends and instructors, warm, vivacious, and hugely popular with his peers; a natural leader; "drop-dead gorgeous"; and a person for whom no one was a stranger. "There was just something about him," said one of his friends. "I don't think anyone could quite pin it down as to why he was so wonderful — he just was." He had been valedictorian of his Wilmington, Delaware, high school; president of both his junior and senior classes; Homecoming King; captain of his sports teams; and an engaging "Mole" in a community production of *The Wind in the Willows.* It was of little surprise to anyone that Drew was offered appointments to both West Point and the Air Force Academy. He had been expected to succeed, and he had.

Drew chose the Air Force Academy, an easy decision for an eighteen-year-old with a passion for all things that fly and a dream and a determination to become a pilot. Yet within eighteen months of graduating from the Academy, Drew Sopirak somehow found his life so painful and his future so bleak that he went to a gun store, bought a .38-caliber revolver, and pulled the trigger. When it misfired, he pulled the trigger again.

He was twenty-three years old: the way down had been long, and it had been fast.

Minds of men fashioned a crate of thunder,
Sent it high into the blue,
Hands of men blasted the world asunder;
How they lived God only knew!
Souls of men, dreaming of skies to conquer

Gave us wings, ever to soar!
Keep the wings level and true.
— "United States Air Force Song"

The Air Force had prepared Drew for many of the things he might expect in life, but it did not, nor could it, prepare him for madness. So when his mind snapped, just a few weeks shy of graduation, he had no equivalent of his earlier survival training to see him through the splintering mania and subsequent, inevitable flameout. His mind pelted first out of bounds and then out of commission; it took along with it his dreams and his life. Manic-depressive illness proved to be an enemy out of range and beyond the usual rules of engagement.

Drew was to mention later that he had experienced occasional problems with racing thoughts and periods of depression prior to his first manic episode. But these he had kept to himself. He was the last person any of his friends would have expected to become psychotic or to have to be confined to a psychiatric hospital. The very unexpectedness and the seeming incongruity, however, were themselves not entirely unexpected, given the nature of the illness that was to kill Drew. Manic-depressive illness usually strikes young, not uncommonly during the college years, and not uncommonly in the apparently invincible — the outgoing, the energetic, the academically successful.

Drew's own academic work, which had been excellent, began to decline significantly during his last months at the Air Force Academy. His roommate noted that at about the same time Drew was making statements "that did not make a lot of sense," and his mother became increasingly concerned that he "sounded paranoid" when she talked to him on the telephone. He was, by his own report, intensely euphoric, sleeping little, and some nights sleeping not at all.

In the midst of his sleeplessness, increasingly manic, Drew became convinced that he had the answers to many or most of the world's problems and that he was a messenger of God. He designed a super spacecraft, based less on his background in aeronautical engineering than on his newly, and delusionally, acquired understanding of UFOs. The spacecraft, as he drew and described it, had spinning lights, a mysteriously increasing energy source, "a new kind of synergy" derived from dry-ice packs and plasma, and a strange force field that created a flow pulse that would somehow "push" the aircraft. The concepts are difficult to follow — indeed incoherent, as manic thinking tends to be — but the notes and drawing clearly had signal importance to Drew as he sketched them out late in April 1994 in his acutely grandiose and delusional state. Painfully, there is also a more personal and prophetic sentence, buried and almost lost in his frenzied notes and sketches: "You will not be happy," Drew had written to himself. "You'll be stressed — about something *important.*" There is no clue as to what the source of the stress would be.

Early in June, while in the mountains, he heard the voice of God telling him to "purify" himself; in response to this commandment, he removed all his clothes and ran naked through the woods. Later, frightened, confused, and covered with cuts and bruises, terrified that the world might be ending, he made his way to his chaplain's house. The chaplain's wife put a blanket around him; then, shaken and very psychotic, he was taken to the Air Force Academy

Hospital. Still paranoid the next morning and agitated that Russian spies at the Academy, having heard about his superplane, were "out to get him," he was transferred to Fitzsimons Army Medical Hospital.

The military physicians who evaluated Drew were psychiatrically thorough, medically rigorous, and compassionate. His brain was scanned to rule out tumors or vascular disease that might cause a mania-like syndrome; his urine was checked for drugs that might cause paranoid, agitated, or manic states; consultations were obtained from both the departments of neurology and medicine. The doctors concluded that Drew had an extensive family history of manic-depressive (bipolar) illness and that he himself had a classic textbook case of the same disease. They also noted in his medical record that he had many friends, was a very good student, and had been an excellent cadet. "His past history," wrote one of his doctors, "is significant for excelling in any activity that he became involved in."

Drew was started on lithium and within two or three days was decidedly better. By the ninth day of his hospitalization he no longer was delusional, although at one point he became frightened that the hospital might try to do surgery on him to "remove important information from his head." He was able to attend the graduation ceremonies at the academy but within a few days' time had to be air-evacuated for continued treatment at Andrews Air Force Base, near Washington, D.C.

Prior to his transfer, a medical board comprising three military physicians was convened. Their final report, written in the impersonal, if necessary, language of medicine and the military, brought to an end

Drew's plans for the future: his commission was denied; he lost his slot in flight school; he would be neither an officer nor a pilot. "This examinee does not meet the medical standards for commissioning due to a mental disorder with psychotic features," wrote the board. The command surgeon agreed, concluding, "I strongly recommend medical disenrollment in this cadet." Drew's active military service was over. His struggle with mental illness was not.

Drew was hospitalized at Andrews for an additional three weeks. The admitting physician, who concurred with the earlier diagnosis of bipolar manic-depressive illness, observed that Drew was still slightly paranoid, anxious, and "trying very hard to make sense of what had happened to him." He noted, as well, Drew's perfectionism (a characteristic mentioned by many who knew him) and the fact that Drew felt guilty about the problems he was causing his family by being ill.

Notes made by the physicians and nurses who treated him throughout his hospitalization make it clear that Drew was struggling to put back together the pieces of his life, struggling to piece together the beginnings of a future. He discussed the possibility of obtaining a Ph.D. in aeronautical engineering, becoming a teacher, or perhaps, he suggested in a less optimistic mood, working at the beach. He didn't know; it was too early to say. He was desperately concerned about paying off the educational debt he felt he had to the Air Force. But his immediate goal was to understand his illness and the medication he was taking to treat it.

Drew's hospitalization at Andrews was difficult, in part because the devastating consequences of his illness were beginning to sink in, in part because it is readily apparent from his medical history that he had a severe form of manic-depressive illness. On his second day at the hospital, one of the nurses found him deeply depressed, rocking in a fetal position. He appeared anxious and stated that he was scared, felt he was being tortured, and was going to die. He was placed on fifteen-minute checks, which ensured that a member of the nursing staff would monitor his safety and whereabouts. His moods cycled rapidly and violently. A few days later, he stated to the other members in his group therapy session that he had the solutions to all of the world's problems, but within a few hours he was tearful and frightened that he could not control his racing thoughts.

Drew's condition gradually improved, and early in July he was given a two-day weekend pass to visit his parents. When he came back to the hospital, he was angry and agitated at having to return to the ward; he thrashed his arms about and shouted to the staff, "No! I'm not staying! No!"

Thirty minutes later one of the nurses found him lying in bed, where he stated, awfully, "I'm all right. It was just so hard to come back."

Within a few hours, Drew was again agitated. The nurse observed that his face was flushed and that he was pacing back and forth in the hallway. Within fifteen minutes he escaped from the hospital — an escape made easier, no doubt, by his survival training at the Air Force Academy — and was on his way to his parents' home in Delaware. He crawled in through a back window; his parents found him the next morning, sleeping in his own bed.

His mother called the hospital to notify it that Drew

had been found and that he was extremely upset by a telephone call he had received. A fellow patient from his days on the psychiatric ward in Fitzsimons Army Medical Center had attempted suicide and been rehospitalized. Under the circumstances, Drew's parents thought it would be better for him to receive his psychiatric treatment closer to home.

Drew arrived home in early July 1994, and his parents arranged for him to get private psychiatric care and counseling. Psychologically shaky for a while, he continued to be preoccupied with guilt because he had been forced to leave the Air Force. He made slow but reasonably steady progress, however, and by midsummer he was feeling better, exercising again, and playing tennis. He had a brief recurrence of his delusions and a short-lived period of sleeplessness, but he was definitely better. In November he began seeing a new psychiatrist, who added an antipsychotic medication to the lithium that Drew already was taking. Both Drew and his doctor noted a dramatic improvement in Drew's mood and thinking, as did his parents.

From late 1994 to August 1995, Drew's mood remained stable and he experienced no psychotic symptoms. He worked at a bank twenty hours a week, was physically active, and talked about going to graduate school. Although he occasionally expressed a desire to stop taking his medications, in the hope that he might someday be able to fly airplanes on a civilian basis, he continued to take his drugs as prescribed.

But Drew's anger about the stigma he felt about having manic-depressive illness was intense, and he felt unable to discuss it with his friends or new acquaintances. "It's the last thing I want to talk about, but it generally comes up when meeting new people or out with friends at bars and parties," he confided to his psychiatrist. He limited his drinking to one or two beers and found that he was questioned about why he didn't drink more. Often asked about why he was no longer in the Air Force, he was too embarrassed to tell the truth and was forced to invent alternative explanations.

Friends were aware that Drew did not want to talk about his problems. One, who went to high school with Drew and described him, as many did, as "Mr. Everything," remarked, "He was still funny and willing to have a good time. I had no idea what he was dealing with inside his head." Another close friend, who is still "looking for explanations I don't even understand," described a change in Drew after his return from the Academy. Drew, he said, had been a loving person, "with a passion for life"; now something had gone wrong; Drew didn't want to talk about it; he "kept a lot of secrets." Still, Drew and his friends were a close-knit, active group. Together they listened to the music of U2, went to rock concerts and the beach, played tennis and volleyball and basketball, yelled exuberantly at ice hockey games, and went to parties in hopes of meeting new women.

Drew remained deeply troubled, however, and utterly convinced that he had disappointed those who mattered most to him. "I never saw bitterness from Drew," says his mother, "only disappointment and regret. He felt he had let everyone down, including the younger cadets, his friends and the Air Force. He was troubled that he could not repay the education he had received. He had a difficult time explaining why he was living at home. He felt he had followed all the rules of the Air Force and still this didn't work out for him. He felt shame at being sick." Like many with manic-depressive illness, Drew had conflicted feelings about his disease. "We told him of all the people who had coped with bipolar disorder and done well," his mother explained, but "he never heard it."

In November 1995 Drew stopped taking his medications and quit his job. For a brief time, it looked as though things might work out. He and two others went to the University of Connecticut to visit a friend, and one of them commented, "Drew was great — meeting people, breaking the hearts of several girls, and generally being Drew." But this same friend also noted, "That was the last time I saw Drew happy."

Drew deteriorated rapidly. "It was during this time that I found out what Drew was really going through," wrote a friend. "We'd talk for hours about his Jesus sightings, UFO theories, or whatever else he was experiencing. Through all his depressive episodes, he still maintained a sense of humor." Another friend commented on Drew's desire for privacy: "He came back from the Air Force broken, I suppose. He was able to hide it pretty well. All I know is that somehow his wings were clipped, and that I shouldn't bring it up — he didn't want to talk about it. It's as if he just didn't want to worry anyone."

Drew's losing battle with manic-depressive illness was profoundly disturbing to the friends who had known, loved, and admired him for so many years. He had been their leader, a person of strong character, an individual of great kindness: he was, said one of them, a person who had "a sweet nature and downright gorgeous looks — a friend we all hope to be, a man who women dream of, and a man who men admire, respect, and almost always befriended." To be privy to such a person's struggle for sanity was almost unbearably difficult and distressing to his friends.

Drew was lucky in these friends, and they in him; their reactions to his sickness are therefore all the more heartbreaking. One who was particularly close to Drew wrote:

"I remember trying to talk to him, but conversations were frightening and confusing. He often talked in circles or made no sense or described that his friends were plotting against him. He described to me in horrid detail what ran through his mind and most of it I choose not to repeat. I simply do not know if there is a way to repeat the awful details, and somehow I feel it is my duty still to protect his honor and his name. He would do the same for me.

"After he was diagnosed with Bipolar Disorder and I began to try to understand the horror in his mind, I knew he might never be the same. But I did not dream he would commit suicide. It simply did not seem possible. For months after he was hospitalized, his family and Drew told no one but family and me. We wanted to protect him, and perhaps we thought he would get better, and we would never have to speak of it. But Drew did not get better, and the more time dragged on, the more I knew he might never recover.

"Drew took his lithium on and off, but I think he never really wanted to believe he needed it. He never wanted to admit it to himself. I think he thought he could recover. But as the months dragged on, I realized that this illness had stolen a part of Drew's soul. It took from him part of his personality and his love of life. I remember when he was hospitalized in D.C. and I went to visit him. His mom left to get dinner, and he laid his head in my lap, curled up in the fetal position. I saw with my eyes the man's face I knew as Drew, but my ears heard another creature. Something else seemed to live in his shell. Someone other than Drew brought words to his lips or created his awkward, disturbing actions. As he rubbed his head, as though to bring his thoughts to some sort of sanity, I looked at him and wondered where my friend had disappeared to. This monster had taken over. He was gaunt and had not shaved in weeks. His skin was sallow and his cheeks sunken; each movement appeared painful. I did not know this person he had become. The more he talked the more my fear for him grew. I went home that evening and cried for two hours straight. Never had I looked horror in the face as I had that evening."

By December, Drew's condition plummeted. He was increasingly depressed, and he kept more and more to himself. The packages he received for Christmas remained wrapped in his room, and he went out with friends only after much inducement and prodding. Temporary solace was to be found in music and in the long baths that he took in a desperate attempt to curb his agitation.

By early January 1996, Drew was almost totally withdrawn from everyone. Finally, he was catatonic in his bed. He was taken by ambulance to a local hospital, where he was admitted on an emergency, involuntary basis. At the time of admission he was mute, his eyes were closed, and he was lying inert on a stretcher. The doctors gave him an antipsychotic drug, which worked rapidly. Indeed, it worked rapidly enough that the next day he escaped from the locked ward and made his way home through one of the worst snowstorms on record. He was taken back to the hospital, where he stayed for another ten days. During this time his physician noted that Drew showed "some improvement," although he was "continuing to struggle with coming to grips with seeing himself as an individual with an illness."

Drew's medical chart paints an unremittingly grim picture. He described himself as "hopeless" to the admitting nurse. His employment history was recorded simply as "unemployed — was working in a bank. Graduated from Air Force Academy." In just over a year and a half, a young man of great promise had gone from a world of academics and athletics, officers and gentlemen, to "unemployed" and "hopeless." Manic-depression had taken no hostages.

Drew was asked during the hospitalization to describe an ideal scenario for his life, once he recovered. He emphasized that he wanted no pity and no medicine. The items he endorsed on a standard psychological test were deeply despairing in nature: "I am so sad or unhappy that I can't stand it," he checked off on the test form; "I feel I have nothing to look forward to." He also endorsed the statement "As I look back on my life, all I can see is a lot of failures" and, most distressingly, "I have thoughts of killing myself, but I would not carry them out."

Drew was discharged to outpatient care five days before he committed suicide. No one knows what he was thinking or feeling during that time, but he did leave behind scattered notes and journal entries. In them, as his mother put it, "you can see him slipping away." The writings are enigmatic, idiosyncratic, flailing; they are at times cohesive, but more often than not the confounding presence of psychosis makes itself felt.

He records unusual dreams, coincidences, and events; there is a sense of a mind trying desperately just to hold on. He mentions falling stars and eagle dreams, dreams of Hell, hurricanes, lightning, jets, death. His instructions to himself compel him to relax, pray, tone down, focus, find peace. He is frightened that his "old beliefs" will come back, and he laments, "I asked God to help me. I didn't deserve his help. Because I cursed God before I asked him for help." His writings are filled with the sense of a world that is lost, a self that is lost, and a hope that has been entirely abandoned. He is guilt-stricken for the pain he feels he has brought upon others, especially his family, and he enumerates at length the problems he must confront: he must pay off his debts, he has lost his girlfriend, he must take medication, he must see doctors. He is convinced that "everyone will label me as having [an] illness until the day I die," yet he also states, "No one knows the special experiences I have had — so they won't hear what I tell them ever."

The final entry in his journal reflects this pervasive ambivalence toward his disease: "Sick or not? —

Medicine reduce[s] symptoms but [I] want [to] be happy."

In his copy of *Moral Issues in Philosophy,* an assigned textbook Drew was reading when he first became ill at the Air Force Academy, different colors of ink accentuate, underline, and emphasize various phrases and ideas. He repeatedly circled and underlined the sentence "There is such a thing as life not worthy to be lived" and underscored yet another sentence, "It is cruel to allow a human being to linger for months in the last stages of agony." Chillingly, the last phrase Drew underlined was "[there is a] moral duty to terminate the life of an insane person who is suffering from a painful and incurable disease."

> *But the souls of the righteous are in the hand of God, and no torment will ever touch them. In the eyes of the foolish they seemed to have died, and their departure was thought to be an affliction, and their going from us to be their destruction, but they are at peace.*
> — WISDOM, 3:1-9, read at Drew's memorial service

A few days before Drew's death, two of his closest friends visited him. They did not know that it was to be for the last time. Only recently released from the hospital, Drew was, one of them observed, "unshaven, in black from head to toe, and very sullen. I'm not sure if he had made up his mind by then or not. All I can tell you is that he didn't laugh or smile. As [we] left that night, Drew matter-of-factly said, 'I love you guys.' It was quite strange, and I didn't know how to respond. Sensing this, he just said again, 'I really love you guys,' and shut the door. As far as I know, that's the last thing he said to anyone."

On January 27, Drew Sopirak left his parents' home in Wilmington and drove to a gun store. The state of Delaware required no waiting period to purchase handguns; the clerk sold him a .38-caliber revolver straightaway. A few hours later, Drew shot and killed himself. The police notified Drew's parents that his body had been found inside his jeep at the entrance to the Pennsylvania Turnpike. He was about forty minutes from home.

"We had been on that turnpike so many times," said Drew's mother. "Both our families live in the Pittsburgh area. That road would have taken him to grandparents, aunts, uncles, and cousins and his brother at Penn State. He just never got on it. He must have run out of hope there."

The family was left to do the unimaginable: identify Drew's body at the morgue, notify other family members and friends, plan a funeral and memorial service, mourn him, miss him.

Drew's parents and younger brother received an extraordinary number of condolence letters from Drew's high school friends and teachers, his fellow cadets and instructors at the Air Force Academy, and parents of friends. In reading through them it is striking how many of the letters are in the form of thank-you letters: thank-yous for his life, his presence, his warmth; appreciation of his vitality, friendship, and influence.

"I cannot begin to tell you how sad it makes me to know the world is without one of its great participants," wrote one friend. He continued, "Ovid once wrote, 'Welcome this pain, for some day it will be useful to you.' I don't know how true that is for you concerning your loss, but I know that each time I remember Drew I hurt. What a wonderful gift you gave all of us in Drew. Thank you."

Another said simply, "May your consolation be that he was truly loved in this life." One of Drew's teachers, an instructor in aeronautical engineering at the Air Force Academy, wrote, "I never really understood his illness and he never used it as an excuse. I don't remember the names of most of the hundreds of students I had in my class but a few do stand out. Drew was a stand out guy. Drew made a difference. Drew mattered. I am proud to have known him."

Consolations were of help, but ultimately it was left to Drew's family and friends to attempt to understand why he had done such an incomprehensible, final thing. One friend tried:

> I do not often say this, but after seeing his suffering for so long, I can see how suicide cured Drew's pain. I am not angry for his decision as I am not sure I would have had the strength to continue as long as Drew did. Many did not know his suffering, and he let few close enough to see it. But those of us who loved him and saw his pain do not fault him for leaving this life behind. Still I hate his illness and still I wish I could hear, if just for one last time, his jeep roar up to my house with U2 blaring and see him jump out suntanned and gorgeous and wanting to go for a ride in the valley.
>
> I will never be the same. As I said before, none

of us who know him ever will. But I know I have been blessed to have known a soul such as Drew. This is a gift few are given.

Drew's family, whose warmth and understanding of him would have been, in a fairer world, more than sufficient to keep him alive, could not compete with a relentless and ruinous disease. Their funeral notes for Drew end with a perceptive, straightforward statement of fact: "On January 27, 1996 Drew took his life. He had stopped taking his medication. His illness moved faster than his acceptance of it." The Christmas before Drew graduated from the Academy, he had placed a small gift for his parents under the Christmas tree — it was the last package to be unwrapped. Inside the box they found a pair of lieutenant's epaulets, which he asked them to pin on his shoulders when he received his officer's commission in six months' time. All the cadets in his squadron received their commissions and epaulets in June. All except Drew.

His parents remedied this by placing the unworn epaulets in his hands the day that they buried him.

And He will raise you up on eagle's wings,
Bear you on the breath of dawn,
Make you to shine like the sun,
And hold you in the palm of His hand.

You need not fear the terror of the night.

The February day of Drew's memorial service at the Air Force Academy was a beautiful, breezy, and sunny one. The flags at the Academy flew at half-mast, and the chapel was filled with young men and women in uniform. They stood, as one, for the opening hymn, "On Eagle's Wings," and listened to their fellow officers and cadets read passages from the Old and New Testaments. The chaplain spoke of Drew's leadership and of how he had been a role model for so many in his class. With obvious emotion, he remarked, "I don't think we know how much pain, how much turmoil, how much anguish Drew experienced as a result of his illness."

Five cadets and officers — sad, young, sober, stricken — went, in turn, to the pulpit to deliver their remembrances. One second lieutenant, a close friend of Drew's, was painfully eloquent: "This chapel," he said, "means a lot to my life. Six years ago I walked in those doors scared as a new basic. A year and a half ago, I walked out of those doors happy as a newly married man. Today, I return to this place sad, as I must say good-bye to a friend."

The young officer paused, his sadness palpable. Then he ended his eulogy with an Air Force pilots' toast that he, Drew, and their fellow cadets had made the night they received their class rings from the Academy. Proposed at the time to the legendary flier and commander of the U.S. air forces in World War I, General Billy Mitchell, the lieutenant now used it to bid farewell to his friend:

As we soar among them there,
We're sure to hear his plea,
To take care my friend,
Watch your six,
And do one more roll. . .
Just for me.

The congregation rose for the final hymn. "We will run and not grow weary," they sang, "For our God will be our strength, / And we will fly like the eagle, /

We will rise again." One by one the young men and women in blue left the jagged triangular chapel.

Their leaving is the last thing you see on the home videotape; there is a terrible sadness in it, even more than you had reckoned on. The only thing that goes through your mind is what you heard a military chaplain say, many years ago:

"I do not know why young men have to die. You would think it would break the heart of God."

THE FIRST TIME

By Sharon O'Brien

DEPRESSION entered my life the summer after tenth grade. By then I was too old for camp but had not yet made the transition to summer jobs. Some of my friends had found work counseling in summer camps in New Hampshire or waitressing at the Cape, but my parents had made it clear I had to stay in Belmont. Perhaps they feared what might happen now that I was sixteen — in 1961 summer jobs away from home meant suntan oil and browning bodies on the beach, dancing to "Rock Around the Clock," wearing shorts and halters; they meant boys, they meant no curfews, they meant sex. There was no way I was going anywhere.

And so the summer of 1961 introduced me to one of the surefire catalysts for depression: unstructured time. Now that school was out, there were no tasks to perform, teachers to wow, A's to be won. I'd lie in bed as long as I could, submerged in a dark, clotted lake. Sounds were muffled, voices remote; I was living under water. I had the sense of life going on elsewhere, and it grated on me like nasty chalk. I didn't like hearing the sharp, relentless ringing of the phone, and I hated it if my mother or father would say, "Sharon, it's for you," and I'd have to drag myself down the hall and listen to the chirpy voice of a friend saying, "Hey, a bunch of us are going to Wingaersheek this Saturday. You want to come?" At first I said yes, because I had nothing else to do, but the trip to the beach would be agony — me trying to pass for normal while my friends talked about the great summers they were having, me pretending mine was great too. Usually I loved the beach, but this summer I hated it. The sun looked down like a fierce, hot eye, not giving me anyplace to hide, and as soon as I got there, I wanted to be back in the cool dark of my bedroom, but someone else was driving, and I was trapped. So I'd lie on my stomach and pretend to sleep or force myself to join the fun. When I got home, I'd wash off the sand in the tub, put Solarcaine on my reddened skin, shut the door to my bedroom, and dive back into bed, waiting for sleep.

I had no idea what was wrong.

I pulled down all the shades in my bedroom to keep the morning sun out as long as possible, trying to sleep forever, but I'd hear my mother rattling pots as she made breakfast, and I knew she'd be calling "Sharon!" in what seemed an accusatory voice but was probably an anxious one. I'd drag myself out to the kitchen, eat breakfast, and slink back into my room, where I'd try to sleep away the day. Sometimes my mother opened my closed door and peered down at me.

"What are are you doing?"

"Nothing...reading. I'm reading."

"What are you reading?"

"A book. I'm just reading."

"Why don't you call one of your friends? All you do is spend the day lying there like a bump on a log."

"They're busy. Everyone's away. Leave me alone, Mom, I'm losing my place." *If she doesn't shut the door and leave me alone, I'm going to scream. Thank God, the sound of the door closing. It's so quiet now.*

Then I'd lie back on the bed in the hot, humid Boston summer, listening to the far-off whine of saws and the rumble of power lawn mowers, hoping my mother would leave the house so I could sink down further into the dark lake without sensing her nervous presence somewhere on the shore, calling to me as she did at the beach: "Sharon, come back in here; you're out too deep!"

Perhaps my mother, who had lived through my father's depression, became alarmed, sensing the connection between my bedroom retreat and his. Or perhaps she just thought I had a case, maybe an extreme one, of the usual adolescent mopeyness and sullen apathy. In any case, by the middle of July, she took charge: She dragged me out of my dark lake by sending me to Massachusetts General Hospital as a candy striper. This got me out of the house, but depression, my sly bedfellow, came with me, sitting next to me on the Waverly streetcar, following me to work.

I spent the remaining summer days numbly pushing people in wheelchairs to their destinations in X-ray or physical therapy, wishing I had the energy for small talk because the patients looked so small and shrunken in their blue-and-white-striped hospital gowns, their feet white and vulnerable inside the standard-issue paper slippers. I'd stare at the patients when they didn't notice, wondering what it would be like to spend my life paralyzed in a wheelchair. I thought I would probably kill myself, although I didn't know how I'd bring it off.

At 4:30 I left to catch the subway at Charles Street, the only elevated station on the line. I'd watch the sailboats dotting the river, turning my head so I could get a last glimpse of the white sails scudding across the blue water before the dark tunnel to Kendall Square swallowed us up. Then I'd catch the Waverly streetcar in Harvard Square, my depression right beside me in the hot subway air, and let it take me home.

Sometimes I'd skip the hospital and go to a 10:00 a.m. movie. You could see a double feature at the Uptown for thirty-five cents. I'd stay in the theater until mid-afternoon and it was time to go home, emerging, blinking and stunned, from the darkness like some hibernating animal thrust into a summer light as sharp and bleak as a razor. Then I'd go home and pretend nothing was wrong. What I was suffering from did not exist or have a voice.

"How was the hospital?"

"Fine, okay. What's for dinner?"

"Barbara Hunter called you. You need to call her back."

"Barbara Hunter is a jerk."

Barbara Hunter was a mild, puffy girl with a pockmarked face, much lower in social status than me. My mother knew her mother, and I could bet that she had arranged this phone call.

"She wants you to do something with her. You call her back."

"I wouldn't be caught dead with Barbara Hunter.

She is the most boring person on earth."

"Suit yourself. Go through the whole summer without seeing anyone if that's what you want."

That really wasn't what I wanted. I wanted, although I didn't know it, to be off working at the Cape with Patty Ramsey, living in a waitresses' dorm, trading makeup tips, going to midnight beach parties with a crowd of teenagers. I didn't want to be having sex, although my parents must have feared this. I'd been more indoctrinated with Irish Catholicism than my sister and was still convinced that it was a mortal sin. But I wanted to be away from home, to be one of a crowd, to be out of the spotlight. If I'd been able to know what I wanted, that would have been it.

August crawled along, me patching together a life out of patient-pushing, daytime movies, candy bars, TV Westerns, and — my only true consolation — sleep. Sometime that month I'd discovered over-the-counter sleeping pills — *Take Sominex tonight and sleep! sleep! sleep!* — and on Friday night, facing the horror of the weekend, I'd start taking them and drift through till Monday morning in a somnambulistic haze. Then, blessedly, Labor Day came and with it all the new, hopeful signs of school — fresh notebooks, keen Number 2 pencils, glossy blue-and-white Belmont High book covers. I went back to the classroom, my real home, and my spirits lifted.

The next summer, depression descended again. I was still jobless. This time my mother enrolled me in a typing course in Boston — she had the same strategy for coping with a depressed daughter as does Esther Greenwood's mother in *The Bell Jar* — and I took the subway in every day to the Copley Secretarial School. There I sat, in a small, windowless room, with six or seven other hopeless girls whose mothers had also decided they had to take typing. I stared at the alphabet soup of the keys and made up nonsense words with the letters in my head ("qwerty," "trew"), repeating them to myself like a mantra when I took the subway home, drumming typing exercises in the air. Sometimes I turned my typewriter words into limericks — anything to pass the time, and a limerick could take me all the way from Park Street to Harvard Square. *There once was a fellow named Qwerty, who never would live to see thirty. It's sad but it's trew, he died at twenty-two, and never got old or got dirty.*

Labor Day finally came round again, and I went back to school for my senior year, my still-unnamed depression lifting like a fog burning off in the sun. I applied to Radcliffe early on and got in, and I knew that in September I'd be living away from home. I couldn't wait.

I didn't name this wretched period in my life "depression" until a few years ago when, going back in time, I was trying to understand where my midlife depression came from. Then those high school summers came back to me, and I realized that this wasn't the usual adolescent moodiness; this was something different. I was experiencing what the *Surgeon General's Report* now calls "early onset depression," far more common in girls than in boys, anticipating women's higher ratio of depression. The sources were multiple. There was my genetic predisposition to depression, all the genes inherited from the O'Briens and Quinlans just lying in wait for what the psychologists call "precipitating circumstances." My mother's banishment of my sister contributed to the fear both Kevin and I felt during these years, and I was more exposed to parental surveillance since he'd escaped to college. And then there was my rocky journey through puberty and adolescence, made even rockier by my mother's fear that each sign of maturing sexuality meant I'd end up a college dropout like my sister. We didn't live in a culture then that easily allowed girls to be both pretty and smart, and it was clear what choice I had to make. "She's the pretty one, and I'm the smart one," I told a family friend, referring to my sister. There were many rewards for being the smart one, and many losses too. One of the results of my inability to integrate these two parts of a female self — and so begin to express what Alice Miller calls the "true self" — was depression.

My first transition into puberty went pretty smoothly. This was before Maureen's defection, so my mother and sister were my mentors when the time came to make the all-important change from undershirts to my first bra, actually something called a training bra, as if my newly emerging breasts were getting ready for some major sports event. I was eleven when my breasts started to bud and get tender and sore. I was sure I had cancer and managed to choke out my fears to my sister, who laughed and said it was nothing to worry about; I was just getting breasts, and pretty soon it would be time to go down to Touraine's and have a consultation with the Bra Lady.

During that year, other girls started leaving undershirts behind and showing off their new bras while we were undressing for gym, so I eventually became impatient for my visit to Touraine's and asked my mother to take me to get a bra. So one Saturday morning, we set off on a momentous journey to Harvard

Square. The Bra Lady, ruler of the lingerie section at Touraine's department store, must have presided over the coming-of-age of thousands of girls in the Boston area in the early '60s, brought to her, half excited, half fearful, by their mothers. The Bra Lady was a bosomy woman in her sixties who swirled her white hair in a wispy bun, swept on top of her head by tortoise-shell combs. She wore berry-red lipstick and nail polish, which you could see up close when she spread the bras out on the glass counter. She would trace her finger over their puckery cups while evoking their virtues ("this one is satin, hooks in the front, sometimes easier for the younger woman"). The Bra Lady glided through the aisles of the lingerie section like a goddess, her bosom preceding her authoritatively, as if saying, "This woman *really* knows about bras, trust us."

When I first went with my mother, the Bra Lady took a kindly look at my flattish chest and recommended a simple cotton bra, 34AA. "Don't worry," she said encouragingly to me, "they'll grow. You'll be back in here for a 36B in no time at all." I liked my new bra because, when I looked at myself in Touraine's three-way mirror, I thought I resembled the lady in the Maidenform ad — the one who, with mingled bewilderment and pride, found herself semi-exposed in public settings. ("I dreamed I conducted an orchestra in my Maidenform bra.") I thought there was something sexy and daring about those ads, those proper '50s women — hair curled, lipstick on, eyes demure — going about their business fully dressed except for the exposed bra, which caused nearby men to stare like idiots and drop their newspapers and their coffee cups while the proper '50s women — in their nylons, heels, tube skirts, and Maidenform bras — never noticed them at all.

Going home with my mother and my new cotton bras, I felt happily indoctrinated into a stage of womanhood that I liked, and even though I never "filled out" enough to earn the Bra Lady's 36B, I felt no regret in leaving undershirts behind. My mother's companionship on this venture smoothed the path. She and the Bra Lady seemed benign collaborators, and the way they nodded when I showed them both my 32AA said they belonged to the same club, one they both wanted me to join.

The next part of the journey didn't go as smoothly. One morning I woke up with blood dripping down my legs. I was terrified, having no idea there was any connection between this phenomenon and those pamphlets from Kotex my mother had given me the year before, when I went off to summer camp. The pamphlets told me something called "menstruation" was coming, and it had something to do with a uterus and eggs and Fallopian tubes, which looked like graceful fringed flowers. And it had something to do with "fluid," which the pamphlets said I was going to "discharge" each month, and that was why these things I had to wear called sanitary napkins featured something called "absorbency." So I was prepared for the napkins, which my mother had bought for me and laid in the bottom of my camp trunk like fat, flat sausages. And I was prepared for fluid. I was not prepared for *blood*. The little pamphlets never mentioned the word "blood."

So when I began bleeding, I was sure I was dying, and my mother's response only confirmed this: "Oh God, and she's not even twelve, she's not even twelve," she moaned to my father.

All that could mean was that I was dying too soon, I wouldn't even live to see my twelfth birthday. Then she told me my period had come and I'd have to go find one of those napkins and put it on, and I was relieved I wasn't dying but still knew that something pretty bad had happened much sooner than it should have.

It never occurred to me that my mother's momentary grieving for my period had anything to do with my sister. But now it all makes sense. My period arrived just a few weeks after my mother learned of my sister's pregnancy and marriage, and she must have feared this irrevocable sign of puberty more than any other because now I could get pregnant; now I could follow, if I chose, Maureen's downward path.

She had never spoken to me about my period — the pamphlets were my source of information — just as she had never spoken to me about sex. I had some vague ideas about sex based on stray comments from girlfriends and the illustrations I came across in a musty old anatomy textbook I found at a yard sale. After I got my period, my mother evidently felt she had to broach the subject, a tough one for most '50s mothers. So after going over the rules for sanitary napkin disposal, she said, "I suppose you know...about the *other thing.*"

I knew almost nothing about "the other thing" except to guess that my mother was referring to sex and that she didn't want to talk about it and didn't hold it in very high regard.

"Yes," I lied, and waited to see if she'd say anything more.

"Well, then," my mother said, "I guess that's it," and went back to her ironing.

Maybe because she couldn't do anything about my period, my mother declared war on my pimples, which had begun popping out all over my face about the same time. My father drove us to one skin doctor after another. He'd go for a walk or stroll over to Brigham's for a coffee ice cream while my mother accompanied me into the doctor's office, sitting beside me while he squinted at my face and hummed under his breath.

The skin doctors all seemed to be cousins — pale, lugubrious, nearsighted men whose glasses magnified their eyes alarmingly. Magnification seemed their *raison d'etre* — they also possessed magnifying mirrors that transformed my skin into a pocked terrain of hills and craters while they talked earnestly about the biochemistry of acne. I'd stare at my skin's moon surface while they told me about whiteheads and blackheads and hot washcloths. After a while, I became convinced that my face had disappeared; when people looked at me, they must be seeing only my pimples.

After the nearsighted skin doctors popped my pimples with a small metal implement they carried in their vest pockets and applied a cotton ball, soaked in a stinging astringent, to my reddened face, they recommended twice-daily drenchings of my face in Phisohex, the recommended medicinal soap of the '60s. "And no peanut butter, chocolate, or sweets," they said to my mother.

When we got home, she would place the new bottle of Phisohex on the bathroom sink and tell me my future complexion was up to me. "Remember, acne leaves scars," she'd warn, and I'd be left confronting the ugly green-and-black plastic dispenser. I'd look at my spotty face in the mirror and resign myself to the disconsolate ministrations of Phisohex. It had a sickly, curdled smell like rotting cottage cheese and didn't even lather like normal soap but felt thin and slippery between your fingers.

I hated Phisohex even more than I hated my pimples, and sometimes, after days of Phisohexing and following the doctor's grim diet, pasted to the mirror in the bathroom, I'd break out on a rampage, stopping at Henry's Bakery on the way to school and stuffing down six jelly donuts at once or consuming a fistful of candy bars on the way home — Kit Kats and Three Musketeers were my favorites, followed by Hershey's Milk Chocolate and Nestle's Crunch. M&M's were good but too small — I'd have to stuff a huge handful into my mouth in order to believe I was really eating chocolate. My mother would find the candy wrappers in my jacket pockets and tell me I'd better be careful about my complexion and my weight.

"You weren't fat," my sister tells me. "Mom was just preoccupied with your eating. She used to talk to me about it. 'What am I going to do about Sharon?' she'd ask. 'I can't keep cookies in the house. She sneaks out at night and lifts the lid on the cookie jar. I can hear it clinking.' But you didn't weigh much more than you do now." When I looked over my old report cards, which chronicle weight and height as well as grades, I see that my sister was right. My weight inched up gradually until tenth grade, when I weighed five pounds more than I do now — and friends sometimes accuse me of being too thin.

So what was it all about? Like the doctors, my mother was magnifying, but what huge pictures filled her imagination? What she feared, I think, was my appetite. Soaping with Phisohex, avoiding sweets, having just one chocolate chip cookie, not eight — this was all good advice, probably the kind I'd give an adolescent daughter too. But I think that my mother was worried about my appetite in a larger sense: She didn't want me developing an interest in *the other thing.*

Unlike my sister, I began dating occasionally in high school. So it must have been easy for my mother to worry — if Sharon begins fooling around with boys this soon, she might fall into darkness more quickly. Every phone call I received from a boy must have grated on her ears and set her heart pounding. *Not this daughter too! This one is going to go to college and set the world on fire, not end up pregnant and married to some man or other. I didn't like the sound of that boy's voice. I didn't like the way he talked. He sounds ignorant and common.*

If my mother thought I was early, I knew I was late. My girlfriends had all done Spin the Bottle in sixth grade at the mixed "boy-girl" parties I wasn't allowed to attend and had gone to dances in junior high school, where they'd danced with boys. I never got asked. I kept hoping that someday things with boys would work out. I was interested, even though I pretended I wasn't, and had a serious crush on Roger Perry. I sat behind him in homeroom throughout junior high and still remember the morning in eighth grade when I realized how beautiful the back of his neck was.

I had to acknowledge that I was seriously backward and behind schedule one day in tenth grade when I read the "Ask Beth" column in the *Boston Globe.*

"Dear Beth," the letter read, "I am sixteen years old, and I have never been kissed. Am I behind schedule? Sincerely, Wondering in Medford." I related to that letter: I was sixteen years old and in the same spot. I was no nearer to being kissed than I was to being an astronaut. I knew what Beth was going to say — something consoling, like, "Of course not, dear, you're just fine, right in the mainstream."

Except that's not what she said. "Dear Wondering: Not to worry. Just relax and enjoy your friendships with girls *and* boys. Eventually you'll catch up!" Oh God, I'm a sexual retard — that's what Beth is really saying. *Dear Wondering: You are, in fact, a pathetic failure. When you get kissed, which could be years from now, you'll still be thousands of kisses behind the other girls. Too bad you're wasting the best years of your life sitting home with your parents, sneaking the occasional midnight cookie when you want a real thrill.*

I stared at the *Globe* for a long time. I resolved I was going to beat "Wondering in Medford." I was going to get kissed first.

The first boy to ask me to a dance was Stephen Antonelli. I was in tenth grade and he was in eleventh, so he had the panache of being an older man. Stephen played the saxophone in the band and had a clever, pockmarked face. He was a little shorter than me, but I liked him. He had an ironic, downbeat sense of humor, he liked jazz, and he wore black turtlenecks, so he struck me as cool without being too scary. "Great," I said. "I just have to ask my parents."

"Mom, I've been asked to a dance," I said, as my parents came in from their Saturday shopping. My mother put down her bags and turned to my father without acknowledging me. "Oh my God, Norb," she said, her voice edged with something more than contempt, something like anger or maybe even hatred, something dark and vicious and unacknowledged, something that lived down below the surface with the thing that frightened me. Then, I couldn't hear the fear.

Then she turned back to me. "What's this boy's name?"

"Stephen Antonelli."

"An-to-nelli, he's I-talian. She wants to go out with an Italian!"

My father shrugged his shoulders and said something mild and placating like, "Now, Jeannie, there are many fine Italian families in our parish," and my mother gave one of her disgusted sighs.

After my mother said the word "Italian," I could see it painted on the wall in our kitchen, dripping with blood and scum, the name of something obscene. I called Stephen back and said I could not go, I'd made a mistake, I was busy.

"Mom, I've been asked to a dance."

"Who is it this time?"

"Adam Schwartz. He's a junior."

"Jewish boy?"

"No, he's Catholic. Isn't it obvious?"

"Don't be fresh with me. Can't you find somebody besides this — Adam Schwartz?"

Then I walked out of the room, aware that my mother was saying the Jewish name as if she were picking up some repellant object with tongs.

This time I wasn't going to back down. I went to the dance with Adam, and he took me to Howard Johnson's afterwards for ice cream — a proper date.

When he dropped me off, he gave me a goodnight kiss — my first! — and I felt I'd crossed an invisible line. I ran to the bathroom and looked at my face in the mirror, surprised to find that I really didn't look any different. For our next date, we went to the Cafe Pamplona in Harvard Square, a funky basement cafe with marble-topped tables and cappuccino, an exotic locale in the early '60s. I was impressed. Then we had a parking double date on Belmont's infamous Somerset Road. We went with Mark and Karen, who had been King and Queen of the Junior Prom. I felt honored by this association with teenage royalty, Cinderella invited to the ball, even though I was terrified by the idea of parking. I'd have to kiss Adam for a long time — I knew that — and since he was driving, I couldn't escape.

It was impossible for me to feel my own desire when Adam turned off the ignition and drew my face toward his. I was conscious the whole time that sex before marriage was a mortal sin, and since the endpoint of intercourse was forbidden, it was hard for me to enjoy the preliminaries, aware as I was that at some point I would have to say, "Stop! I have to go home!" I hated the parking date. I waited patiently while Adam explored the territory underneath my bra and panties, kissing me strenuously in the meantime, sticking his tongue in and out of my mouth with rapid darting motions like a restless lizard. "At least I'm doing French kissing," I said to myself, one more thing to check off my list. *Take that, Wondering in Medford!*

Meanwhile, I kept my right arm tensed to push his hand away if he went "too far." I had to keep him in venial sin territory, the Catholic Church's equivalent of a misdemeanor. I had only the vaguest notion of where the crossover into mortal sin might be, but I knew that mortal sin was a felony and that if you died in a state of mortal sin, you'd go straight to hell. I wanted to leave after five minutes, but Adam had clamped onto me with unsettling permanence, and Mark and Ellen were moaning and breathing heavily in the backseat. I could not ask to go home as this would be sure to anger Adam, who'd already spent ten dollars on dinner, and would let the King and Queen and then the whole school know I wasn't okay about sex. Then Adam changed tactics, putting my hand on *his* crotch, and I said I had to go home. "My mother's really strict about time," I said. "She'll kill me if I'm not back by midnight," for once telling the truth.

I took Catholicism very seriously when I was a teenager. I wasn't pious, and I didn't love God, but I believed everything the Church taught, particularly about sin. I memorized the Baltimore Catechism, which consisted of questions asked by some anonymous source and answers you were supposed to give the nuns, and I passed all the tests. I even became a Catholic Youth Organization leader and received a dictionary, first prize for the eleventh grade test. "God Bless You, Sharon," was the inscription, signed by Father Griffin, the elderly, melancholic priest who was in charge of us. I collected Catechism prizes the way I collected merit badges and A's — I wanted to do well.

The one lesson in the Baltimore Catechism that really wormed its way into my soul was the one on sin. The different levels of sin were illustrated by milk bottles. I can still see them today — a pure white milk bottle on the left, illustrating the cleansed soul after baptism or confession; a graying milk bottle in the middle, filled with spotty, disgusting milk, the soul stained with venial sin; and on the right, a midnight-black milk bottle, the soul after mortal sin, the soul headed straight to hell. I knew that dating was what the Church called an "occasion of sin" because you could be tempted to go "all the way," which was definitely a mortal sin and would turn your soul into the solid-black milk bottle and mean that you'd go straight to hell if you died before you could get to confession.

It never occurred to me then to question the authority of the church; I'd been programmed by all those Q's and A's. The Baltimore Catechism asked *me* questions; I didn't get to ask any back. There was no option then of the kind of "cafeteria" Catholicism that evolved after Vatican II, with Catholics rejecting some beliefs of the church and still considering themselves Catholics. Fifties Irish Catholics didn't allow negotiation. You either accepted everything, or you weren't a Catholic at all. This made sense to me. Being a Catholic was an either/or proposition, just like being a member of my family. You either toed the line and belonged, as Kevin and I did, or you rebelled and got thrown out, like Maureen. You want to have your own opinions? Follow your own inclinations? Go *all the way?* Fine, stay out in the cold.

When my mother told me I had to stop going out with Adam, I did not protest. We were standing in my parents' bedroom, both of us looking into the full-length mirror. "That Adam Schwartz is Jewish," my mother's reflection said, "and you've been going out with him a lot."

"I guess. What difference does it make?" my reflection said.

"I don't want you seeing him anymore," her reflection said.

I left the mirror and went to my room, driven by the coiled-up energy of my mother's fear and my own — far more powerful forces than the desire I couldn't allow myself to feel. When Adam called a few days later to ask me to the graduation dance, I told him I wouldn't be seeing him again. I felt relieved that I wouldn't have to wait in the sunroom for him to pick me up again, my mother hovering in the living room, looking out the windows at each passing car, not speaking to me as I sat in my new dress with my hair curled and sweaty hands, the atmosphere in our house crackling with unspoken words. My mother must have been relieved too.

A few weeks later, school let out, and I got depressed.

> *"Once you make a decision,
> the universe conspires
> to make it happen."*
>
> RALPH WALDO EMERSON

RECOVERY: EMBRACING YOUR DEMONS

By Beth A. Baxter, M.D.

RECOVERY is a concept that has many definitions in our society today. All of them represent a process of healing and restored functioning, whether referring to the economy, a rosebush in our yard, or a bone in our body.

When a part of our body is physically wounded, it can heal almost completely, given the technology of today's health care system. Bones become strong again, skin grows back, and many organs can be replaced.

When we are faced with the problem of recovery from serious mental illnesses, things are a bit different. These illnesses include major depression, bipolar affective disorder, schizophrenia, schizoaffective disorder, obsessive-compulsive disorder, and panic disorder. While medical research has made it possible to improve the lives of about ninety percent of these persons, less than forty percent will actually accept treatment. This is directly due to the stigma in our society about mental illness. People would rather suffer alone in silence than to identify themselves with any of these illnesses.

It is important to acknowledge that a person recovering from serious mental illness is rarely cured. But symptoms of mental illnesses may be minimized by treatment with medications and psychotherapies. Chemical receptors in the brain that are up or down can be regulated as neurotransmitters are taken in or released. These chemical changes can result in stimulated or reduced functioning of certain areas of the brain, and mental processes and physical behaviors are suppressed or activated. As a result, the symptoms of serious mental illnesses are minimized, and functioning is at least partially restored.

The concept of recovery from serious mental illness is also part of the field of psychiatric rehabilitation. Medical treatments do minimize signs and symptoms of these illnesses, but once this is done, a person is often left with social and occupational disabilities. A person would normally develop these skills in their adolescence and young adulthood. However, when people suffer from serious mental illness early in life, their social and occupational growth is stunted by the loss of this developmental phase. This problem can be compared to the fable of Rip Van Winkle. Once the person "wakes up" from the slumber (or recovers from signs and symptoms of their illnesses with medical treatment), the individual finds an unrecognizable world, with little knowledge of the way it functions. The social and occupational disabilities the person faces must be countered by specific rehabilitation that will restore part of this functioning.

Recovery from serious mental illness is also like recovering from a spinal cord injury. A person who sustains a spinal cord injury may lose the function of both legs and find oneself confined to a wheelchair. While the spinal cord injury will never heal, symptoms of the physical injury can be stabilized by medical treatment. When the person wants to get on with his or her life, sooner or later, this will entail a different kind of work. The person, now confined to a wheelchair, must compensate for his/her new social and occupational disabilities. The change from the previous level of functioning must be acknowledged and grieved, just like any other significant loss or illness. He or she must then learn how to function socially and occupationally with the new disabilities. The person has survived the injury. However, life has been forever changed, and nothing will ever make things the way they used to be.

Similarly, the symptoms of serious mental illness may be reduced by medical treatment. However, mentally ill persons will also likely continue to suffer from significant symptoms. They must then grieve their loss of functioning and get on with their lives. Through the process of psychiatric rehabilitation, mentally ill persons can adapt to the symptoms that still exist and their related social and occupational disabilities.

Even those without serious mental illnesses must face difficult losses throughout their lives. These may take the form of a lost relationship through death, divorce, or separation. This loss could also be another form of illness that saps time or physical functioning that we once had. We must then acknowledge the loss, grieve the loss, adapt to the loss, and then get on with our lives. Nothing will ever change the fact that the loss has occurred. This example can also help us to understand the plight those persons with serious mental illnesses face in their recovery.

The first symptoms of my own serious mental illness began in college. Starting in my sophomore year, I had consecutive yearly depressions. Each year I told myself that it couldn't get any worse, but it did. Despite my erratic behavior, no one said anything about my problems to me. I got the message that it was something that people did not talk about. I was able to hide this unnamed problem by a flurry of extracurricular activities, which also included being the president of my student body during my senior year. It was ironic that despite my public position, I was very much alone with my suffering.

I had grown up a lot like many others my age. My younger brother and sister and I did our share of fighting, though we loved each other immensely. I had a standard adolescence including being known as very mature. I had wanted to be a doctor for as long as I could remember. As a child, I would even hide behind the couch after bedtime to watch "Marcus Welby, M.D."

Though I never took a psychology course in college, I knew by the end of this time that something was definitely wrong with my brain. At Vanderbilt University Medical School, during my first behavioral science course, I found out my problem had a name. When I learned about the symptom of "early morning awakening," my years of this experience crystallized before me, and things suddenly seemed to make sense. By this time, however, my depression had begun to include psychotic dimensions. At one time, a representative from my class sat down with me to tell me about their concern for me. However, I was already very ill. I took a leave of absence during my second year in medical school and went to Texas to live with my grandparents. I was tortured during this time by psychotic symptoms, which appeared as personal messages I thought I was receiving from the TV and radio programs. I was living in an old cabin on my grandparents' cattle ranch, where I had very little contact with other people. One day, I packed my car to supposedly meet a group of people from Nashville who had (I thought) come to meet me at a nearby lake. After I failed to meet my grandparents at church that day, they put out a missing persons report. I was found on the side of a road far away and then taken to a nearby hospital.

I slowly recovered from this psychotic break and returned to medical school the next fall to repeat my second year. The experience of taking care of my illness during this time was like pursuing my training while managing a full-time job elsewhere. I hired a tutor for each class to help me "talk through" the material I had to learn. While this experience may have seemed unnecessary to some, it was the only way I could think of at the time to master the material in front of me. And it worked.

After slow, steady work, with a good share of setbacks and hurdles, I graduated from medical school in 1990 though I had been diagnosed with Bipolar Affective Disorder. My first residency year was spent at a medical internship in Memphis, Tennessee. After this, I entered the psychiatric residency program at the University of Rochester in Rochester, New York. I was finally in a position where I would be able to give others some of the help that I had been given.

During this time, however, my illness progressed again, and my psychotic symptoms became prominent. I was hospitalized for psychiatric treatment once during my residency and then again a week after completing this training. Though I had begun a job as an attending psychiatrist at the State Psychiatric Hospital in Rochester, I was quickly sinking into a world that existed only in my mind. Not only did I continue to receive messages from the radio and TV broadcasts, I was also tormented by otherwise normal sounds and objects in the environment that directed my thoughts and actions. The sound of a bird singing or the direction of a nearby car's movement would tell me the answer to a question or would direct my thoughts one way or the other. My pain worsened as the noises and objects told me when to speak, what to eat, and where and when to move. My days were filled not with words but with chaotic stimuli that lured me in unsafe ways to unknown places. The only activity that calmed me was walking long distances, as is true with many other persons with serious mental illnesses.

After my third hospitalization, I remained largely in my world of sights and sounds as I tried to return to work. My life seemed far removed from enjoyable and productive times I had previously known, and there seemed to be no end in sight.

One day in November of 1994, I decided I could go on no longer. I attempted suicide by trying to sever the carotid arteries in my neck. Miraculously, I survived this attempt and figured that God wasn't through with me yet.

After my suicide attempt, it was time to let my parents know just how bad my circumstances had become. My mother came to see me in Rochester about two weeks after my attempt, and I was quite a sight. I had lost about fifty pounds, I had bright red scars across the width of my spindly neck, and I had chopped off all of my hair close to the scalp. I imagined that when my mother came, she would take one look at me, turn around, and take the next plane back to Nashville.

Instead, she came to me, took me in her arms, and sat down to hear whatever I had to say. The more I shared with my mother, the clearer it became just how distant my relationship with my parents had become. Throughout my mother's visit, we seemed to become closer than we ever had been before. We battled the "war" of the health care system around us, which drew us even closer. As we faced the unknown struggles of each day, we shared parts of ourselves that each of us had never seen in the other. Because of this, I actually came to cherish these times.

My father soon became involved as we tried to figure out what, where, and when my next medical and psychiatric care needed to be. Long-term disagreements seemed to melt away as we worked together through the morass of mental health care services we encountered. A doctor told my parents that I would never recover the health I once had. They were told that, at best, I would only be able to do simple repetitive tasks in a sheltered workshop, such as putting items in boxes.

Though this prediction was incorrect, it fueled our efforts to work toward my recovery. It seemed I was caught in a system that sought to either take away all of my decision-making power or give it entirely back to me. Both of these extremes were determined to be "in my best interest." My friends came forward to advocate for me when my caregivers told me I had no part in making these decisions. When the process of my care was left solely to my family and myself, we groped our way along the darkness of uncertainty and the misunderstanding of my mental illness. For example, most caregivers in the health care systems that we encountered abandoned us in the process of family therapy or even in discussions about the impact of my mental illness upon the rest of my life.

Every night on the phone, I kept my parents, brother, and sister up to date with all of my psychotic musings about the events of my day. It was hard for them to sort out what actually happened from what I thought had happened, though they all wanted so badly to help. While they could only occasionally visit me, these times in New England became more treasured than any other of our times together had been. The process of groping our way along through many of these health care systems was difficult but allowed us the opportunity to get to know each other more than we ever had before. My "baby brother" in Boston often visited me and was my sole source for passes outside of the hospital grounds. My sister and I became more patient with each other than we had ever been before.

The nightly phone calls between us brought emotional healing. As my parents discussed with me how things were going, I, in turn, asked the same thing of them. What had they done today to take care of themselves? Each person had to report on what uncharacteristic fifteen-minute activity of self-care they had done that day.

Recovery was a slow process, and I was a long way

from being well. It was initially difficult for me to find reason to continue to live as I recovered physically from my suicide attempt. I was unable to love myself enough to justify this self-care. Again, my parents intervened to help. "If you can't love yourself enough to go on, then do it for me. I love you, and this will never change," my mother said. I finally believed her, and I began to try to move ahead as if I did love myself. One day, during a discussion with one of the nurses on the floor, I said spontaneously that I loved myself. When I realized what I had said, I ran to the phone to call my mother, who was as overjoyed as I was. From that point on, things progressed rapidly. My parents and their supporters came to help me as I moved through this barrier. When I was told that I had no part in the decision-making about where I would be receiving the next phase of my care, my family got help from Nashville and Rochester. When we were told that it would be impossible for my family to afford the next phase of my treatment, my family advocated with my health insurance company and took up a collection within our extended family.

Ultimately, I moved on to a private and noteworthy facility in the northeastern U.S. to continue my treatment. But not before crashing and becoming hospitalized again at a local public hospital. I developed a habit of walking away from my parents while their attention was elsewhere. I was not doing this with any intention to fill them with fear and anxiety; I was simply following the messages I received from various noises in my environment. I could no more ignore these noises than I could make myself well, as many of my caregivers expected me to be able to do. Again, my parents were utterly patient. When I was found after these journeys, they welcomed me with tearstained but smiling faces.

I moved to Nashville to be with my parents, as my support system in Rochester was exhausted. I was still suffering from psychotic symptoms that had been largely denied by my professional caregivers. Soon after moving to Nashville, I took a spontaneous car trip to Rochester, starting in the middle of the night. I ultimately ended up in a different state, hours away from my Nashville home. Again, my parents patiently drove the distance in the middle of the night to bring me home.

I was in and out of a Nashville hospital several times until an undaunted psychiatrist prescribed a trial of Clozaril, a fairly new antipsychotic that was largely reserved for people who had not responded to any other substances. After finding a good set of modern medications, a lot of other good things happened. I rapidly began to improve physically, emotionally, and spiritually. I initially worked in sheltered employment at a local greenhouse. Then I learned about the mental health care consumers' movement. I made my first speech about my experiences as a mental health consumer to a Nashville Rotary Club and, from there, began to attend and speak at national mental health care conferences. Though I was yearning to return to the practice of psychiatry, I wisely began to work as a consumer advocate with a TennCare BHO. There, I was able to represent the views of mental health care consumers and help my company develop appropriate programs and policies. I simultaneously began to travel the country, on behalf of my company, to tell people about my recovery from serious mental illness. I sought to give hope to other consumers who had experienced the same mental torture and psychiatric disability as I had and encourage them to believe that they too could function despite serious mental illness. I was not cured, but I had gone farther up the road of social and occupational functioning than anyone would have predicted, and I wasn't stopping there.

As I improved clinically, I developed a closer relationship with my parents, with whom I was living. We became close friends during the four and a half years I lived with them. When I bought my first home, we experienced mixed emotions as I celebrated another milestone of my recovery yet had to leave the daily contact with them.

Journal articles became another opportunity for me to share my story of pain and hope. I began a mental illness ministry at my church. I worked to collect biblical references about mental illness and the process of battling adversity.

All this time, I was hoping to return to the field of medicine. The managed care company I worked for was bought by another company, which provided me an opportunity to begin working at the Mental Health Cooperative to serve persons with severe mental illnesses like my own. Today I am the psychiatrist for the PACT Program, a mental health cooperative program serving some of the most treatment-resistant persons in our community. I have passed the first part of my Psychiatry Boards and am working to complete the second half. I continue to speak publicly and write articles, though at a slower pace than I did previously. I am thankful to be back to practicing psychiatry. This time, I am truly able to care for myself and, in turn, care responsibly for others.

During the first part of my illness, I had strongly wanted my parents and siblings to understand what was happening to me. I felt like a victim of a cruel fate and didn't want to be alone. My family had first become involved when I felt incredibly devastated and almost without hope. Rochester had been a beginning for their understanding, which grew exponentially as I moved back to Nashville. Throughout their advocacy, they continued to learn about mental illness and the injustices served to those who suffer from it. As my recovery continued into years, they demonstrated an understanding that I could have never expected or hoped for. Soon, my mother became president of Nashville NAMI (National Alliance for the Mentally Ill), and my father began to serve on the board of directors for the mental health agency that served all of middle Tennessee. They both followed editorials and local and national mental health legislation, and fought against stigmatizing entertainment.

All of us now possess an understanding of and the passion for working toward recovery from serious mental illness. We have seen this happen in our lives and those of countless others. As we share our story and advocate for others, we are blessed with an even stronger recovery and greater emotional health. It shows that what you give to others comes back to you manifold. My recovery would not have been possible without the love and support of my family. From this, I am blessed with peace that I never could have imagined.

Today I know that I am one of the lucky ones.

(1) I have schizoaffective disorder and am thus saved from the pain of psychotic symptoms at

least some of the time. I still can occasionally assign special meanings to sounds and sights around me, but I know that this perception is part of my illness and an incorrect interpretation of these environmental stimuli.

(2) I had a positive clinical response to the trial of Clozaril I was given in 1995. This does not happen for all treatment-resistant mentally ill persons, who are left in their tortured world of misperceptions.

(3) I have a loving family who has supported me on every step of my way. My recovery would not have been possible without their loyalty, patience, and inspiration.

(4) I have an excellent team of health care providers who have never given up on me and have provided me with the best care I could have received.

(5) I survived my suicide attempt. This is a miracle that I have remembered most every day of my life since that time.

(6) I am able to work in the profession of my choice. Sheltered workshops do provide opportunities for many persons who could not work otherwise. A lot of recovery is due to the excellent medical and therapeutic services I have received. But it was also due to the fact that I refused to give up and hung tenaciously to the fact that I was alive. That was hope in itself.

(7) My recovery has also involved spiritual growth. I have a peace and serenity that began soon after I physically recovered from my suicide attempt. This serenity has grown every day that I have shared my recovery with others.

During my recovery, I have become very aware of the spiritual growth that is possible for me through battling adversity. Dr. Patricia Deegan is a psychologist who received her degree after recovering from schizophrenia. She states that recovery is only possible as we "try and fail and try again." The book of Romans in the Bible tells us that it is through our suffering that we gain spiritual fruits of perseverance, character, and hope. Those of us with serious mental illnesses have battled adversities all of our lives. We gain a type of strength that most "normal" persons in our society find difficult to achieve. Persons with serious mental illnesses are today's heroes, fighting adversity with bravery and perseverance and showing others miracles can occur.

Chapter Two

SCHIZOPHRENIA: THE ADVENTURE

By Rebecca Stevenson

I just finished reading the book *Living with Schizophrenia — A Guide for Patients and Their Families,* by Alexander P. Hyde, M.D. In it, the author noted that the adventures that schizophrenic writers relate about their illnesses are rare. Most schizophrenics experience their illness as boring and unhappy, like their boring and unhappy lives. Well, I'm a born writer. I decided I wanted to be a writer at age eight, got published the first time at age ten, began to get serious about doing it for money at seventeen, and made it a lifelong career at thirty. Now I'm forty-one. So when I began to break down with schizophrenia at fourteen, I was primed for "writer's schizophrenia," the adventurous type.

There is no way I can tell my adventure without mentioning Kathy, my best girlfriend ever since the sixth grade, as she lived through most of the adventure with me (although we didn't recognize it as schizophrenia in the beginning). We met in the spring of 1971. I was eleven; she, thirteen. We were both shy and lonely, and in P.E. class neither of us could hit the ball or ever be chosen for any of the teams. So we made our own team, just the two of us. In the seventh grade, we were separated as I went into the gifted classes and she, into the average classes. In the eighth grade, we found ourselves in the same music class and picked up our friendship just as if we'd never been separated. By the ninth grade, we were having sleepovers as often as our mothers would permit and generally hanging out, to the exclusion of everyone else. And talking constantly of music and boys. We had classes together all the way through high school, and she knew me better than anyone else. She was more like a sister than my real sister.

It wasn't until college that I switched "best friend" allegiance to Carol, which lasted until Judy took over, and then Ruth and Alice, and on from there. I am still in touch with Judy, but not the others, and I am still in touch with Kathy, as ever.

The schizophrenia? It was around my fourteenth birthday, July 22, 1973, that the change began. I became obsessed with the number thirteen, wishing to stay that age, as the eighth grade had been so much fun. I was sad to be leaving it behind and scared about the future, about growing up. I was leaving behind Barbie and childhood. My sister, Jeanne, and I weren't on speaking terms. In the eighth grade, we'd been good friends. As the ninth grade progressed, the depression deepened, fueled by being beaten up on the school bus daily and constantly harassed in my science class. I hid my feelings from everyone, including Kathy. Her noisy, raucous home (she had a brother and three sisters) was a balm to my hurting soul and an antidote to the emotionally cold atmosphere of my own home.

High school started, and my depression became severe. In January, 1975, I dreamed I was walking along a lonely beach. In the sand I found a large moss-covered rock on which was written, "Hold your breath for twenty-two seconds." I awakened with the feeling it was some sort of instruction for my life. So I started practicing holding my breath. I easily conquered twenty-two seconds, then one minute. At first I kept the "secret" to myself; nobody would understand it anyway.

In February another rapist tried to "do" me (I'd been attacked before), and I told Kathy. Because I didn't show any feeling as I related the story, she didn't realize the reality of the situation. In fact, she thought it was a joke and started teasing me about it. That shut me up as far as sharing my painful feelings was concerned.

Meanwhile, the breath-holding thing got jump-started by a science lab studying the respiratory system, in which we were required to hold our breaths as long as possible under various conditions. My record was one minute, fifty-five seconds. The next day, I found out that was one of the best in the class. Wow, I thought. Of course, my secret activities became known to Kathy, and I continued doing it. Two minutes, thirty-five seconds; two minutes fifty-five seconds; three minutes, fifteen seconds. I began to wonder, "What is the world record for doing this?" And of course, Kathy heard all about it. We did another lab in another class, testing yoga exercises to see how they affected breath-holding capacity. They worked! Kathy was satisfied with three minutes, forty seconds, but I pressed on. I wanted more.

In September, 1975, my depression bottomed out, and overnight, in early October, I started to climb to the dizzy heights of mania. I also found out the world breath-holding record: Thirteen minutes, forty-two and a half seconds. Wow again! Instead of being discouraged by the gap between 3:15 and 13:42.5, I decided to try harder. After all, I was on a mission — a mission for God. That, I was sure of. It was my sole purpose in life. But knowing there was a huge gap, I tried other ways of entering the Guinness Book in case breath holding didn't pan out. I tried card houses, coin stacking, sunflower growing.

Many changes were taking place on the inside — and rapidly. My identity became "Guinness Book Challenger" instead of "rape victim." I was beginning to see myself as acceptable, free of the filth of the past. I was, in my own thoughts, "joining the human race." And in my joy, I wanted to take my best friend and fellow outcast, Kathy, with me, but she didn't follow. After joining me in a few record attempts that failed, she dropped out. So I went it alone. By then, I was getting messages in the songs on the radio, all telling me: *Go for your dream. It's your purpose in life, your mission from God.* By the beginning of 1976, I was deep into it, the songs propelling me — "Do it Again," by the Staple Singers, after a failed attempt; "Right Back Where We Started From," by Maxine Nightingale, to remind me of my original inspiration; and many others. I didn't notice it at first, but I was becoming edgy — angry — and it grew, little by little, as part of the backdrop of my frenzied efforts, my frenzied life. I joined the Art Club in my junior year, and in my senior year, I joined other clubs and sports as well. It was all part of "joining the human race" and becoming that beautiful, clean, acceptable teenager I so wanted to be. I hit four minutes, five seconds in breath holding in August, 1976, and that's when my world began to crumble.

My enrollment in clubs and the swimming team in the fall of 1976 pleased neither Jeanne nor Kathy, who joined forces to stop me (for once they stopped hating each other). When I started making new friends, including a boyfriend (gasp!), Kathy must have felt threatened, so she stopped speaking to me and started hanging around with Dianne. Author's Note: Kathy didn't stay mad at me forever for having a boyfriend in high school. We are good friends now by long distance. She's in Council Bluffs, Iowa, where we grew up; I'm in Columbus, Nebraska, and married with four grown stepsons — Orlando, Will, Pat, and Chris.

It was then that the anger bubbling under the surface started to erupt in self-injuring incidents, usually triggered by noise. However, I continued my quest to be "acceptable." And I continued the breath holding. By then, I was beginning to see "colors" in my mind, all around me. In April, 1976, I had noticed that the blossoms and fragrance of the flowers and trees were more intense, sounds became louder — all my senses seemed to have awakened. My feelings had become more intense and powerful also. In October, 1976, the mania had faded, and I felt like I was falling into a hole. I was scared. My boyfriend Jay and I were doing the Guinness Book things by then, but he made it clear his halfhearted participation was for me; he wasn't interested for himself. Jesus was his thing. So I got more involved in church activities — for him.

I was having trouble sleeping, and it was getting worse. I often slept every second night, and it was common for me to stay awake for thirty-six hours at a time. My inner tension grew. Meanwhile, my frenzied pace continued.

It was on a Sunday, December 12, 1976, that I held my breath for my "mission" for the last time. Six minutes, forty seconds. It was as if someone had slapped me in the face then dumped ice water over my head. What!? The record done without hyperventilating with oxygen was six minutes, twenty-nine point eight seconds. Oh, man, I had cheated on it too! I had broken the record, but I had cheated. No way could I repeat the performance — honestly — with all the TV cameras, radio personalities, and other witnesses necessary to get in the book! I wanted to die. And not only because of the 6:40. I also realized there was something wrong with my head, something seriously wrong. I plunged into a black depression.

I struggled to survive the rest of my senior year, graduated, then spent the summer in Arizona with Grandma and Uncle Steve, recovering my physical health, sunning and swimming, and wondering why my life had fallen apart. I hadn't felt I had really "joined the human race"; in fact, I felt the whole school had been laughing at me behind my back!

Colors swirled in my mind — blues, grays, black, rose, purple. I thought I had a brain tumor. I worried about brain damage from the 6:40. A "structure" seemed to have formed during my Guinness Book days, and now it was breaking down, decaying. It had fit over my whole body, tight as cellophane wrap, and now it was tearing, coming unraveled. I was terrified. The structure held in the "good" me and held the "bad" stuff out, and now it was leaking! I was going crazy! At the end of the summer, I said good-bye to my unfulfilled Guinness Book dreams and entered college. My new identity? "Schizophrenic." Yes, that had to be it. I felt it in my bones. I steeped myself in my new identity by reading books such as *I Never Promised You a Rose Garden* and other literature on mental illness. The strange things continued happening in my mind. The structure became a huge umbrella — rose, blue, and purple. It hovered over me everywhere, protectively, like a guardian angel. My emotions were pipes going into and coming out of the walls. Sometimes they were red and purple snow piled in my dorm room, on the furniture. My head felt stuffed with cotton, and there were little tiny panes, in different shapes, that I could move around with my thoughts. I was obsessed with mental illness and tears and emotions. I felt I had to talk about it to everyone I met to make sure they "really" cried and "really" had human feelings and "really" expressed them, so it was okay for me to do so.

Frankly, I don't know how my new friends, Carol and Kat and the gang, put up with me. But they had been in therapy themselves, so they recommended it to me. In November, 1977, I started therapy. With therapy, the acute phase of the schizophrenia passed in a matter of months, and all I had left were residual symptoms, dull and boring, repetitious and painful. The colors disappeared, the intense feelings disappeared; the adventure was gone. All I had left were the self-injuring impulses and the noise sensitivity. Even the crying obsession was gone; it disappeared in 1989. I have one new symptom, hearing voices. More like occasionally hearing one voice in my head, always a male voice, calling my name or asking me a nonsense question.

I am now on medication and still in therapy, or I'd have most of the acute symptoms back in a hurry. I am, as the old Paul Simon song says, "Still Crazy After All These Years."

When I read that book by Dr. Hyde, I found out not only that I have a rare case of schizophrenia — one that isn't boring, at least at first. I also discovered what my doctors didn't tell me about recovering: Number one, it is possible, even for severely ill patients; number two, it can be accomplished in as little as six months; number three, how it's done. The cure is more than a bottle of pills. What follows are the fascinating bits of information I gleaned from the book, the ten commandments for managing schizophrenia (what you can do for yourself beyond doctors, pills, and therapy):

(1) Get at least eight hours of sleep every night. This is very important. Some schizophrenics need as much as eleven hours a night.

(2) Do not use stimulants of any kind, not even that "innocent" cup of coffee or can of regular pop.

(3) Do not drink alcoholic beverages. They are a poor mix with psych meds.

(4) Don't use marijuana or any other recreational

or unprescribed drug. The effects can be disastrous. Marijuana got me into my first hospital.

(5) Eat a minimum of foods containing white flour or white sugar. It's empty calories, and the average schizophrenic is fat enough already, due to side effects of their meds.

(6) Don't eat junk food (see #5).

(7) Don't live in a toxic atmosphere. This goes for both physically polluted and emotionally stressful and unhealthy situations. I couldn't live at home, as my Dad had a drinking problem, but the boarding homes were a poor substitute. This is something that needs to be looked into.

(8) Have more than one loved one. If you lose your only friend, you are up a creek without a paddle.

(9) Don't live alone. Schizophrenics need someone around to ground them in reality; also, everyone needs companionship.

(10) Get plenty of moderate exercise every day. Exercise relieves stress and keeps the body fit. Do something you enjoy so you'll keep doing it.

Besides these ten, it is important to have a comfortable, low-stress, easy-going, but satisfying lifestyle. Schizophrenics can work, have social lives, and basically be "normal" — IF they mind their P's and Q's (the ten commandments). Volunteer work is a good start, then part-time paid work, then full-time paid work. Once schizophrenics are stabilized, they can drive, provided they don't have other handicaps, such as epilepsy. Schizophrenics often have poor people skills. They usually "break" in their teens and stop maturing emotionally until they recover. Still, once they are mature enough, they can marry and even have children. (Some doctors advise against children because of the heredity factor, but diabetes is hereditary, and I've never heard of doctors encouraging diabetics to remain childless. Leave it up to the individuals and their mates; they know what they can handle.)

How to handle doctors? To find a good doctor, ask around. Especially ask other schizophrenics and their families. Once you have a doctor, appreciate him or her. They'll work harder for you if they know they're appreciated. Butter them up a little. Don't do what I did with one of my doctors: When I ran out of medicine and was manic, or frenzied, I went into his office and lambasted his entire profession to his face! Anyway, once a positive rapport is established, you can bring up med problems or other problems. No counselor has all the answers. It is actually the patient's job to solve problems; the counselor's job is to guide them through the process. If a good rapport simply can't be accomplished due to clashing personalities or values (I had a counselor say, "God is irrelevant," and I am very spiritual), find another counselor. (I did.)

About drug side-effects: There are many, and most are short-lived and minor (as long as the patient isn't overmedicated), like dry mouth or mild constipation, but some are cause for concern and should be brought to the doctor's attention. They are:

(1) Akathisia — the "walkies" — inability to sit still, constant pacing.

(2) Dystonia — stiffness, drooling, eyes rolling upward.

(3) Akinesia — the "zombie" effect — looks a lot like the apathy some schizophrenics experience as part of their illness.

(4) Photosensitivity — extreme sensitivity to sunlight. Five minutes in the sun can cause a severe burn.

(5) Tardive dyskinesia — smacking of the lips, chewing the tongue, jerking the arms — all involuntary. If this isn't caught early, it becomes permanent, even if meds are withdrawn.

(6) Increased psychosis — ironic, isn't it?

(7) Suicide attempts.

(8) Trouble reaching orgasm.

(9) Seizures.

(10) Neuroleptic malignant syndrome — starts with stiffness and fever. If this isn't caught early, it leads to death!

(11) Weight gain.

Normally, a med change will solve all these problems! Bring the problem to your doctor. If he doesn't listen, fire him! Get another doctor! In 1980, when Hyde wrote the book I got all this information from, there were three categories of schizophrenia — one, paranoid schizophrenia; two, process schizophrenia; and three, acute schizophrenia. The first two are long-term illnesses; the third comes and leaves in a matter of days or weeks, with or without treatment. But schizophrenia is usually such a frightening and painful experience that therapy is needed to help the patient cope. It is critical that the patient feel respected and taken seriously no matter what they say, or trust will not be established. It takes a skillful therapist to deal with a schizophrenic patient! Paranoid and process schizophrenics usually don't improve without intervention; they get worse.

One final note: There is still a stigma surrounding "having a nervous breakdown" or "going crazy." It helps if the patients dress normally, keep up hygiene, and act as "normal" as possible. Early on in recovery, they may not be able to do that. So if teased, they'll have to "sweat it out." It helps to remind themselves of people who use wheelchairs or are retarded or have epilepsy — any serious handicap. It's no more shameful, but it's often perceived that way by an ignorant public. They CAN do what I do — join consumer groups to advocate for themselves and educate that ignorant public! Author's note: Common statistics say one third of schizophrenics recover completely, one third partially recover, and one third stay the same or get worse.

In the twenty-three years since my original diagnosis of schizophrenia, I have also been diagnosed with thought disorders, mood disorders, sleep disorders, eating disorders, character disorders, personality disorders, even a seizure disorder. I have been on many different medications and had most of the side effects mentioned. I have also been to many doctors and therapists, had many treatments, both outpatient and inpatient, and been in five hospitals for a total of fourteen stays between them. I have learned from this that warm, loving support is one of the most important things a mentally ill person needs to recover. The other is hope.

When Jim, a friend who also has a handicap (in his case, blindness), told me I "have what it takes" to make a life for myself beyond doctors and pills and sitting in front of the TV all day, I took the job he offered and later, wanting more, went back to school and launched my dream career, being a writer. I am not rich. I've so far completed only one novel, and it hasn't sold (yet), but I am doing what I love and have had many articles, essays, short stories, and poems published. From this I derive much joy and satisfaction, and it adds a touch to my identity. Now I'm a "writer," not just a "schizophrenic." I also know I'm educating the public about mental illness and helping people realize that the "dangerous mental patient" stereotyped in the movies is just a person, not so dangerous at all, like you or me. He or she is ordinary and could be your next-door neighbor.

I mentioned support. I have found some very good support groups over the years. Recovery, Inc., is the one that helped me the most. I have also been a member of Al-Anon, Codependents Anonymous, Schizophrenics Anonymous, Emotions Anonymous, and the Mental Health Association of Nebraska. I am currently a member of this last one. The wonderful thing about a support group is you find out you're not alone in your "weird" experiences. And you make friends, and you gather information. I am also currently a member of an on-line support group for people with epilepsy. I am finding out loads of information my doctors didn't take time to tell me! It's so wonderful to be understood when you find out others were also rejected by friends, fired from jobs, asked to leave schools, picked up by the police, and even locked up for having seizures in public! This story is about mental illness, so I won't belabor epilepsy, which is not a form of mental illness.

I believe the three most important things mental patients need are the three most important things all of us need: faith, hope, and love. I've mentioned hope and love (in the form of loving families, friends, and support groups); now I will end with this: If it weren't for my faith that God is still running things and allowed my illness to come to bring me to Himself (make me see my need for a Savior and that it was all for my GOOD), I wouldn't have much of a leg to stand on. Since I became a Christian on May 13, 1994, I have found a spiritual stability that has reduced my symptoms considerably, although I am still under a doctor's care. This care is not a sin, despite what some pastors preach. Even St. Luke, who wrote the book of Luke in the Bible, was a doctor!

STOPPING THE WAR

By Jack Kornfield

*When we step out of the battles,
we see anew, as the* Tao te Ching
says, "with eyes unclouded by longing."

THE unawakened mind tends to make war against
the way things are. To follow a path with heart, we
must understand the whole process of making war,
within ourselves and without, how it begins and how
it ends. War's roots are in ignorance. Without understanding, we can easily become frightened by life's
fleeting changes, the inevitable losses, disappoint-
ments, the insecurity of our aging and death.
Misunderstanding leads us to fight against life, running from pain or grasping at security and pleasures
that by their nature can never be truly satisfying.

Our war against life is expressed in every dimen-
sion of our experience, inner and outer. Our children
see, on average, eighteen thousand murders and violent acts on TV before they finish high school. The

leading cause of injury for American women is beatings by the men they live with. We carry on wars within ourselves, with our families and communities, among races and nations worldwide. The wars between peoples are a reflection of our own inner conflict and fear. My teacher Achaan Chah described this ongoing battle:

"We human beings are constantly in combat, at war to escape the fact of being so limited, limited by so many circumstances we cannot control. But instead of escaping, we continue to create suffering, waging war with good, waging war with evil, waging war with what is too small, waging war with what is too big, waging war with what is too short or too long or right or wrong, courageously carrying on the battle."

Contemporary society fosters our mental tendency to deny or suppress our awareness of reality. Ours is a society of denial that conditions us to protect ourselves from any direct difficulty and discomfort. We expend enormous energy denying our insecurity; fighting pain, death, and loss; and hiding from the basic truths of the natural world and of our own nature.

To insulate ourselves from the natural world, we have air conditioners, heated cars, and clothes that protect us from every season. To insulate ourselves from the specter of aging and infirmity, we put smiling young people in our advertisements while we relegate our old people to nursing homes and old-age establishments. We hide our mental patients in mental hospitals. We relegate our poor to ghettos. And we construct freeways around these ghettos so that those fortunate enough not to live in them will not see the suffering they house.

We deny death to the extent that even a ninety-six-year-old woman, newly admitted to a hospice, complained to the director, "Why me?" We almost pretend that our dead aren't dead, dressing up corpses in fancy clothes and makeup to attend their own funerals as if they were going to parties. In our charade with ourselves, we pretend that our war is not really war. We have changed the name of the War Department to the Defense Department and call a whole class of nuclear missiles Peacemakers!

How do we manage so consistently to close ourselves off from the truths of our existence? We use denial to turn away from the pains and difficulties of life. We use addictions to support our denial. Ours has been called the Addicted Society, with over twenty million alcoholics, ten million drug addicts, and millions addicted to gambling, food, sexuality, unhealthy relationships, or the speed and busyness of work. Our addictions are the compulsively repetitive attachments we use to avoid feeling and to deny the difficulties of our lives. Advertising urges us to keep pace, to keep consuming, smoking, drinking and craving food, money, and sex. Our addictions serve to numb us to what is, to help us avoid our own experience, and with great fanfare our society encourages these addictions.

Anne Wilson Schaef, author of *When Society Becomes an Addict*, has described it this way:

"The best-adjusted person in our society is the person who is not dead and not alive, just numb, a zombie. When you are dead you're not able to do the work of the society. When you are fully alive you are constantly saying 'No' to many of the processes of society, the racism, the polluted environment, the nuclear threat, the arms race, drinking unsafe water, and eating carcinogenic foods. Thus it is in the interests of our society to promote those things that take the edge off, keep us busy with our fixes, and keep us slightly numbed out and zombie-like. In this way our modern consumer society itself functions as an addict."

One of our most pervasive addictions is to speed. Technological society pushes us to increase the pace of our productivity and the pace of our lives. Panasonic recently introduced a new VHS tape recorder that was advertised as playing voice tapes at double the normal speed while lowering the tone to the normal speaking range. "Thus," the advertiser said, "you can listen to one of the great speeches by Winston Churchill or President Kennedy or a literary classic in half the time!" I wonder if they would recommend double-speed tapes for Mozart and Beethoven as well. Woody Allen commented on this obsession, saying he took a course in speed-reading and was able to read *War and Peace* in twenty minutes. "It's about Russia," he concluded.

In a society that almost demands life at double-time, speed and addictions numb us to our own experience. In such a society it is almost impossible to settle into our bodies or stay connected with our hearts, let alone connect with one another or the earth where we live. Instead, we find ourselves increasingly isolated and lonely, cut off from one another and the natural web of life. One person in a car, big houses, cellular phones, Walkman radios clamped to our ears, and a deep loneliness and sense of inner poverty. That is the most pervasive sorrow in our modern society. Not only have individuals lost the sense of their interconnection; this isolation is the sorrow of nations as well. The forces of separation and denial breed international misunderstanding, ecological disaster, and an endless series of conflicts between nation states.

On this earth, as I write today, more than forty wars and violent revolutions are killing thousands of men, women, and children. We have had one hundred fifteen wars since World War II, and there are only one hundred sixty-five countries in the entire world. Not a good track record for the human species. Yet what are we to do?

Genuine spiritual practice requires us to learn how to *stop the war.* This is a first step, but actually it must be practiced over and over until it becomes our way of being. The inner stillness of a person who truly "is peace" brings peace to the whole interconnected web of life, both inner and outer. To stop the war, we need to begin with ourselves. Mohandas Gandhi understood this when he said:

"I have only three enemies. My favorite enemy, the one most easily influenced for the better, is the British Empire. My second enemy, the Indian people, is far more difficult. But my most formidable opponent is a man named Mohandas K.

Gandhi. With him I seem to have very little influence."

Like Gandhi, we cannot easily change ourselves for the better through an act of will. This is like wanting the mind to get rid of itself or pulling ourselves up by our own bootstraps. Remember how short-lived are most New Year's resolutions? When we struggle to change ourselves, we in fact only continue the patterns of self-judgment and aggression. We keep the war against ourselves alive. Such acts of will usually backfire and, in the end, often strengthen the addiction or denial we intend to change.

One young man came to meditation with a deep distrust for authority. He had rebelled in his family — understandably, for he had quite an abusive mother. He had rebelled in school and dropped out to join the counterculture. He had fought with a girlfriend who, he said, wanted to control him. Then he went to India and Thailand to find his freedom. After an initial positive experience in meditation, he signed up for a period of practice in a monastery. He decided to practice very strictly and make himself clear and pure and peaceful. However, after a short time, he found himself in conflict again. The daily chores didn't leave him enough time to meditate nonstop. The sounds of visitors and an occasional car were disturbing his meditation. The teacher, he felt, wasn't giving enough guidance, and due to this, his meditation was weak and his mind wouldn't stop. He struggled to quiet himself and resolved to do it his own way but ended up fighting himself.

Finally, the teacher called him to task at the end of a group meditation. "You are struggling with everything. How is it that the food bothers you, the sounds bother you, the chores bother you, even your mind bothers you? Doesn't it seem odd? What I want to know is, when you hear a car come by, does it really come in and bother you, or are you going out to bother it? Who is bothering whom?" Even this young man had to laugh, and that moment was the beginning of his learning to stop the war.

The purpose of a spiritual discipline is to give us a way to stop the war, not by our force of will, but organically, through understanding and gradual training. Ongoing spiritual practice can help us cultivate a new way of relating to life in which we let go of our battles.

When we step out of the battle, we see anew, as the *Tao te Ching* says, "with eyes unclouded by longing." We see how each of us creates conflict. We see our constant likes and dislikes, the fight to resist all that frightens us. We see our own prejudice, greed, and territoriality. All this is hard for us to look at, but it is really there. Then, underneath these ongoing battles, we see pervasive feelings of incompleteness and fear. We see how much our struggle with life has kept our heart closed.

When we let go of our battles and open our heart to things as they are, then we come to rest in the present moment. This is the beginning and the end of spiritual practice. Only in this moment can we discover that which is timeless. Only here can we find the love that we seek. Love in the past is simply memory, and love in the future is fantasy. Only in the reality of the present can we love, can we awaken, can we find peace and understanding and connection with ourselves and the world.

A sign in a Las Vegas casino aptly says, "You Must Be Present to Win." Stopping the war and becoming present are two sides of the same activity. To come into the present is to stop the war. To come into the present means to experience whatever is here and now. Most of us have spent our lives caught up in plans, expectations, ambitions for the future; in regrets, guilt, or shame about the past. When we come into the present, we begin to feel the life around us again, but we also encounter whatever we have been avoiding. We must have the courage to face whatever is present — our pain, our desires, our grief, our loss, our secret hopes, our love, everything that moves us most deeply. As we stop the war, each of us will find something from which we have been running — our loneliness, our unworthiness, our boredom, our shame, our unfulfilled desires. We must face these parts of ourselves as well.

You may have heard of "out-of-the-body experiences," full of lights and visions. A true spiritual path demands something more challenging, what could be called an "in-the-body experience." We must connect to our body, to our feelings, to our life just now if we are to awaken.

To live in the present demands an ongoing and unwavering commitment. As we follow a spiritual path, we are required to stop the war not once but many times. Over and over we feel the familiar tug of thoughts and reactions that take us away from the present moment. When we stop and listen, we can feel how each thing that we fear or crave (really two sides of the same dissatisfaction) propels us out of our hearts into a false idea of how we would like life to be. If we listen even more closely, we can feel how we have learned to sense ourselves as limited by that fear and identified with that craving. From this *small* sense of ourselves, we often believe that our own happiness can come only from possessing something or can be only at someone else's expense.

To stop the war and come into the present is to discover a greatness of our own heart that can include the happiness of all beings as inseparable from our own. When we let ourselves feel the fear, the discontent, the difficulties we have always avoided, our heart softens. Just as it is a courageous act to face all the difficulties from which we have always run, it is also an act of compassion. According to Buddhist scriptures, compassion is the "quivering of the pure heart" when we have allowed ourselves to be touched by the pain of life. The knowledge that we can do this and survive helps us to awaken the greatness of our heart. With greatness of heart, we can sustain a presence in the midst of life's suffering, in the midst of life's fleeting impermanence. We can open to the world — its ten thousand joys and ten thousand sorrows.

As we allow the world to touch us deeply, we recognize that just as there is pain in our own lives, so there is pain in everyone else's life. This is the birth of wise understanding. Wise understanding sees that suffering is inevitable, that all things that are born die. Wise understanding sees and accepts life as a whole. With wise understanding, we allow ourselves to contain all things, both dark and light, and we come to a sense of peace. This is not the peace of denial or running away, but the peace we find in the heart that has rejected nothing, that touches all things with compassion.

Through stopping the war, we can embrace our own personal griefs and sorrows, joys and triumphs. With greatness of heart, we can open to the people around us, to our family, to our community, to the social problems of the world, to our collective history. With wise understanding, we can live in harmony with our life, with the universal law called the Tao or dharma, the truth of life.

A Buddhist student who is a Vietnam veteran tells a story about a meditation retreat where he experienced for the first time the terrible atrocities he had witnessed as a soldier. For many years he had carried the Vietnam War inside himself because he hadn't had a way to face the memories of what he had been through. Finally, he stopped.

I had served as a field medical corpsman with the Marine Corps ground forces in the early days of the war in the mountainous provinces on the border of what was then North and South Vietnam. Our casualty rates were high, as were those of the villagers we treated when circumstances permitted.

It had been eight years since my return when I attended my first meditation retreat. At least twice a week for all those years, I had sustained the same recurring nightmares common to many combat veterans: dreaming that I was back there, facing the same dangers; witnessing the same incalculable suffering; waking suddenly, alert, sweating, scared. At the retreat, the nightmares did not occur during sleep. They filled the mind's eye during the day, at sittings, during walking meditations, at meals. Horrific wartime flashbacks were superimposed over a quiet redwood grove at the retreat center. Sleepy students in the dormitory became body parts strewn about a makeshift morgue on the DMZ. What I gradually came to see was that as I relived these memories as a thirty-year-old spiritual seeker, I was also enduring for the first time the full emotional impact of experiences that as a twenty-year-old medic I was simply unprepared to withstand.

I began to realize that my mind was gradually yielding up memories so terrifying, so life-denying, and so spiritually eroding that I had ceased to be consciously aware that I was still carrying them around. I was, in short, beginning to undergo a profound catharsis by openly facing that which I had most feared and therefore most strongly suppressed.

At the retreat I was also plagued by a more current fear, that having released the inner demons of war, I would be unable to control them, that they would now rule my days as well as my nights; but what I experienced instead was just the opposite. The visions of slain friends and dismembered children gradually gave way to other half-remembered scenes from that time and place — the entrancing, intense beauty of a jungle forest, a thousand different shades of green, a fragrant breeze blowing over beaches so white and dazzling they seemed carpeted by diamonds.

What also arose at the retreat for the first time was a deep sense of compassion for my past and present self — compassion for the idealistic young would-be physician, forced to witness the unspeakable obscenities of which humankind is capable, and for the haunted veteran who could not let go of memories he could not acknowledge he carried.

Since the first retreat, the compassion has stayed

with me. Through practice and continued inner relaxation, it has grown to sometimes encompass those around me as well, when I'm not too self-conscious to let it do so. While the memories have also stayed with me, the nightmares have not. The last of the sweating screams happened in silence, fully awake, somewhere in Northern California over a decade ago.

Lloyd Burton, now a father and a teacher, stopped the war in himself through an uncompromising courage to be present. And in that process a healing compassion arose for himself and those around him.

This is a task for all of us. Individually and as a society, we must move from the pain of our speed, our addictions, and our denial to stop the war. The greatest of transformations can come from this simple act. Even Napoleon Bonaparte understood this when, at the end of his life, he stated, "Do you know what astonished me most in the world? The inability of force to create anything. In the long run, the sword is always beaten by the spirit."

Compassion and a greatness of heart arise whenever we stop the war. The deepest desire we have for our human heart is to discover how to do this. We all share a longing to go beyond the confines of our own fear or anger or addiction, to connect with something greater than "I," "me," and "mine," greater than our small story and our small self. It is possible to stop the war and come into the timeless present — to touch a great ground of being that contains all things. This is the purpose of a spiritual discipline and of choosing a path with heart — to discover peace and connectedness in ourselves and to stop the war in us and around us.

A Meditation on Stopping the War Within

Sit comfortably for a few minutes, letting your body be at rest. Let your breathing be easy and natural. Bring your attention into the present, sit quietly, and notice whatever sensations are present in your body. In particular, be aware of any sensations, tensions, or pains you may have been fighting. Do not try to change them; simply notice them with an interested and kind attention. In each area of struggle you discover, let your body relax and your heart soften. Open to whatever you experience without fighting. Let go of the battle. Breathe quietly, and let it be.

Then, after a time, shift your attention to your heart and mind. Now notice what feelings and thoughts are present. In particular, be aware of any feelings or thoughts you are now struggling with, fighting, denying, or avoiding. Notice them with an interested and kind attention. Let your heart be soft. Open to whatever you experience without fighting. Let go of the battle. Breathe quietly, and let it be.

Continue to sit quietly. Then cast your attention over all the battles that still exist in your life. Sense them inside yourself. If you have an ongoing struggle with your body, be aware of that. If you have been fighting inner wars with your feelings, been in conflict with your own loneliness, fear, confusion, grief, anger, or addiction, sense the struggle you have been waging. Notice the struggles in your thoughts as well. Be aware of how you have carried on the inner battles. Notice the inner armies, the inner dictators, the inner fortifications. Be aware of all that you have fought within yourself, of how long you have perpetuated the conflict.

Gently, with openness, allow each of these experiences to be present. Simply notice each of them in turn with interest and kind attention. In each area of struggle, let your body, heart, and mind be soft. Open to whatever you experience without fighting. Let it be present just as it is. Let go of the battle. Breathe quietly, and let yourself be at rest. Invite all parts of yourself to join you at the peace table in your heart.

SURVIVING SUICIDE

By Richard O'Connor, Ph.D.

I recently passed my forty-eighth birthday. No big deal, except that for years I believed I wouldn't live past my thirty-eighth. That was the age my mother was when she took her own life, and I was obsessed with the idea that I couldn't outlive her, that whatever drove her over the edge would catch up with me. I've since learned that this is not an uncommon belief with the children of suicides.

When I was fifteen, I came home from school one day to find that my mother had bolted the doors and taped up a note saying she was out shopping and I should wait at a neighbor's. I knew something was wrong and was climbing in a window when my father came driving in after work. We discovered her body together. She had gone to the basement to commit suicide.

She had put a plastic bag over her head and sat down at the table where I played with my chemistry set. She ran the gas line from my Bunsen burner into the plastic bag and turned on the gas. Later we learned that she had also taken a lethal dose of a sleeping pill that my father sold in his job as a pharmaceutical representative. Her body was cold, so she must have started to set things up soon after we had left the house in the morning. This was not any cry for help; she took great care to make sure she would end her life.

Children of suicides have a lot of trouble with grief. As Freud made clear many years ago, the more ambivalent our feelings about the person who has died, the more difficult our grieving is. Besides the expected feeling of loss, the hole in your heart that appears with any death, besides the fear and sense of vulnerability that strikes any child who loses a parent, we have more layers added on. We feel hurt and rejected because our parent has chosen quite deliberately to end life rather than be a parent for us. We feel angry — a very mild term for the kind of rage I felt — and betrayed by the selfishness of their act. And of course, we feel guilty because of our hurt and anger, because part of us understands our parent's pain and because we wonder if we're not responsible.

This still haunts me. Today something made me remember the general lack of physical contact in my family. I realized that I always blamed myself. I thought of myself as a stiff, aloof little kid who sent out antihugging vibes. Today I know children can't do that, but my reflexive thought is that I could and did.

After my mother died, what I felt, consciously, was anger. I blamed her for being selfish, and I could not believe that she had ever really cared about me. My father and I grew apart; he quickly remarried, and I had a new family before I was ready. Rather than let myself feel rejected by my parents, I rejected them. I developed an icy armor. I threw myself into the one thing I knew I could do well — school. I had terrific grades, terrific SATs, was editor of the yearbook. I won a scholarship to a college a thousand miles from home. I told myself I'd never look back.

But I was unprepared for the fact that there would be many people as bright as I attending college. It turned out everything I'd accomplished in high school was easy; now that I didn't stand out, things were tough. I got scared. I became desperate to fit in. My grades were lousy. I wasted four years of college and a few years afterward, scared and depressed. I had this self-image as a misunderstood genius who was going to write the great American novel or accomplish something else earth-shaking. But I didn't write or do anything else constructive. My idea of myself as a misunderstood genius was a pitiful attempt not to need anyone. I didn't realize my real fear, that if I let myself depend on someone again, I could lose them again — *and of course it would be my fault because deep down inside, I was truly unlovable.* I started mixing alcohol and pills, the same sleeping pills my mother had used. There were nights when I didn't care if I woke up the next morning.

Something motivated me to get help. I went to see a therapist a friend recommended. It turned out to be a husband-and-wife team, practicing some of the gimmicky Transactional Analysis-type stuff so popular in the '70s. They passed me back and forth between them and had me join a group they were running. It was pretty hokey but very helpful. They really helped me realize I needed to change my life, to stop hanging back and embrace living. During this time, I changed careers and got married.

I went to graduate school and did pretty well, but I had a problem with stage fright; I couldn't speak up in class. I told one of my professors about it and also a little about my background. She recommended that I see a colleague of hers, a psychoanalytically trained psychiatrist. I thought I was moving up in the world. I had learned enough in graduate school to look down on the therapy that I had thought had helped me as not scientifically respectable. Also, the husband-and-wife team were social workers; the new guy was a psychiatrist. Despite the fact that I was in training to be a social worker myself, I caught the profession's own doubts about its self-worth and the popular perception of the pecking order in mental health.

But I ran into trouble in my therapy. When the work of mourning is complete, we put a picture of our loved one on our mantelpiece, and sometimes we look at it and cry, but we get on with life. When mourning is incomplete, as is usually the case with survivors of suicide, we can't put the picture on the mantelpiece because the person is still within us. We become the person we lost, as I was doing. I had recurrent dreams of being trapped in basements. And my symptoms got worse.

Just after my first appointment with the new psychiatrist, he came down with a serious illness that laid him up for several months. When he came back, he seemed weak and frail. In his office on the twenty-third floor, he sat between me and the window. I had a full-blown anxiety attack in his office, feeling that something was drawing me out the window. It was devastating, the worst feeling that I ever remembered, and it happened every session after that for three years. I had no conscious desire to die; rather, it was as if there was a little demon within me that would force me out the window to join my mother.

You could call this an iatrogenic problem, or you could say I was making him a present of my symptom, giving him the opportunity to help me. Whatever it was, it didn't work. Perhaps if he hadn't been sick, if he hadn't presented himself as so gentle and tentative anyway, I would have felt safe. As it was, I couldn't feel comforted in his presence. This was despite the fact that I consciously liked and respected him, and still do.

My life on the outside went along pretty well — my wife and I had children, and I discovered I was a good father. I did well in graduate school and began to enjoy my work. But every week I would be sweating bullets in the psychiatrist's office, convinced I was doomed. My phobia generalized; soon I couldn't go up in any tall buildings or cross bridges.

Perhaps this helped me by confining my depression, as it were, to this one symptom and letting me get on with my life. Even if this were true, though, it's not how therapy is supposed to work. Besides, those weekly episodes of pure terror were eating away at my self-esteem, making me feel as if there was a demon inside me I couldn't control. It seems incredible to me now that both the psychiatrist and I let this drag on for so long. I hope that if I were the therapist in this situation, now I would say, "Look, this is crazy. Let's try something different. Let's try some medication or behavior therapy, or let me refer you to a colleague for a fresh start."

I was thirty-five and still believed time was running out for me and that I wasn't getting the help I needed. I extricated myself from the situation by getting accepted as an analytic subject at the Chicago Institute for Psychoanalysis. I knew this was something my psychiatrist couldn't argue with. We parted company.

When I met my analyst, I was somewhat disappointed that he wasn't much older than me — how much could he know? But he was a psychologist, which seemed like maybe a good compromise between psychiatry and social work, and he had already published with some high-powered thinkers in analysis. I kind of liked him — he was pretty unstuffy for an analyst, had a quirky sense of humor, and seemed to respect me. I stayed with him for another five years, getting through my thirty-eighth birthday unscathed, with a real sense of relief. We worked on my phobia together, and I felt comforted and supported. I enjoyed the analytic process and recommend it highly as a growth experience.

Somewhere along the line, I learned to understand my mother, to forgive her a little. She knew what her choices were. She had seen her older sister impoverished by divorce, finally forced into another abusive marriage as an economic necessity. Isolated from her family, stuck in a loveless marriage, my mother could see no alternatives. Her suicide was both a result of despair and a gesture of defiance. She was so far down in the well, her vision so distorted, that her decision made sense at the time.

I identify myself now as someone with depression, a "recovering" depressive. I have a psychiatrist I trust prescribe my medications and a therapist I see regularly. I'm still working on all this; in discussing my book with my father, he gave me still another perspective on my mother. He reminded me of how much she had loved me and how guilty she felt about being depressed, the horrible debt that the cost of her treatment had placed upon them. In a sad, twisted way, her suicide was also a self-sacrifice. She saw herself as a burden on us; removing that burden was, in her mind, a gift to us. I'm trying to digest this point of view, and it certainly helps me feel less anger toward her, but the terrible implicit sadness is something I can only take in small doses.

Last year my analyst sent me a copy of a paper he was writing. He used an incident in my analysis to illustrate a point he wanted to make. In doing so, he had to summarize my background and treatment. I was knocked for a loop. There was much in the analysis that I had repressed. I had forgotten all the times I spent on his couch, writhing in terror and anxiety, trying not to hear what he had to say. We had gotten past my height phobia. There were times when I felt very safe with him and times when I didn't feel safe at all. And seeing my case history laid out in objective clinical terms, I was overwhelmed with feeling for myself: pity, but not self-pity in the usual sense, more the kind of objective empathy we might feel for a stranger. Also, I could see that while he had a particular theoretical point of view about my problems, I had a different one. This wasn't news. We had often disagreed, during the analysis, on this subject, but both felt we were in good agreement as far as the practical implications for me. But it got me thinking about how doctrinaire I used to be and how I seem to have gotten away from that.

What all this has made me realize is that therapy — and probably medication — doesn't really work for the reasons professionals think it does. My first therapists, with their naíve enthusiasm, helped me greatly using methods that no one takes seriously now. My second, with all his expertise, did me more harm than good. My analyst helped me a great deal, but I think he did it by treating me like a caring, respectful friend I could lean on, and he thinks he did it by helping me feel safe with my impulses. Psychopharmacologists think that Prozac reduces rejection sensitivity and enhances self-esteem, but they can't say how it works or even design an experiment to show exactly what it does. The therapists at the clinic where I work — from a variety of training, backgrounds, and disciplines — are very often quite helpful with their clients, but all have different explanations for how therapy works.

So it doesn't matter how you get better, as long as you get better. The wiser, warmer, more experienced therapists can probably help you more reliably, but I think it's like teaching a child how to ride a bicycle. You can explain how to steer and how the pedals work, but you can't explain balance and momentum. You have to hold the bicycle up while the child learns these things for himself.

We toss around the word "denial" like everyone knows what it means. How's this for an example: A well-trained psychotherapist, head of a clinic, who diagnoses people every day, has had at least three year-long episodes when he's had suicidal impulses; been self-destructive; couldn't sleep; and felt hopeless, helpless, and guilty. He is the son of a suicide and takes antidepressant medication, yet he doesn't recognize that he has depression. But I'm far from unique; we see two or three people like me in our clinic every week. People call us because things are falling apart — there's a psychosomatic disease, a marital problem, their kids are out of control, they're in trouble at work. But it often doesn't take much digging to find that the caller has been depressed for some time; the presenting symptom, the family problem, or the job problem is a manifestation, not a cause, of the depression. These are people who feel almost no joy in life; who have no hope, no ambition; who feel stuck, powerless, and perennially sad — *and who think this is the normal way to feel.* Depression grows in us so insidiously that it feels like our core self, and we can't imagine alternatives.

My work has helped me mourn. I have a depression self-help group. When TWA Flight 800 went down over Long Island Sound, some of the members confessed with shame that their first reaction was envy for the victims, who don't have to suffer with life anymore. My first reaction was shock; I've been depressed, but I've never felt that bad. Then, maybe that's how my mother felt. Then, how can I blame her?

Depression is a complex condition, and we still have a lot to learn about it. There is no doubt that it is somewhat hereditary and no doubt that something goes haywire in the brain chemistry of depression. But there is very often a history of loss in childhood and a recent traumatic loss that sets the first episode in motion. And there is a whole set of self-destructive defense mechanisms we learn in a futile effort to avoid further pain.

We try to control our grief. Because we fear that powerful emotions can permanently destabilize us, we seek to deny, rationalize, isolate, and "stuff" our feelings; but doing so just perpetuates the fear that emotions can destroy us. We don't display our feelings and so don't elicit comfort from those around us, and we continue to believe that we are strange. It's a short step then to believing that we are unworthy of love. We end up looking at life from the outside, feeling as if we are essentially different, hopeless to do anything about it, and ultimately at fault for our own suffering.

Now I find I have to practice being spontaneous, feeling my feelings, being present in the moment, and not always thinking that happiness will come in the future or feeling bitter about the past. I know this sounds awkward and forced, perhaps just psychobabble, to people who never lost these childhood skills. But learning any new skill is awkward at first, and it seems to be working for me. Recently, I've started dreaming about climbing *out* of basement windows.

Richard O'Connor's story, which can also be found in his book, Undoing Depression *and on his Web site (http://www.undoingdepression.com), provides us with an example of someone who suffers from depression, studies it, learns how to control it, and helps others in their effort to do the same.*

> ***"The journey of a thousand miles begins with a single step."***
>
> Lao-Tse

Chapter Three

POST-TRAUMATIC STRESS DISORDER

By William P. Whelan, Jr.

CURSE of the adult survivor of child abuse and the precursor to depression.

Hey, Mom, I love you! Man, did I ever. But she was so cruel to me. When I was ten, as long as my little mongrel dog, Blacky, was under the bed, Teddy under my arm, and my little blankie over me at night, all was bearable. Then Blacky was run over, and Mom made fun of me for crying.

Shortly after, she decided I was too old for a teddy bear and a blankie, so in front of my brothers and sister, she threw them into the fireplace. As I screamed hysterically, we all watched them die. It was truly the all-time worst thing she ever did to me. All the beatings, all the days she told me I was a mistake and shouldn't have been born, that I was worthless, were nothing compared to this. My little heart was broken. I was stripped bare and barely functional.

A few weeks later, I was hospitalized with rheumatic fever, resulting in damage to my heart. But alas, after a long recovery, like all of us, I grew up.

When violence becomes the model in a family, children spend most of their time, energy, and thoughts on survival rather than growth and development. They develop a sort of violence-oriented ESP, an early warning system that provides split-second notice for self-protection. In order to stay alive in that unlivable reality of depressing, traumatic circumstances, at a very young age they learn the technique of numbing.

Post-Traumatic Stress Disorder (PTSD) used to be called "shell shock." It's a condition that occurs as a response to the horrors of combat on the battlefield.

Statistics from the military indicate that fifty percent of PTSD cases will develop during the first week of combat. By the fourth week of combat, ninety-eight percent of the active troops will suffer the psychological injury called post-traumatic stress.

Many of our troops who fought the Vietnam War were treated for PTSD overseas. Hundreds of thousands of Vietnam vets were sent from jungle combat directly to their hometowns without any treatment. Today, many years later, some still suffer tremendously, both physically and psychologically, from PTSD.

Benjamin Colodzin, Ph.D., who has worked extensively with Vietnam vets and is a leading authority on PTSD, describes the disorder as "a sane reaction to an insane situation." He adds that having "strong reactions to ugly events doesn't mean you're crazy." War is an extreme and ugly event to experience.

Dr. Colodzin suggests that PTSD is "combat mode" behavior, but that behavior, which is necessary for survival in war, may become a hindrance in civilian life. A vet described his experience this way: "There are reactions that sometimes go on inside of me — in my feelings, my thoughts, my ways of acting — that have something to do with combat reflexes. Sometimes I may react to situations happening now with a way of acting that is meant to be used in survival situations, even when what is happening now isn't a question of survival."

Andrew Vachss, in his novel *Down in the Zero*, describes emotional abuse as the systemic diminishment of another. It is designed to reduce a child's self-concept to the point where the victim considers himself unworthy — unworthy of respect, unworthy of friendship, unworthy of the natural birthright of all children: love and protection.

Emotional abuse can be verbal or behavioral, active or passive, frequent or occasional. Regardless, it is often as painful as physical assault. And the pain lasts much longer. A parent's love is so important to a child that withholding it can cause a "failure to thrive" condition similar to that of children who have been denied adequate nutrition. Even the natural solace of siblings is denied to those victims of emotional abuse who have been designated as the family's "target child." The other children are quick to imitate their parents. Instead of learning the qualities every child will need as an adult — empathy, nurturing, and protectiveness — they learn the viciousness of a pecking order.

Whether as a deliberate target or an innocent bystander, the emotionally abused child inevitably struggles to "explain" the conduct of his abusers and ends up struggling for survival in a quicksand of self-blame.

Emotional abuse is unique because it is designed to make the victim feel guilty. Its effects are rarely seen because the emotionally abused tend to implode, turning the anger against themselves. Some depressed, emotionally abused children are programmed to fail so effectively that a part of their own personality "self-parents" by belittling and humiliating themselves. The primary weapon of emotional abusers is the deliberate infliction of guilt.

Part of one's recovery may be obtained through "forgiveness." For the victim of emotional abuse and the ensuing depression, self-help, through forgiveness, is a viable method to recovery. Adult survivors have only two life choices: learn to self-reference or remain victims. When your self-concept has been shredded, when you have been deeply injured and made to feel the injury was your entire fault, when you look for approval to those that cannot or will not provide it, you play the role assigned to you by your abusers. Victims carry the cure in their own hearts.

Salvation means learning self-respect, earning the respect of others, and making that respect the absolutely irreducible minimum requirement for all intimate relationships. For the emotionally abused, healing, in part, comes down to "forgiveness, for you and your abuser."

This description applies equally to the experience of the "survivor of family violence," specifically the people who were continually abused even when specific causal events are not totally remembered or cannot be verbalized because they occurred before the survivor developed language skills.

Our prisons are full of grown-up survivors of child abuse, many of whom suffer from PTSD and depression.

Children and adult survivors of childhood abuse also particularly evidence PTSD behaviors when they begin to confront their early experiences, either in re-emerging memories or sharing what happened with someone else, such as a therapist.

As so often happens in the course of confronting and disclosing traumatic events of childhood, the survivor will experience additional trauma as family members deny the survivor's memories, deny their own behaviors, and begin to scapegoat the survivor for being the bearer of bad news. Under these circumstances, PTS behaviors are likely to increase, at least for a while.

Usually the coping behaviors of PTS develop in late adolescence or young adulthood, when there is already a foundation to the personality structure. Many adult survivors of child abuse live various forms of dysfunctional lives, from alcohol and drug abuse to all the unfortunate methods of domestic violence.

Statistics prove that people who are raised in loving homes with appropriate discipline, who feel good about themselves, usually do not grow up depressed or become abusers.

Benjamin Colodzin, Ph.D., in his book *Trauma and Survival*, lists the following symptoms of PTS:

- Vigilance and scanning: watching out as if something dangerous were about to happen to you.

- Elevated startle response: being jumpy when something unexpected happens or when someone touches you from behind.

- Blunted affect or psychic numbing: reduction or

loss of the ability to feel and to be close to others, to experience happiness, love, creativity, playfulness, and spontaneity.

- Aggressive, controlling behavior: acting with violence (physical, mental, emotional, and/or verbal).

- Willingness to use force to get your way, even when it is not a survival situation.

- Interruption of memory and concentration: difficulty concentrating and remembering under certain conditions that activate survivor stress.

- Depression: in PTS the condition can reach an extreme and is marked by exhaustion, negative attitude, and apathy.

- Generalized anxiety: tension in the body, such as muscle or stomach cramps, headaches, etc.; worried thoughts, such as the belief that someone is after you; sustained feelings of fear and guilt; and low self-esteem.

- Episodes of rage: not to be confused with ordinary anger, this is a violent outburst marked with real danger for all present. Often more likely to occur after use of drugs or alcohol.

- Substance abuse: self-soothing with drugs or alcohol (use of prescription drugs as directed not included). Many PTS survivors use no chemical substances and do not drink.

- Intrusive recall: probably the most significant indicator of the presence of PTS. Old, usually ugly, memories that come to consciousness without warning. Happens both awake and asleep, in dreams. Night sweats often accompany intrusive recall in dreams.

- Dissociative experiences: memory of a traumatic event so powerful that present reality fades into background and is perceived as less real than the memory. In this state, one might believe that one is back in the old situation and begin to act, talk, and feel in ways that helped one survive in the past.

- Insomnia: difficulty falling asleep or staying asleep. Brought on by fear of intrusive recall in nightmares and high levels of pain and anxiety.

- Suicidal ideation: thinking about and planning one's death.

With society's focal point of attention on child abuse, more concentration needs to be on the "grown-up survivor of child abuse." This is where parental education needs to be channeled, to break the brutal aspects of family violence and to alleviate society of the tremendous financial burden associated with depression, drug and alcohol abuse, prison and court costs, and all the peripherals associated with this disorder.

This article was excerpted from the book *Friends of the Children,* the true story of a home for severely emotionally disturbed children on a Southern New Mexico ranch, founded by a New York saloonkeeper.

(The book may be previewed and ordered at www.billyskids.org.)

> *"Every child is an artist.*
> *The problem is to remain an artist*
> *once you grow up."*
>
> PABLO PICASSO

A MASK OF AUTHENTICITY

By Rev. Janet S. Oliver, NCC, LMHC

Lies, Secrets and Shame

I rest in reverie, coffee in hand, as I think about this article I have been asked to write. I am fifty-four years old, a Licensed Professional Mental Health Counselor, and an ordained minister. Married thirty years, I have had a successful private practice for over twenty-five years. I have served in churches, taught in colleges, and been a national lecturer on a multitude of subjects in practical psychology. I am physically healthy, and on Prozac. If I were not on Prozac, I might be dead. Where do I start?

"Shame on you!" Mother said harshly, failing to note my gleeful smile. "Look at you. You're filthy! You're a bad girl. I can't leave you alone for a second. What would the neighbors think?" I didn't dare answer as a tight knot of fear grew in my three-year-old belly. My smile faded. "Shame on you. You are a bad girl," she kept yelling, making sure all the neighbors could hear.

Pushing the memory aside, I took another sip of coffee. No, I don't want to write this story. Not today anyway. Then I noted the unwelcome tightness pressing in my midsection, "Damn!" I said out loud, wondering if one ever recovers from these painful childhood memories. "How many times?" I blurted angrily into the silence of the morning. It was a shock to hear my voice for the first time since waking, but the memory refused to fade.

Happily covered in thick, gooey mud, surrounded by eight carefully constructed patties drying in the sun, I turned to look at the angry, frowning mouth and red puffy nose looming high above. Mother smelled funny again, like when she and Dad came back from their cocktail parties at the Country Club. I wondered what was coming next, knowing she didn't smell like that when she put the clean blue overalls on me before telling me to go out and play.

It was hot in the Albuquerque sun, and the shade of the apple tree was cool. The hose watered its thirsty roots, and the warm clay mud felt squishy through my little fingers.

I was confused. I was a "bad girl." I was always a bad girl for something, but mostly I never knew why. I was just bad. And I was always sick too. Why was I always so sick? I guess I was just bad. How do I not be so bad? I looked down at my muddy overalls.

"Look at me when I speak to you," she demanded as she yanked my arm from the water as though she had forgotten a body was attached.

Mother took a lot of white pills and was always depressed. Sometimes she was nice, but not for long. It wasn't okay to have fun, even when she told me to go outside and have fun. It was always okay to be quiet, though, but not too quiet. Mother had headaches, and quiet was just fine for her, unless I was too quiet. Then she would get suspicious and hunt me down, yelling at me for being lazy or sneaking around behind her back. I never thought she liked me much, but Dad would always say, "Your Mother loves you so much."

"Damned if you do, damned if you don't, huh?" said Frank, my gentle therapist, thirty-five years later as I sought to sort out my confusion and depression. "Sounds like years of double messages, lies, and secrets. How did you make it?" he asked with a deep and sensitive compassion. I started to cry.

I sipped the sweetened coffee, allowing the thoughts to drift in. I know I don't want to do this article, but I said I would. Damn! It may again mean sleepless nights as the "stuff" still has the power to cause pain.

Those of us who have managed to overcome depression, or are at least in a remission of sorts, don't relish the idea of reliving memories which could become triggers for further discomfort. We know that facing the triggers is part of healing, but when wellness is present, why rock the boat? Do I stay behind my mask of authenticity and competency, a safe place to reside, or do I once again challenge myself to a deeper understanding by engaging the lies, secrets, and shame?

What We Live With

"What we lived with, we learned. What we learned, we practiced. What we practiced, we became. What we have become, we can change."
— *Earnie Larsen*

These powerful words from a lecture given by noted author and speaker Earnie Larsen in 1988 rattle around in my head as I seek to put some order to my ancient memories. These words became the key to my personal and therapeutic philosophy for many years, prior to Prozac.

In the late '80s, a slew of workshops were presented nationally and internationally for adult children of alcoholics. This cult of thousands flocked together to try to learn what healthy was after years of learning to do life in the midst of lies, secrets, shame, fear, and sadness. Surviving a childhood of abuse is a unique journey, but not all effects were learned. Chemical addiction is a physical disease, and studies indicate that tendencies are genetically passed on. An important symptom frequently inherited with this disease is the tendency toward depression.

Although we were financially comfortable, Mother was constantly depressed and tried many things to feel "up." She could get "up" by creating an argument with my Dad. She could get "up" by making herself upset over something I had done that she disapproved of. She could get "up" by going on a spending spree, which would leave us in debt for months. Generally, she settled for alcohol as her drug of choice to numb the unacceptable feelings of depression and other emotional agonies that tortured her soul. Although she sought psychiatric care, the analytic psychotherapies of her day didn't help. When I was fifteen, the ravages of a difficult menopause tore into her life, and she chose an ugly suicide.

Healthy people don't commit suicide, but children don't know this. They only know what they see and experience. At fifteen life seemed heavy. I was a social outsider at school. The frequent allergies and colds kept me tired and weak, and I was terrified to go to medical doctors, having seen horrid medical abuse of my Mother. I was emotionally exhausted from years of inconsistent, unpredictable chaos, hiding, lying, and faking a life I had not been taught how to live effectively. Secretly, I was thrilled my Mother was dead and totally ashamed of the feeling. Completely relieved, I did not cry. Instead, I turned to the safety of silence.

Honest feelings were unwelcome in our family. Blame and shame was the game. Lies and fake smiles were expected, and guessing about what to do right was the way to survive. I was supposed to know what was *normal* and just do it, even though I hadn't a clue.

"You are the coldest young lady I have ever known," said my never-present Dad on the day of the funeral. "Can't you even shed a tear for your Mother? Didn't you care for her at all?" I was silent. "You never cared for anyone but yourself. You are so damn selfish. You're going to turn out crazy just like your Mother. Just you wait and see," was his guilt-ridden, grieving edict to me.

"So, not only am I bad, but I am going to be 'crazy' too, just like my Mother. I guess I am crazy, or I wouldn't be here, huh, Doc?"

Frank smiled gently, "So you got to carry on all the family guilt and shame too?" He paused. "Has it ever occurred to you that you may have also inherited some tendencies to her chemical imbalances?"

In my mid-forties, with a successful private practice, I didn't want to hear this. I went into the professions of counseling and ministry to prove to the world (and mostly myself) I wasn't crazy, and I kept proving this over and over again. I felt my mask of authenticity cracking. *No, no, don't look any further inside, please!* I screamed in silence, though my face wore a mask of the calm listener. My thoughts raced. I've done the proper degrees, therapeutic journaling, individual and group work. I've seen the shadow and the face of God in my soul. I know the sadness and the shame, but don't look any further — please.

It is amazing how good we can be at hiding from ourselves. Therapists in the '70s and '80s were far from immune to the erroneous and ignorant social stigmas attached to the new powerful and effective antidepressant drugs that emerged heavily into public awareness in those years. Like most therapists, I was doggedly devoted to the concept that the majority of depressed individuals could be and should be effectively treated without these drugs.

"Yeah, but..." was my defensive reply to Frank's suggestion. This was followed by a ton of logical, intellectual, professional bullshit justifications as to why my depression was anything but a "chemical" imbalance. I didn't want to think I needed antidepressant medications. The not-so-subtle cultural shame attached to antidepressant meds in the late '80s was not something I wanted to be a part of, even though it was okay for my clients to be on them. I was better than that and wanted nothing to do with more shame. Cognitive behavioral thought change techniques were for me, not drugs. On top of that, I had just graduated from, and been ordained by, a Christian seminary that specialized in a positive-thinking and God-centered focus as the answer to all healing needs. Frank sat silently, never pushing, respecting my background and allowing me to reflect. It was all too much. I quit therapy instead.

My depressions weren't that bad anyway, I reasoned. I can handle it, always have. No biggie! Life had always been lived with this persistent heaviness that never fully reached joy on a day-to-day basis. I knew no different. Therein lies the problem for most of us. We cannot change what we don't know, and we can't know what we didn't learn. We didn't learn what healthy was, so we had nothing to compare our feelings to.

The Plexiglas Shield

I never knew that what I was feeling had a label, "dysthymia." It escalated to a black place from time to time, making me feel insecure, powerless, and wondering about the suicide my Mother had chosen. I was so angry with her for her stupid, wasted life that I swore I would never do something like that. This saved my life.

As a Boomer, the late teens and early twenties were filled with sex, drugs, and rock and roll. Mostly I sought excitement to keep the invisible, black dysthymia at bay. I forced my body to create antidepressant chemicals by doing exotic and wild things. I joined sports car clubs and raced cars. I partied and ran with the bikers. Being a professional go-go dancer in the late '60s and early '70s kept the highs going; later, ramp and TV modeling; and there were always men, sex, and changing relationships; finally, marriage to another adult child, to assure frequent fights and chaos — all of which kept the depressed brain frequently bathed and charged with epinephrine and serotonin. I never realized other people felt differently. Their lives just looked boring to me. How could I know there was a better way to feel? Then one day I began to wonder how the Buddha could have such a peaceful smile.

Settling into life by my forties, I found more conventional ways to gain the excitement "ups" I needed to stay comfortable. An active private practice, teaching college, and community leadership was fun. I liked the stage and was in high demand as an entertaining speaker. I was a good actress, comedian, and improviser and watched myself with amusement behind my invisible Plexiglas shield. Who was this clever and cunning woman whose wit brought much joy and laughter to others in the practical skills she taught? The outer adulation effectively kept the pain of depression at bay. It also kept most joy at bay too. Run, Jane, Run. See Jane Run. See Jane Run Fast.

Although antidepressant drugs had been on the market since the '60s, they were not used liberally until much later. Like many therapists of the '70s and '80s, I was doggedly devoted to the concept that the majority of depressed individuals could and should be treated without drugs. Initially, I gave only lip service to the value of antidepressant drugs and the new research. I sent only my most severely depressed clients to local psychiatrists for "med evals," preferring to treat the others with alternative methods. But as the years progressed and I saw the miracles they produced, I became a believer.

In time, the results were so stunning that some docs became devoted to drugs as the answer and almost quit doing talk therapy altogether. All-or-nothing types, I called them.

These docs brought a lot of criticism on themselves

from psychologists and mental health therapists. That bias still exists today to some degree, as I frequently hear, "Oh, yeah, him — he just puts them on drugs; don't go there."

Later I was to learn many of my colleagues had taken these drugs on and off since the '80s, but did we talk about it with each other? No.

The Future

The years continued into the '90s, and my depressions deepened. Life was functional but faked. I lived behind my Plexiglas shield and mask of authenticity, suspecting I should be on an antidepressant but too ashamed to find out. The silent critic in my head whispered, *If you need an antidepressant, you will prove to everyone, colleagues included, you really are as crazy as your mother.... Shame on you!* Although Frank was a wise psychologist, unafraid, and well ahead of his time in suggesting I might have a chemical imbalance, he had no idea of the exquisite power of shame.

I watched my clients blossom into full recoveries, patted away their grateful hugs, and held doggedly to the belief that my personal recovery could happen completely as a result of practicing self-reflection, thought change, self-acceptance, positive thinking, and prayer. By the mid '90s I had taught positive thinking fifteen years, grieved for my inner child, vomited all my ills in journals and on the couches of other therapists, prayed myself into being an ordained minister, and I was still depressed.

The coffee is cold as I begin putting order to this reverie. I guess that is about it. I knew the Buddha had a smile I wanted at any cost. When menopause hit, the depression became unbearable, affecting all around me. I wanted to die. Hormones didn't help, so I bulldozed my way through shame and demanded my gynecologist put me on Prozac. It worked. It not only worked, it saved my life. It not only saved my life, it gave me a life I had never known before. That was four years ago. The future is good...very, very good. The Buddha's smile lies peacefully within my heart.

There are many ways we find our way through what we have learned and what we have become to what we must transform. There are many ways to find out there is something other than a mask to wear or a Plexiglas shield to hide behind. There are many ways to learn to touch life with our hearts. The Bible says, "Seek and ye shall find" (Mt 7:7). I add, "...and do so doggedly until you find peace. It is there for each one of us if we are persistent enough."

In life, you must be willing to do whatever it takes to find and be yourself. You are all you have. In expressing your courage to be you, you provide others the courage to be themselves.

—Terry Cole-Whittaker
Retired TV minister and author

SURVIVAL

By Mary Yerkes

"CRASH" goes the sound of the glass shattering and falling to the floor. Hiding behind the arm of my father's favorite chair, I crouched down, shaking uncontrollably, trying to become smaller and smaller. "Maybe if my mom doesn't see me, she'll stop throwing things," I thought. "Maybe if I just disappeared forever, things would be better." Sounds of shattering glass and profanity continued to punctuate the air. Then it was quiet, except for the sounds of my sobbing against my father's chair. My father tried to comfort me by telling me not to worry, that Mom was just a "little upset." I was not convinced.

As you can probably tell from this one incident, I grew up in a dysfunctional home. Incidents like this happened more often than not as I grew up. My father just pretended like it never happened. And we went from day to day, walking on eggshells, wondering when the next eruption would occur.

I was raised Roman Catholic and went to parochial

school as a child. If anyone dared talk during class instruction, the nun would quietly glide down the aisle clutching a ruler and, after instructing you to hold out your hand, strike you across your knuckles with it. *Swat!* went the sound of the ruler as it stung the skin, leaving a red mark. The paddle was left up in the front of the room for more serious infractions of the rules. Usually it was the boys who got paddled for fighting in the coatroom or saying a bad word. The children lived in mortal fear of the nuns. If we really misbehaved, they would take away the bathroom privileges of the entire class. Once, a first grader wet her pants after the class's bathroom privileges had been taken away. The nun, after noticing the mess, yelled at the embarrassed girl to go get a mop and clean up the mess she had made. She was publicly humiliated in front of the class, even though it had been six hours since our last bathroom break.

Very early on, I decided the only way to avoid emotional or physical pain at home and at school was to be "perfect." People surely couldn't get upset with me if I never did anything wrong.

I spent most of my school years getting straight A's and trying hard never to make a mistake or make anyone angry. But no matter how hard I tried, it seemed like I could never quite manage to be perfect all the time.

I remember once, when I was about twelve years old, we were getting ready to move. My mom wanted me to help pack and clean the house before the movers came. She picked the next Saturday as the day we would try to get most of the job done. I awoke early that morning not feeling very well. Within a few hours, I had a temperature of about 102 degrees, had the chills, and was nauseated. I laid down on the sofa to rest for just a minute. Try as I might, I just couldn't get the strength or energy to get back up. My mom came in and started yelling and cursing at me. She was gritting her teeth so hard in anger and yelling at me so loudly, I could feel her spit on my face as she leaned close to me. She told me that she was very angry with me and accused me of getting sick "on purpose" just to get out of helping clean. She once again reminded me that I was worthless and would never amount to anything. How could I forget when she took every opportunity to tell me?

I somehow made it through the rest of my school years, and in high school I met Paul. It wasn't long before I thought I had met my one true love. We started dating, and as he saw what was going on in my home, he assured me that there was nothing wrong with me but that my mom was crazy. I spent time with his family — well, most of his family anyway — and felt for the first time that this is what a normal family was. It wasn't long before I learned that his family had not always been like this. In fact, his father was an alcoholic and would often come home drunk and abuse his mother. He told me that one time, when dinner was not cooked to his liking, his father over-turned the dinner table and broke a plate over his mom's head. Well, at least the effects of the alcohol were behind this family for now. Or so I thought.

We continued to date, and I began to see that Paul did have some faults that I was unaware of at first. He did like to be in charge of everything all the time, or so it seemed. Whenever I spoke up with a differing opinion or thought, he would tell me that he knew best and, since I didn't really understand the way things were, we were going to do it his way. He made all the decisions, including what he liked me to wear. I could see that there were problems, but reflecting on my childhood, I recognized that I had some problems from growing up in an abusive home and there was probably no one else who would ever love me or want me. So I decided to marry him.

Things went well at first. Along came our son, and with him, the dream that I would finally have a normal life. I wanted so much just to be "normal." Finally, it seemed to be in reach.

It wasn't long before I found out my husband didn't quite share my desire for a normal life. In fact, he was feeling very trapped and regretted marrying so young. He regretted that he was forced to be so responsible so early, to help care for his mom after his parents separated. He was tired of being mature and responsible.

One night, I decided to show him how wonderful family life could be by preparing his favorite meal for him when he came home from work. Everything was ready and waiting, only he never came home, and he never called. Six o'clock rolled around to seven; seven turned to eight. Before long, it was eleven. By this point, I was devastated. I was crying and convinced he didn't love me, convinced that I was worthless — just like my mom had always told me.

Somewhere around eleven, I heard the key turn in the front door. Paul stumbled in, and I realized he had been drinking. He looked at my tearstained face and started yelling and cursing at me. He asked me what was wrong with me, why was I so upset; other wives understand their husbands' need to be out with the guys. He looked at me in disgust, turned his back, and walked away from me. He told me he was sorry he had ever married me.

Unbeknown to me, that one night, in conjunction with the abuse of my childhood, would be the start of a journey that I never could have imagined in my wildest dreams. My husband talked very little to me for six months. The few times he did talk to me, he was always verbally and emotionally abusive. At the end of those six months, any love I had once had for him had died.

In fact, it felt like I had died inside. I could no longer experience any emotion, whether good or bad. I was just numb inside — all the time. I could no longer think clearly. Things that had been so easy for me suddenly became very difficult. I had a difficult time carrying on a conversation with friends. I would get lost in the middle of the conversation and forget what I was saying. I would forget simple things, like my phone number or my address. My mind just didn't seem to work any longer. Driving was extraordinarily difficult for me. I could not mentally process how far away a car was and if it was safe to turn. I would either wait an excessively long time or go when in actuality I was in danger of being hit. There were many occasions that I was nearly struck. Other times, I would have reckless thoughts. *Maybe I should just drive into that oncoming traffic, and it will all be over. I'm so worthless. No one loves me. I'm just a burden to my family and to society. My family would be better off without me.*

Somewhere around that time, the numbness I had felt turned to excruciating emotional pain. I had just gone through natural childbirth, but the emotional pain I felt was far greater than giving birth with no medication. I had undergone several surgeries as a child, but this emotional pain was much greater than any physical pain I had ever suffered. In fact, I was certain that the emotional pain I felt was the worst pain that could be felt by man at any time.

A quote I had found by Abraham Lincoln describes well what I was feeling:

"I am now the most miserable man living. If what I feel were equally distributed to the whole human family, there would be not one cheerful face on earth. Whether I shall ever be better, I cannot tell. I awfully forebode I shall not. To remain as I am is impossible. I must die or be better, it appears to me."

My marriage continued to deteriorate. My husband was unable to forgive me for that one night when he came home late without calling and found me upset. Eventually, he did start talking to me, but usually to berate me or humiliate me. It seemed that I just couldn't do anything right for him. It got to the point that I was the one not talking. It seemed the only way to protect myself from the verbal abuse was to not say anything. The less I said, the worse I felt, and the more confused I became. I was either not sleeping at night or sleeping all the time. When I did sleep, I was often jarred awake by violent nightmares. I had a recurring dream that I was in a war and I was running and running, trying to find a safe place from the exploding gunfire around me. I was thinking more and more that life was not worth living.

One afternoon, I was lying on the sofa, reading a magazine. I didn't have much energy and spent most of my time either lying down or sleeping for long periods of time. It was not uncommon for me to sleep twelve to fourteen hours a day. I came across an article that seemed to perfectly describe what I was going through! Maybe there is an answer to this hell on earth I was experiencing. The article went on to ask several questions of the reader: "Do you have fatigue and a loss of energy?" "Do you have trouble thinking, concentrating, or making decisions?" "Have you lost interest or pleasure in almost all activities?" "Have your sleeping patterns changed?" "Do you have feelings of worthlessness or excessive guilt?" "Do you have recurrent thoughts of death or suicide?" I answered "yes" to every question. Based on the test, the article said that I was likely experiencing clinical depression and to immediately seek medical help. Seeking medical help was totally out of the question! There was no way my husband would pay for me to go to a counselor or psychologist! I decided to just deal with the symptoms on my own.

A month or two after reading the article, I was having a birthday party for my four-year-old son. My sister stopped by to bring her children to the party. She took one look at me and decided to stay. I was having a hard time thinking clearly and would stop in mid-sentence, unable to remember what I wanted to say. During the party, while the children were playing, my sister bluntly told me she felt I needed to leave or I was going to end up in a hospital. After the party, she waited while I packed a bag. Then she took my son and me back to her house.

Shortly after, I made arrangements to stay with some friends. When I told them I was thinking that my family would be better off without me, they immediately called a counselor and made an appointment for me. I felt so relieved. Maybe I would finally start to feel better and be able to get on with my life.

Things with the counselor went well at first. But before long, there seemed to be some tension between us. Shortly after that, he announced that he was terminating our counseling because he felt my problems were so deep that he was unable to help me. He gave me the name of a psychiatrist that he had already spoken to, who had agreed to take my case. Rejected by a therapist. How bad was I that even someone who helped people for a living couldn't help me? Had I gone too far to be helped? Needless to say, I was devastated.

I made an appointment with the psychiatrist for the following week. I entered his office and sat down opposite him in a large leather chair. It was then that I saw IT. Next to him sat a long leather couch with no back and no arms. It was not the kind of couch you sit on, but the kind you see patients lying on in the movies every time they show a psychiatrist's office. Did he think I was going to lie on that couch? Forget it!

He gently asked me to tell him what the problem was. Crying, I poured out my heart. I was relieved to see a box of Kleenex on the table next to the chair. I took one and wiped the tears streaming down my face. Apparently, I wasn't the first patient to cry in his office. After listening attentively, he told me that, based on what I had told him and based on what he had learned talking to the other therapist, he felt that I was probably going through a major clinical depression. I asked him if he thought I could be helped. Without hesitation, he replied, "Definitely." For the first time in months, I felt hopeful. I agreed to meet with him once a week.

Things were going very well. So well, in fact, that I reconciled with my husband and moved back into the house. Things went well at home, too — for a season. But it wasn't long before that season passed. Old patterns started surfacing, with Paul yelling, cursing, and berating me. The nightmares started once again. My thinking was becoming more and more confused. Realizing that I did much better when I was out of the house, I decided to find a part-time job. The problem was I was so nervous and so jumpy, I wasn't sure anyone would hire me. I talked to my therapist, and he prescribed a very low dose of Valium, two-milligram tablets, to help get me through the interview and through any particularly stressful days. I was hired within a few days as a salesclerk at a local women's clothing store.

My marital relationship continued to worsen. I picked up more hours at the store. So many, in fact, I began missing some of my therapy appointments.

One evening I had a particularly bad argument with my husband. I was feeling very anxious and took a Valium. Still feeling anxious, I took another one a few minutes later. *That should hold me until my therapy appointment tomorrow morning,* I thought.

However, during the night I was still anxious and took a few more Valium. By morning, I realized I wasn't feeling well. I was really, really tired and could barely keep my eyes open. I decided to call my therapist and cancel; I was just too out of it to drive. I left a message on his machine that I would not be coming in. He called me back in a few minutes and told me that it was very important to come in right now. I told him I couldn't drive. He told me to get a friend to drive me, but that he must see me. My sister drove me, and within an hour, I was in his office. Nothing prepared me for what happened next. He told me that he felt my life was in danger and that he wanted me to go to a psychiatric ward at a hospital nearby. I told him I wouldn't go. He told me he would have me committed, that legally he could do that. Trying to maintain even a small amount of dignity, I told him I would go of my own volition.

The hospital was a very scary place for me. When I arrived, they told me to empty my purse, and they confiscated every medication and nonprescription drug in my purse along with any sharp objects that I might try to hurt myself with. I arrived just in time to see the other patients lined up at the nurses' station, waiting for their afternoon medications. *They look like a bunch of cattle. I definitely do not belong here,* I thought. But my doctor had prescribed Prozac for me, so I had to join the herd at the counter. That night, I slept without any nightmares for the first time in a long time. When I awoke, I realized that I felt very "safe" and that I was actually glad to be there.

We were expected to maintain a strict schedule while we were there. In the morning, there was group therapy. In the afternoon, we had art therapy and recreational therapy. My therapist also came by daily to talk with me. After two or three weeks, my doctor, not happy with the way I was responding to my medication, increased the dosage of Prozac. In addition to the daily schedule of therapies, my doctor insisted on marital therapy and family therapy for me. I spent a total of six weeks in the psychiatric ward. I was released and went back home and resumed my prehospital therapy schedule with the addition of marital therapy.

Somewhere around the time of my hospitalization, my husband came to the realization that this was a very serious situation indeed. This stark realization was the beginning of the healing process that was going to occur in our relationship. Little did we know at the time, but the process of healing would not come easily or quickly. Rather, the healing process would be a journey that continued on for many years. At times I would grow weary on the journey, but I continued pressing forward, taking my medication, going to therapy, learning new things.

I cannot tell you the exact moment when I was no longer depressed. But I can tell you that at some point, it did happen.

It is now twelve years since my hospitalization. Our marriage is far from perfect, but we have learned to accept each other, enjoy each other, and yes, even love each other again. This summer, we are planning our second trip to the Bahamas. Things would really be good except for the fact that a few years ago I was diagnosed with a chronic illness for which there is no cure and usually is progressive. We are facing this as another journey, and though we don't know where it will take us, we are confident that we will make it.

It seems that nothing that is worthwhile comes easily.

> ***"This above all:***
> ***to thine own self be true."***
> WILLIAM SHAKESPEARE

Chapter Four

A STRANGE TRIP IT'S BEEN

By Catherine Nelson

I was born into a family that, from the outside, appeared happy and wholesome but on the inside was seriously dysfunctional. In the 1950s and '60s my grandfather was a highly respected obstetrician/gynecologist and active leader of our community, an upper-class society man, loved by all. Grandma ran the household lovingly but formally — we learned our manners there. They had two beautiful children — a girl (Mom) and a boy, both adopted. To everyone, the family appeared "perfect," but in reality this beloved man was molesting his daughter on a daily basis. She endured the abuse her entire childhood (he even secretly performed two abortions on her, the first when she was twelve, the next when she was fourteen). And, although he was older at the time and getting ill, he still managed to abuse and harm his grandchildren, my sister and me, as we grew up.

Mom and Dad met and married in their early twenties, and by the time she was twenty-five, they'd had three kids. My mother is a beautiful person, inside and out, and somehow had luckily held onto her sanity, but she suffered from such depression and confusion over God, who she felt had failed to answer her repeated and desperate prayers, that she was quickly drawn toward an alternative religious sect. Dad was never interested in the group, but it and its followers increasingly engulfed our whole lives.

Unfortunately, my mother never shared the pain of her childhood with my father, and they drifted apart. In 1976, when my little sister was six, my brother was seven, and I was eight, my parents got divorced. Mom left us kids with Dad and went off to live her life with her cult friends. As much as a young child could, I tried desperately to involve myself in her life, embracing the religion and her friends, in order to be as close to her as possible.

Soon, however, Mom's religious leader was requesting her to move to Los Angeles, two hours away from where we lived, so that she could better serve the needs of the organization. Of course she went. Let's just say the next seven years were hell for us kids. Dad worked hard and loved us deeply but, as a child of neglectful and abusive alcoholics, was emotionally distant and a hard-to-please perfectionist to boot. We had a succession of live-in nannies that quickly came and went. We were now only seeing our mother once a month or so via an unsupervised and unnerving trip on the Greyhound bus. Needless to say, the whole arrangement was quite difficult for three little children who so very badly needed extra love and attention from their mommy and daddy.

After my mother moved out, my list of friends dwindled down to only one, as it was just too painful and embarrassing to share my situation with others. Sadly, my pain manifested as anger and aggressiveness toward my siblings (whom I wish I'd instead been able to embrace as a surrogate mother), and I was punished almost daily for it, being sent to my room for hours at a time. To divert my attention, I became completely obsessed with a boy in my class. I was madly in love with him for two years but never let him know it. My infatuation was so intense that I still dream of him to this day, though I now recognize the obsession for what it was — something to take my mind off my home life. During this time I also suffered from frequent nightmares and cried constantly. However, crying to my father was like crying to a wall, and this only further served to increase my feelings of being alone and abandoned, with nobody in my life who could just hold me, sympathize, and tell me everything would be okay. I was very, very sad and deeply depressed. This was the first time I entertained thoughts of suicide, but luckily, at the age of twelve, I was way too unsophisticated to figure out how I could possibly accomplish such an act.

By the time my sister was twelve, she was also suffering tremendously, to say the least, and after years of begging, she finally convinced my mother and her second husband to let her move in with them. Once I heard this, I immediately made the same request, and soon we both made the move to the big city, leaving my brother with my dad (we had been living with his girlfriend and her fifteen-year-old son at the time). Sadly, our move, I learned later, devastated both my brother and my dad, but it was something my sister and I desperately needed to do, and so we went, convinced that greener pastures lay ahead.

The next year was the happiest of my young life. We had a close-knit community of friends and active social lives through the religious organization, and I was thrilled to be living with my mother again. I had never known any other children who lived with their fathers after their parents were divorced, and our living arrangement had always embarrassed me. Now I felt like a normal kid again. I immediately made many friends in my new high school and thrived there. Unfortunately, the happiness was not to last.

The next year, Mom and her husband learned some awful truths about their esteemed cult leader and left the group. He quickly announced our family had been "infected with evil," and all of our friends immediately cut all ties with us. Mom and her husband soon divorced as well, and we were basically forced to start our lives completely over. This was a terribly difficult time for all of us, especially Mom. At least my sister and I had a life outside the cult; Mom did not.

My sister never completed school and was in and out of drug, alcohol, and eating disorder treatment centers her entire teenage life, becoming dangerously self-destructive and rebellious. Interesting enough, if the focus had been on treating the roots of her depression and her post-traumatic stress rather than the outward manifestations of it, I believe her treatment would have been much more successful. However, she still suffers to this day. During those years I was the middleman between her and my mother. I was glad to help, but my feelings and problems seemed minor in comparison and were consequently ignored in the midst of all this turmoil. One day, when I was sixteen, about the same time as our association with the religious cult fell apart, my sister and I sat down and, for the first time, started comparing notes on Grandpa. When my mother overheard us, she sat down crying, and we soon discovered the truth about her horrible past. We were hurt and angry beyond belief, but by this time he had severe Alzheimer's disease and was in a nursing home. He died not long after, and we were never able to confront him. However, I comfort myself with the belief that he has been reincarnated into a life of hell of some sort or another and fully understands the harm he caused to so many.

Anyhow, our lives soon took a turn for the better when a wonderful man came into my mother's life — a kind, spiritual man, whom she ended up marrying, and they remain happily married to this day. He took the three of us in and helped support my sister and me in a lovely home for the next few years until we were old enough to move out. However, by that time I'd become entirely overwhelmed and emotionally distraught as a cumulative result of all the traumas I'd been through (made worse by the extreme fluctuations of teenage hormones) and slipped into a deep depression. I strongly felt I had no one to rely on but myself, and once again the feelings of being alone in the world intensified.

Somehow through all of this I continued to do well in school, had a good job, and was generally very responsible (I give credit to my father's perfectionism for this); but at the same time, I did drugs, drank a lot, was sexually promiscuous, and partied till dawn on a regular basis. Mom had never given me a curfew and never really asked what I was doing. We had more of a friendship relationship than a traditional mother-daughter relationship. I often spent my days alone, hysterically crying and pacing around, just passing time until the night, when I would join my friends again and escape into the comfort of drugs and alcohol. My journal entries at that time were full of rage and pain and sadness that I didn't understand. It's hard to see the big picture when you're in the midst of such deep despair. I was convinced I was just an alien, living on this planet to observe but never really belonging here.

After high school, my best friends went away to college, and I was left at home since the college money Dad had supposedly saved for me had been spent on other things, and we couldn't qualify for financial aid. I think it was because he was so hurt that I had moved away from him, but he only told me, "I supported myself through college, and you can too."

I was devastated. I felt so alone and abandoned — a familiar feeling, but now the pain inside my heart became simply unbearable. Way deep down, I knew I had hit rock bottom and life was bound to improve, since how could it possibly get worse, but I REALLY wanted to die. I wrote several wills, comforting myself with the thought that I would soon be able to escape the pain. I did try to commit suicide several times but fortunately never actually found the nerve to go all the way. This probably sounds silly, but I honestly believe it was our dog that saved me, because I loved that dog more than anything, and he was always with me in my darkest moments of despair. He was the only living thing who I felt had ever given me unconditional love, and I couldn't leave him like that.

Despite doubting the existence of God (because if

He in fact did exist, how could He possibly let me suffer as I had) and lacking any kind of spiritual guidance, I did continue to pray. Finally, I decided to have a "reading" with a gifted psychic. I know to some it will sound strange and unconvincing, and it was something I'd initially resisted and was skeptical of, but honestly, the reading changed my life dramatically. Finally I had someone reassure me that it wasn't in fact my destiny to die by suicide, as I had believed, but rather that, as a soul, I wouldn't have chosen to live my life if I weren't strong enough to overcome the difficulties placed before me. Much more was said, but these were the words I most needed to hear, and I resigned myself to the fact that I was going to survive this madness after all.

Shortly afterwards, I think because I was working almost full time at that time (in addition to attending the local college) and living a substantially independent life, Mom told me to start paying rent or I'd have to move out. The ultimatum felt like rejection to me, and my pride would not let me argue. I was nineteen years old, and I knew if I was going to pay rent, I certainly wasn't going to live at home. Within a month I had moved into an apartment with a girlfriend. I believe everything happens for a reason, and it just so happens there was a very good reason for this move — my future husband was living in the apartment twenty feet across the courtyard from ours. Our bedroom windows faced each other, and I later learned that I wasn't the only one with a pair of binoculars!

Although we got off to a rather rocky start, our relationship blossomed after I began attending weekly therapy with a wonderful woman referred to me by my adored physician, in whom I had confided my past. The doctor also put me on an anti-anxiety medication called BuSpar, which I took for a year or so. The medication helped me cope with my heavy burdens overall, but I believe it was the therapist who was the most important catalyst in developing my relationship with my husband. My longest previous relationship (by far) had lasted just five months, but because she practically walked me through the first three years of our courtship, my husband and I were able to survive the toughest tests, and we have been together for twelve years now, married for almost seven.

I have to say that letting someone love me unconditionally was the most important thing I could ever do for myself. Opening up and being vulnerable, while it seemed impossibly difficult at the time, is so crucial to being functional in a love relationship. In the early years I responded to our difficulties with frustration, aggressiveness, and flat-out rage. I was highly sensitive (actually, I still am) and defensive. I laid the truth of my past out right away, figuring if he was going to leave me because of it, better he do it sooner rather than later. Fortunately, he did not leave me, and finally, as I began trusting him not to abandon me, I was able to start lifting myself out of the darkness and into a world of light and love.

In 1993, after more than five years of dating, I not only married, I also began my hard-earned but exciting and wonderful career as a court reporter. When our healthy and gorgeous son was born three years later, being self-employed, I had the luxury of being able to stay at home with him. I was the happiest I'd ever been in my life, feeling that I had overcome the most tremendous difficulties and that I was going to live happily ever after. Unfortunately, however, that fantasy was not to be, as bad luck struck once again.

In November of 1997, I was rear-ended in a car accident and suffered serious career-ending back and neck injuries. The next two and one-half years were comprised of little more than doctors' appointments and tremendous physical suffering. My life had changed dramatically in the course of an instant of someone else's carelessness. It suddenly became extremely difficult to care for my highly active toddler, who was big enough to run around but small enough to still need to be lifted into his highchair, car seat, and picked up constantly. The thought of the impending lawsuit also weighed heavily on my mind, even though I was not at fault. As a former court reporter and legal secretary, I know you can never predict what a jury will do, and I knew my entire medical history and life would be up for public scrutiny. Worst of all, I was a victim once again, and all the feelings of being taken advantage of came rushing back with a vengeance.

I tried every conceivable medical treatment under the sun, with short-lived or disappointing results; I was in an endless cycle of high hopes and devastating letdowns. To compound matters, under severe physical and mental stress, I came down with a bad case of the Epstein-Barr virus several months after the accident and became very ill for a long time. A few months later, my beloved grandmother was ill and dying, but by that time the sciatica I had been experiencing had become so bad that driving the two to three hours it would take to go see her was impossible. I was unable to be there for her before she died, and I was very upset and angry over that. About a month later, having already delayed a much-wanted second pregnancy due to the back injuries, I consulted two doctors to discuss my situation. I was told by both of them it would be extremely difficult to carry, deliver, and care for another child and that I'd better think long and hard whether I felt it would ever be worth it. The news was devastating. And all the while, my relationship with my husband became more and more strained, as I felt he didn't understand what I was going through (nobody did!) and was unsympathetic to my pain. Again, there I was, feeling completely alone and abandoned in my misery.

As I became increasingly aware of how the accident had permanently changed my life, I became more and more distraught. My attorney advised me that private detectives hired by the insurance company could be spying on me, and I was constantly looking over my shoulder, though I had nothing to hide. In addition, I began to have extreme anxiety whenever driving or riding in a car, and I spent more time looking in the rearview mirror than looking ahead, always certain I was about to witness someone plowing into me again.

Somehow during all of this, I managed to take care of my son full time, but to this day I don't know how I did it. I still feel sad that I could never be the pain-free mother I feel my son deserves. I also believe it was due to my growing inability to properly handle the stress that my son started stuttering (now resolved, thankfully) at the age of two and one-half, as it began after I lost my cool one day. My guilt over this was the final straw. It became nearly impossible for me to cope, and I felt myself breaking apart, losing my sanity, if you will.

Thankfully, in January of 1999 my pain management doctor recognized my distress (not hard to do since I had a breakdown in his office) and put me on the antidepressant Elavil. While the medication did help to ease the severity of my depression a bit, I continued to suffer terribly over the next few months. After my deposition was taken for the lawsuit in June of 1999, it was the lowest point I'd ever known. For weeks I was totally obsessed with thoughts of failure and embarrassment over what I'd said and what I should have said but hadn't. I was at the point where I was literally paralyzed with fear, anxiety, and anger and could do little more than lie in bed, for the most part. I was in a complete preoccupied daze while taking care of my son's basic needs and not there for him in the slightest way emotionally. Thank goodness he was too young to remember.

During this time I felt myself withdrawing more and more from my husband, and I knew from my past habits that I had the potential to create a permanent separation, emotionally and physically. It scared me. I knew I had to take action or the marriage could crumble. Finally one day, during the heat of an argument, I got up the nerve to tell him exactly how I'd been feeling. I mean everything. I couldn't believe it hadn't already been painfully obvious to him how I felt, but apparently it hadn't. Luckily, after an initial angry withdrawal, he quickly turned around and made a significant change in his behavior. Our marriage was saved, and we continue to be even closer to this day.

However, as I continued to suffer from severe physical pain and the lawsuit was still ongoing, my problems remained. I was miserable beyond belief. Every day was torture, and I felt I just could not endure another day of such unrelenting pain! I almost certainly would have been suicidal had it not been for my absolute resolve not to purposefully leave my son without a mother. Desperate and suffering terribly, I prayed, as there was nothing else left to do.

One day by chance (or more likely, God's guidance) while surfing the Internet, I happened upon a Web site called restministries.org. Rest Ministries is a Christian organization for people with chronic illness and pain. Although, up to that point, religion had not been particularly important to me, I found that the Web site and, subsequently, the newsletters contained articles that helped me begin to see and feel the presence of God through my suffering and despair. I suddenly had hope where I'd had none before, and I saw I was not alone in my feelings. I began praying to God like there was no tomorrow, and I literally got down on my knees, begging and pleading for relief day after day.

Within weeks (in July of 1999), God once again answered my prayers by bringing a very special therapist into my life who used a fast-paced method of therapy called EMDR (eye-movement desensitization and reprocessing) that truly heals like no other. What followed was, for me, nothing short of a miracle. While I'd spent most of my life working diligently toward healing and personal growth, before I tried EMDR, I was in worse shape than I'd ever been. I first went to this therapist to treat my increasingly severe post-traumatic stress and car anxiety, but imagine my surprise when, after only a few sessions, I began to feel dramatically better physically as well as emotionally! We started by working with my feelings of loss and stress concerning the accident, but then we necessarily worked backward and revisited every serious trauma I've ever had in my life. The results were incredible. For reasons still scientifically undocumented, the EMDR worked extremely well to ease my physical pain as well as the depression and post-traumatic stress. As I sat in her chair, my body tingled, and I could literally feel the rush infusing my body like medication. I also saw clearly how my intense overreaction to the present difficulties was a cumulative effect of every major trauma I'd ever been through. Feelings of anger and sadness I'd repressed my whole life were dealt with and dissipated.

Today, a year after completing the therapy, I feel like I have been given my life and my sanity back. I will never again be the person I was before the EMDR. Every day is not perfect, but I feel I can handle any obstacle that comes my way. I am completely weaned off the antidepressants and looking forward to getting pregnant soon. I have no residual driving anxiety whatsoever (and the lawsuit was settled out of court). I still suffer from back pain, but it is not unbearable like before. Best of all, after years of doubting, I now enjoy a close relationship with God and Jesus (a support system I can always depend on). It is impossible to deny the spiritual intervention I've witnessed in my life, and exploring Christianity has become very meaningful to me. To that end, I would encourage anyone to pursue their own spiritual path as an important part of healing and growth.

I think it is important for people who suffer from depression to understand that they are not alone. Outward appearances are deceiving. They must realize they are not the only ones who grew up with a dysfunctional family or are suffering inside and walking a difficult path. They may feel, as I did, they are the only ones who feel like they do and no one else could possibly understand what they are going through. This is not true. There are many people who can understand and empathize with them, and help them as well. But they must reach out and speak about their pain, and get to the true root of it, if they ever hope to get past it. Pushing painful feelings down inside will never get rid of them; it only adds fuel to the fire.

Also, it is imperative for people who are seriously depressed to obtain professional help from a qualified individual that they trust and can connect with. If medication is recommended, take it! Chemical imbalances occur when sadness persists, and sometimes medication is necessary to foster healing. There is much more shame in holding your thoughts and feelings in, and letting them alter your life for the worse, than in needing help to face them — which takes tremendous courage, strength, and determination and is something to really be proud of.

Finally, the power of prayer is never to be underestimated. Miracles can and do happen.

I have a special message for those suffering with sexual abuse issues:

For those of you who are too young to escape your abusive situation: My heart and prayers truly go out to you. You may feel hopeless and desperate and suicidal now, but please know that it WILL end. You can make it! You will become old enough to go out on your own, and you can choose two roads — continue the cycle of destruction or break it. But to break it, you will need help from someone you trust (hopefully a qualified professional). If you can't get it now, get it as soon as you are able. In the meantime, don't lose touch with yourself and your true inner nature, which is goodness. People survive and thrive after going through the worst kinds of abuse...you can too. Your abuser is sick, and it has NOTHING to do with you.

For those of you who are also adult survivors: It can and will get better for you, but you too need to talk about your pain with someone you trust. That is crucial. You CANNOT do it alone. And, it was NOT your fault. Hey, like me, you may even find you are a more "well-rounded" person for it, for better or worse. You can do something good with your experience by helping others who are suffering — if not now, then maybe someday. Our souls have NOT been damaged by what we have lived through. And...you **ARE** living through it. If you are reading this, then you are **LIVING** through it. Although it can seem impossible, the pain you feel is temporary. When you die (at a ripe old age, please!), what matters will not be so much what others did to you, but rather the love in your heart and the courage you found to be able to face your fears and overcome your pain and difficulties. It was **NOT** your fault. You **ARE** worthy of respect and love no matter what. You deserve no less.

I know. I am a survivor. If I can make it, I believe anybody can. The key is love — first yourself, then others, and surrounding yourself with people who love you just the way you are.

I would also like to express my heartfelt thanks to my incredible family, especially my Mom and Dad, for their courageous encouragement and support for this project. We have been through so much together, and I love you all dearly!

Thank you for reading my story, and God bless you all.

"There is a guidance for each of us, and by lowly listening we shall hear the right word.... Place yourself in the middle of the stream of power and wisdom which flows into your life. Then, without effort, you are impelled to truth and to perfect contentment."

RALPH WALDO EMERSON

THE WAY WE WERE

By Pamela West

CRACKED, chipped, or broken — my sister used to say that described our possessions because we had furnished our homes with garage sale items and the inherited pieces that were "too good to throw away."

But one day when she made the comment, we laughed and said it referred to the members of our family too — the cranky aunt, the ornery old great-grandfather, our grandmother who didn't walk, cousins who were "slow," and all the others who were "peculiar." Then we paraphrased the old Scottish proverb into, "Everyone's a little crazy except you and me, and sometimes I wonder about you."

I thought about that again this morning when the calendar reminded me that it was Sis's birthday. She would have been sixty-nine years old. But she has been dead for twenty-two years.

When we were growing up, we shared so much that we were like twins, and even now, her shadow-self seems to be with me. No day goes by without thoughts of her. I see a rainbow, and an inner voice says, "Sis should see how beautiful this is." Her grandson gives me a roguish grin, and I think, "Sis should hear him call her 'Grandma.'" Instead, he gives that title to me. I want to tell Sis what happened this morning, or yesterday...and on and on.

There is a picture of us standing together beneath a lilac bush in our grandmother's yard when we were about seven and five. I am holding myself very erect, being aware of the constant admonishment from Mother and other family members to "straighten up." Sis is only slightly shorter than I but relaxed and sturdy looking, with a mischievous grin on her face.

Eventually, we were the same height and constantly taken for twins, though she was much prettier and more blonde, with Aryan features, while our paternal family sometimes referred to me as "the little Chinese." We grew up during World War II in a small agricultural-manufacturing town in the center of Iowa. We ran around with a gang of boys and girls, kids who lived nearby, in grade school days. During all those years, Sis was a brave, cheerful, wisecracking, mischievous girl. Nothing seemed to get her down. She and I shared clothes, activities, secrets, and sometimes slept together in each other's beds so we could talk long into the night.

There are pictures of us during our teens laughing and horsing around — mostly with girlfriends because when Pearl Harbor was bombed, the guys in our gang enlisted. We had lots of slumber parties and swam at the local pool in the summer. Late in the afternoon each weekday, we went with friends from the "Y" to the train station to do our patriotic duty and pass out used magazines and treats to the soldiers and sailors passing through to the coast and shipping out. We slipped them our names and addresses and wrote to some of them during the war.

We volunteered as nurses' aides at the local hospital. We played on three basketball teams. Sis was an aggressive forward and the star of many games. We attended school events and sucked down thousands of Cokes at Lillie Mae's store. We sang in the church choir. Sis had a strong alto voice and joined a sextet, which sang for many community affairs.

Both of us started dating "Baxter boys," those guys who lived in a town about twenty-five miles away and were friends of the uncle who was just our age. Those boys had cars. Some were farm boys and could get gas and come to see us, when we didn't take the train to Baxter for a visit. Barb also dated a guy in my class at school. He was a farm kid too, and one of her ambitions was to eventually live on a farm and have lots of animals.

Barb had also dated one of the boys from our old gang while he was home on leave from the Navy. Then one night he called her all the way from Pearl Harbor to say he was coming home. When he did return and separated out of the Navy, they became a steady item.

Meanwhile, I graduated, got married, and was pregnant. Sis and her boyfriend were really serious. They wanted to get married too, but she was barely seventeen and still a high school junior. I helped persuade our parents to give them permission. Mother made a wedding dress out of a silk parachute for Sis, and they were married in "our" church around the

THE GIFT OF DEPRESSION

corner. A big reception was held in the beautiful home where we grew up.

The newlyweds miraculously found an apartment, and within a short time, Sis became pregnant and delivered a big baby boy. While he was still a toddler, our mother broke her hip. Since Daddy was working out of town as a millwright much of the time, Sis and her family moved into the family home to help care for her. It was several years later, when Daddy and Norman took jobs there, that they all moved to Minneapolis.

After a short time of living in the city, Barb and Norman bought a nice home in a suburban tract and became a "normal" American family, raising their kids in a new neighborhood. They made many friends there.

Up to this time, nothing had ever seemed to get Sis down, but after she gave birth to their second son, the crack appeared. Postpartum depression was the diagnosis, and she was hospitalized longer than normal for recovery from childbirth and given Valium.

She continued with that drug on and off through the rest of her life. There was one episode when we were all made very aware that she was being medicated. She had gone back to bed — she always seemed tired (what busy mother is not!) — when her youngest son climbed the sink and swallowed a number of her pills. He had to be hospitalized and have his stomach pumped.

Her marriage started to fall apart. By the time their sons were grown and on their own, she and her husband were separated, then divorced. There were some bitter accusations made, and Norman moved back to Iowa. Sis and their young daughter moved to the small town where our parents were living. Sis bought a house there and found a job. Though she had family, she was no longer close to old, supportive friends — except one couple, and eventually Sis began an affair with that man.

There were some good years. Sis finished her GED, received training as a medical assistant, and continued to work. We saw a lot of each other, went on weekend "junking" trips to furnish our homes, went camping on an island in the St. Croix River with our kids, and did things with our parents.

Then our mother became ill and suffered terribly in the hospital for three months, even begging one of us to kill her. Until then, I had not realized how emotionally dependent my sister was on our strong, sometimes controlling, mother. We were all devastated when she died, but losing Mother seemed to affect Sis even more than it did Dad or me.

And now that Dad was alone, and because he lived near her, Sis had the brunt of the burden in looking after his welfare while she had to take care of and provide support for herself and her daughter.

And her romance was not going well. The man was, in reality, dallying with her. He got tired of Sis's pushing to make a permanent alliance and had started to pull back. She was losing control of the situation, and her resentment at his actions was compounded by the knowledge that I had entered a seemingly strong relationship with a man I met after my divorce.

After our divorces, Sis and I would joke about the old Prince Charming story. After a mutual complaining discussion about our lack of money and male relationships, we would strike a chorus-line pose with our arms around each other and sing, "If I had a rich man..." It was a joke, but I think she half meant it and did want a Prince Charming to take care of her.

Then Dad broke his leg, and she was sure that he would want to come live with her. I kept reassuring her, telling her I had made all the arrangements for him to keep on living alone in the home he and Mother had shared, that Meals on Wheels would deliver food to him, I would come every weekend, etc., but she became more and more upset, almost hysterical.

Sis had continued with the Valium over the years. The last six months of her life, she often seemed like a zombie. We trusted her doctor, but I found out after her death that he often gave her another prescription without monitoring the amount she was taking. He had signed for and she had filled two prescriptions in the last three days before she killed herself.

The phone rang in the late afternoon. When I answered, the voice I heard was incoherent, but I finally realized it belonged to my niece, Stephanie, and made out what she was trying to tell me. My sister was dead — shot herself. My stunned brain's first thought was, *Impossible; she didn't have a gun.*

But my concern then was for my hysterical niece, and I asked her to put someone else on the line. Her neighbor told me my sister was truly dead and the police were there. I replied that I would drive to Lindstrom immediately and asked her to try to calm Stephanie down. Next, I realized that Daddy was still in the hospital and someone was going to have to tell him his beloved daughter was dead. I made it up north to Lindstrom in less than an hour.

Stephanie was able to tell me what happened. She had returned home from school and was eating a snack at the kitchen table. As she sat there, she realized her mother's purse and car keys were on the table too. That was strange. That must mean her mother was home and hadn't gone to work that morning, but she had heard no sound from the upstairs bedrooms. Steph slowly mounted the stairs to check on her mother. Maybe she had one of her terrible sinus headaches and she could get something for her....

She quietly opened the bedroom door and saw her mother lying in bed. The gun was still in her hand. Sis had put it under her chin and pulled the trigger. The wound was horrible. Steph turned and ran, crashing down the stairs and through the screen door, to her neighbor's home. There, she grabbed the phone and called me.

While I contacted my nephews, my daughter and her husband went over to the hospital to tell my father what had happened, but when they arrived, they found that the doctor had already bluntly informed him that Sis was dead. He had not been kind or tactful.

We learned that the gun Sis used had been the one Daddy had borrowed the year before from my ex-husband. Bill had quite a firearm collection, and Daddy, who barely knew how to load a gun, had borrowed it "in case of prowlers" and hidden it in a closet. Sis had found it when she was cleaning and took it home with her.

Then I realized Sis had planned her death for quite some time. I had visited Daddy at the hospital the day before and called Sis, saying I would stop to see her on my way home. She asked me not to come, citing a bad headache, and asked me to tell Dad she wouldn't be driving over that day to visit him. Perhaps she thought she might break down and change her mind if she saw us.

In many ways, her suicide was her way of saying, "F— you!" to the world and, unfortunately, some people in her life. I believe she was carrying resentment for many reasons and decided she would have the last word.

There had been nothing in our lives as we grew up to indicate the depression which followed Barb as an adult. For years after she succumbed to the urge to end the pain, I ascribed her death to a part of our maternal heritage, "the black dog of the Irish." But in later years, as her children and my own manifested signs of this condition, I've looked more closely at the trail it's left in three generations, and I see it — not in the Irish side, but the German. I now realize that our beloved daddy was probably depressed a good share of his life, and maybe his mother suffered from it. Could that be one of the reasons she "took to her bed" and didn't walk? We have cousins who are fighting it along with bipolar disorder, but sufferers now have the advantage of finding more doctors who understand this condition and can offer medication that was not available twenty years ago, and there are now many medications that can help.

Sis was a beautiful, multitalented person. When grown, she looked like Grace Kelly and had style that was unsurpassed. There was a sweetness in her, a toughness, and a sense of fun. But circumstances and that imbalance of chemicals in her brain caused her to end her life. Such a waste and heartache for those who loved her. There was so much we should have shared together and so much left for her to enjoy, and if she had just hung on and received proper treatment, she could see that rainbow and hear her grandson's laughter.

*"Everything has its wonders,
even darkness and silence,
and I learn, whatever state
I may be in,
therein to be content."*

HELEN KELLER

A RIDE IN THE BACKSEAT

By James L. Rodgers

THE amazing alignment of family disease.
"Jesus Christ," bellows this recovering alcoholic at his lovely, whimpering wife. "I grew up with this crap; my mom took the pipe. If you're going to have a breakdown, go have it somewhere else."

This was in response to a desperate, slow-motion, nervous clinging and a long, depressed face made compelling by a frantic "please see and hear me" stare. There was an agonizing explanation that January is not a good month, and could I please practice some of that "infamous patience, tolerance, kindliness, and love that you so glibly advertise to your friends in recovery."

She announces that the month will be spent in bed praying and meditating, but I don't buy it, and a flag pops up in the mind, spelling in red, wavy letters, "*depression, self-pity, poor me*," and I react not from thoughtfulness or intuition, but from the cold, steely taste of fear.

This unhappy scene, accompanied by musical snapping and rattling of pills in little brown bottles, finally drones the wife into a medicated zombie-like state. This further releases deep-rooted fears and resentments planted in my childhood and nurtured for forty years. Yes, I finally married my mother, in a grandiose way, after three failed previous attempts.

My mother was absolutely stunning in appearance, even after many years into an abysmally rotten marriage. I was told that she had the best legs on campus at the large, rich-in-tradition Eastern university she had attended and that the honor was confirmed "by student vote." Her picture appeared in a Vogue Scrapbook of Modeling, printed by the big city newspaper, using locally famous architecture as background. What a catch she was! And wonderfully vulnerable. Perfect for a guy like me. She was the daughter of a recently dead alcoholic (from pneumonia, as the result of a drinking binge just prior to the availability of penicillin). He was a "brilliant man, an inventor from Vermont — why, the United States still uses his patent for tin plating."

Mom was sent away to boarding school as far as Belgium to avoid some of the damage unintentionally wreaked by the strikingly handsome, loving, powerful, brilliant, cocksure, snappy dressing, Vermont-style, garden-variety *drunk*. What emerged was a guilt-ridden, remorseful, naive, bewildered, Irish-Scandinavian beauty, with blue "doe-eyes" the size of saucers, who married, in the Catholic forever-tradition, another alcoholic. Except now penicillin was readily available.

"If my dad would have been alive," says she, in a depressed state, to her boys, "he *never* would have let me marry your father."

The chaos that ensued conspired with the alchemy of the already-damaged psyche to manifest what I would misperceive as something weak, shameful, untidy, and selfishly inconvenient — depression.

"Jimmy, be quiet. I'm nervous and depressed." How I grew to despise that obtuse reference to why she was the way she was. What the hell does that mean? It was easier to accept my father's observation on depression and the people who attempted to treat it: "You're all nuts. Snap out of it." What I didn't know was that that was like telling my dad to snap out of it and quit drinking.

My mother was trapped inexorably. No family. The church could not, would not, put the charade aside even in matters of life and death. The representative for the church told my mother to "go out and buy some new perfume." Think about that. Think about that as a solution to living every day forever on this earth with a battering, emotionally cruel and calculating, tortuous hulk of a drunk man.

More Depression...

"Jimmy, promise you will stay at home and go to college here, live here, help me here in this house." I heard this repeatedly, with her holding a death grip on both my arms. Imploring and genuinely frightened — no, terrorized — she was unwittingly helping to pull me, this teenage juggernaut of frenzied fear and confusion, into the web of disease.

I resented her for these events and this condition in my life, so that I grew to hate. Clearly, my needs and a healthy nurturing were not only not being met, but now I felt trapped also in the melee of incessant, impending doom.

Consider the insidious creeping of all the family diseases in this house to manifestation and final fruition. The firm grip of active alcoholism by my father; Mother's relentless depression, in part related to horrific codependence on his drinking; his hostage-like security; and my happiness. Her depressed helplessness and despair were infectious and provided the fodder so that I took on the role of the victim, reveled in it so as to gravitate to this perverse security, and I created enablers of the textbook variety. Even my father knew that the relationship with his family was based on a hostile dependency. He was fearful of the day he would be alone with his wife.

I resented this situation fiercely, that I should shoulder responsibility for emotional support due from a spouse, that I was a surrogate husband while my dad was alive and came home every day, albeit drunk.

My mother's depression worsened. What an enormously strong-willed woman she was. This ceaseless, unholy barrage of doom, conditions at home in her marriage, and unimaginable near-future events would conspire to bludgeon this now mortally wounded individual into a slow and still more agonizing downward spiral.

My opinion of women, dads, moms, psychiatrists, religion, and doctors in general deteriorated, and I began to develop a lifelong habit of fear-based condemnation when confronted with someone's depression. My brother complained of "being depressed" like Linus in the Peanuts cartoon. It became a catch phrase. I saw clinical depression as being laced with extravagant bills and pills, of many alluring colors, to sleep, eat, function, change the mind and the mood. Mother was so desperate for the gloom to cease, she "volunteered" for electric shock treatment. I found this sad and embarrassing — so why did I tell everyone I know?

I began to watch my mother change size and shape frequently with each new drug, all the while her frantic, frenetic pleas falling on deaf, resentful, ignorant ears. I could not find compassion because I was too damned scared. I would flee at the sight of her open arms imploring a life-giving hug, her hope for tomorrow. I was utterly useless in this situation. I could see the monster ruminating at will inside her precious skull, just behind those gorgeous blue eyes.

Of course I became alcoholic and proceeded to carve out my own path of destruction familiar to those actively addicted and medicating the daily shame, cowardice, guilt, sadness, self-pity, disappointment, and abject terror at the prospect and reality of feeling. Shortly after leaving this thickly-laden, grotesque atmosphere and the unconditional love I used and squandered, it happened.

The sunshine of my mother's life was her two boys, especially my brother. Whereas I was repulsed by her neediness, my brother relished the time he spent alone with my mom. Besides, I had exhibited a degree of toughness and immunity to this thing called depression that my brother had not. A relationship flourished. Just at this time, my brother, who was very much like his mother in thought and mind, was mysteriously and violently murdered. Envision, if you will for a moment, the ballistic effect this had on the three of us and the new dimensions now possible for our diseases to explore! Incomprehensible, unless of course, you have the experience.

Now even more desperate for compassion, consolation, answers, love, revenge, and the end, my mother reached out, and I grew further away. I could not fill this void, this yawning maw of need. We didn't know these incredibly horrific circumstances could ever be successfully worked through. I could not conceive that anybody anywhere could. I became a walking, talking, frozen, hate-filled, and dangerous drunk.

Miraculously, Mom's tenacity, prayers, and hope in me — "You are the only reason I don't kill myself, Jimmy" — kept her alive for eighteen more years. I became further imprisoned by my anger at her inability to elude the monster that descended upon her and darkened her world forever. This depression all the time that I knew her, her clawing pleas to help make it better, left me helpless, hopeless, plagued by demons, repulsed, and squirming. I loved her deeply, and I still do; however, I did find her to be entirely alien in her separation from reality by the prescription drugs and the toll that decades of depression, abuse, and circumstances had exacted.

My fears, lack of learned healthy intimacy, and my perception of women, in their various depressed states, throttled my attempts at relationships with people in general. All of my wives, significant others, friends — anyone who was close to me — were all very ill, a like-consciousness attraction. My mother began to speak endlessly of suicide and once discharged a .38 caliber pistol into her bedroom wall. Her nervous system started to break down from the burden of untreated or mistreated or misdiagnosed or exacerbated depression so virulent as to resist all medical treatment. The physical debilitation and the mental ravings began to unfold. That fearsome and effective telephone "weapon," which closed the fifteen-hundred-mile gap between us, cheerfully carried the suicide message to me on a biweekly basis as my guts writhed and heaved with revulsion and I pulled straight whiskey out of a bottle.

Her depression and broken brain manifested physically in an ever-worsening neuropathy in the extremities of her legs — an inexplicable and untreatable pain and burning of the legs that was, quite literally, maddening. If you can imagine, the gloom and mental anguish worsened. Painkillers were not prescribed because of quick and inevitable addiction. The phone calls and illegible notes pleading for help, imploring, "What am I going to do?" became more frequent and always fell on drunken ears, both mine and my dad's.

During this final period, I came to a bottom, where even I knew that for me to continue to drink was to die very shortly. I watched my life and my health unravel in amazement as alcohol and drugs waltzed me around mercilessly, gleefully leading me in a hideous, incestuous dance of self-destruction.

The seeds of AA had been planted firmly in my first inpatient treatment facility. I began to surrender, do the psychological gymnastics, housecleaning, sponsorship, literature studies, tapes, meetings, meetings, meetings, and even joined the Fellowship. I was desperate.

I shared with my mother, when I was eight months

into recovery, that something was happening to me that I could not quite explain but that, as a result of this work and effort, I was going to get sober and I *knew* it.

During my first, and ultimately only, attempt at making amends to my mom in person, I gave her a copy of the *Big Book of Alcoholics Anonymous* and convinced her that this was what is changing my life. An avid reader, she devoured enough of the message to also know that I was in God's hands and I *knew* that! Her mind told her that her job with me was over, that God was my parent now and she could exit, that Jimmy would be all right!

She called me a few days prior to "the colossal act of self-pity," or what sometimes happens to depressive types, and mentioned that there would be no more doctors, no more prodding and poking. I thought it odd that she was happy when she made this declaration. On Saturday my father left for one of his day rides in the van. She padded to the garage in nightgown, slippers, and robe, turned on her car, and nestled into a bench van seat that had been removed and stored under cabinets which, from her vantage point, were now covered with little spidery critters. My mom loved critters. She had displayed no fear of spiders for quite some time, as I recall, and certainly not now. It all went as she planned.

That van of my dad's and the bench seat from the back ended up with me in a small Western mountain town. I sold that van to a wonderful family, and quite frequently I see my mother's little bed tooling about town, holding shiny packages and laughing children, and I crack a wry smile. See, only I know this fact, and the alcoholic in me wants to shout, "Hey, do you know that seat you're sitting in is where..." Then I realize I'm in recovery and become aware that grieving with sardonic, unhealthy humor just hurts me and everyone within earshot.

Immediately after I heard about the death via telephone ("James, come home, your mother killed herself"), I experienced a profound sense of relief that the pain was over. I had recently started praying for an end to her emotional and physical pain and wondered if the power of prayer extends to the realm of the mad courage required in this effort. Is it allowed? Does God condone?

I wax and wane in sobriety, of course, paying rapt attention to those who speak of "another disease" at meetings and their recovery from depression. I *know* in my soul that strong Al-Anon, step work, fellowship, the open-mindedness to dump all her old ideas, and maybe the right meds, could have shown Mom a way out thirty years ago. I see women in recovery, coarse women, that would have gone a long way toward helping my classy and proper mom receive the miracle of recovery — and I hurt that these worldly women could not meet her because they would have liked each other and things could have been different and not so terribly sad.

Then I become aware of her spirit and her journey that continues and her soul that has learned, by her son's experience, where to go and what to read and what to do. Wherever and whenever that spirit is in this eternal "now" moment, it becomes all right with me. Because of my experience — in part with her depression and because, in part, I was thrust into a caretaker and protector position as a small boy — my emotions, my instinct for sex, power, and money, and my whole attitude toward life, God, and people are in need of a complete rearrangement. Refocusing my desires and energy is taking all of my time; in fact, this will take more than one lifetime, and therein lies the adventure. What a compelling journey to begin to understand the fears that have motivated me and continue to exert themselves. What joy in the fact that I am detaching ever so slowly from these self-centered fears toward true freedom of spirit.

So here I am, fifty years old, with four children with three different moms, each mom attracted to me from a level of like-consciousness (a nice way of saying, if you got mixed up with me, there is definitely something wrong with you). One perfectly lovely daughter was abandoned by me but reunited for the first time eighteen months ago with her dad. As an example of Divine Synchronicity, her mother had taken ill and died seven months later. She still only has one biological parent; however, the opportunity for me to demonstrate those living amends may soften her grief.

Fifty-seven months into recovery, I'm posturing and lecturing wildly at my fourth wife to "get some f— help! One of us is into recovery, and one of us is not, and if this gap grows much wider, I don't know, blah, blah, blah, blah, blah, blah." This tirade of "professional" advice, "strewn," as my mother would say, "with gratuitous expletives," is terror, of course, that this ugly reminder of depression is all about what I'm going to lose and how all this affects me.

And so I pause to try to get myself out of the way

momentarily, for that *is* the problem. I must ignore my bad brains and ask my heart to tell my mind to shut up so as to let God and the intuitive wisdom within me come into my awareness and bring with it some accurate, spontaneous, and compassionate contributions. Shortly thereafter, everyone in the room, the house, the neighborhood, and the entire world is just a little bit better.

> *"My imperfections and failures are as much a blessing from God as my successes and my talents, and I lay them both at His feet."*
>
> MAHATMA GANDHI

Chapter Five

I CAN SEE

By Pamela Palmer Soward

WHEN you've hit the very bottom, there's nowhere else to go but up. Lessons have to be learned, and new patterns of thought and behavior have to be put into place. This is no easy task after years of finding ways to escape pain instead of preventing it in the first place; old habits die hard.

My first bouts of depression started when I was in my early twenties, just after college, during my first marriage. I had no idea what was happening. I just knew that in the fall, a black mood would come over me. Food had no taste. I no longer had interest in anything I used to enjoy. My mind was fuzzy, and I felt as if my intelligence was leaking away. I was immobile.

I couldn't go to the grocery store; I couldn't go anyplace where there were other people. I became afraid of my husband and everything he said and did. The only place I was not afraid was at home, preferably in bed. I lost a considerable amount of weight. Somehow I made it through the winter.

My mood lightened, my energy was restored, and I enjoyed doing things and being with people again. My self-confidence returned. By February or March, I was like a bright, shining star. I was outgoing to the point of being overbearing. I wanted desperately to run workshops, sell cosmetics, volunteer at the community theater, and work a full-time job. I did them all. I had absolutely no idea this was a manic phase and, unless I was treated, I would crash and become severely depressed again. I didn't know it then, but I was beginning on a roller coaster ride that lasted for more than fifteen years. In the fall I would want to hide from the world, and in the spring I thought I was on top of the whole world.

Psychiatrists would give me antidepressants and talk therapy in the fall, because I seemed just fine in the spring. I got fired several times in both moods. The eighteen months of major depression drove me to a suicide attempt and a month in a psychiatric ward. The psychiatrist was so much like my husband in demeanor and looks that I forced myself to get better just to get away from him.

Prozac pulled me out of the darkness and into the brilliant light of mania within three months. I didn't sleep. I ate very little. I had the energy of a toddler and the sexual drive of a seventeen-year-old boy. The light was so bright within me, I attracted men like bees to the hive. I spent my inheritance on nothing — I bought a six-hundred-dollar gym/spa membership and have no idea where the rest went. I was fired again. Even though I was twenty-eight years old, my family urged me to enter another psychiatric hospital.

Another month in the safe cocoon of quietness, talk therapy, groups, and all the art supplies I wanted.

Fortunately, the psychiatrist diagnosed me as manic-depressive, which we now call bipolar disorder. I began on lithium and very slowly came down from my mania and didn't go into a depression.

I felt like this doctor saved my life. Now I had a disease I could tackle, that I could research, that I could put a name to, and to which I could connect my entire bizarre behavior. Then that savior of a doc moved out of the state because of the stringent health insurance laws at that time. I thought my world had just deflated. I didn't have a therapist, I didn't have a psychiatrist, and I didn't have that face or that ear to listen and help me.

I became pregnant from a man I barely knew and now had to change my whole life. I was twenty-nine and extremely happy because I was pregnant although my entire family tried to talk me into an abortion or at least a private adoption. This was not an option for me. I didn't know if this would be my last chance to have a child.

I was living in supervised housing for the mentally ill and had, through services by the state, a wonderfully capable therapist and a psychiatrist. The pregnancy went by without incident, and I was stable until the next fall, when the baby was turning one. I had started working full time, but money never seemed to stretch far enough, and I became depressed again. I had no desire to plan or even have a first birthday party for my daughter. I temporarily moved in with my folks since I couldn't work full time and take care of my baby and myself. Another change in antidepressants, continued therapy, and eventually the mood lifted.

Stability for any of us with a mental illness cannot

be taken for granted. After three years of single motherhood (and level moods), I treated myself to a Halloween party hosted by some coworkers. There I was a witness to a savage beating. The assailant was a coworker, and the man hurt was another coworker's husband. He suffered a broken nose, broken jaw, amnesia, and a personality change! They had a little boy the same age as my daughter, and emotionally I got extremely drawn into all of this. The police called me at work, made inquiries, and asked me to be a witness. I had to appear in court, and the assailant (who was a cocky young bastard from a well-to-do family) knew he could get away with anything, including intimidation.

I left my therapist's office just a few days after the court appearance, and during the drive home, a black shadow seemed to float down my eyes. I knew I would attempt suicide when I got home. I took a full month's supply of lithium and antidepressants, turned the oven gas all the way up, sat on the door, and pulled a blanket over me to try to breathe the gas in faster and deeper. Somehow during this time, I changed the message on my answering machine to "I'm sorry."

My babysitter called, then called my Dad. He called 911, and I made another trip to the psychiatric ward for three days in intensive care, then three days on the ward. That was all my insurance would allow. I'm glad I have insurance, but it did not allow me to stay as long as I needed. Of course, another change was made in the antidepressants administered to me.

I remained stable for about three years with a different therapist and strictly followed my med schedule. I moved into a townhouse owned by HUD on a lease/purchase grant and worked very hard to pay off my debts. I loved my job and had the kind of position and responsibilities I could be very proud of. I started to lose weight and began a sexy relationship that I thought would end in marriage, though he was already married. (It took me about a year and a half to know that this was never going to bring what I wanted, and I finally ended the relationship.) He continued to pursue me, writing me letters and e-mails.

Within two to three months, I had a total job change. I also helped my stepmother move out of my Dad's house. I made no suicide attempt this time but suffered severe anxiety, slept very little, and had no concentration. I was admitted to the hospital for five days and had yet another change in antidepressants. The lithium was still monitored for toxicity, but the dosage was rarely changed. My Dad let us move in for a few weeks and took care of my daughter so I could keep going to work. I did not have to worry about preparing meals or shopping for groceries.

I spent another year working back to stable moods, making changes to my lifestyle, and getting plenty of sleep. I had met my current husband while I was still dating the married guy. We became friends immediately, and I spent time at his summer parties, having no idea he was in love with me. He came to see me at the hospital but had absolutely no clue about depression or bipolar disorder.

I fell in love with him in December, we were married in March, and by July my anxiety level was so high, I couldn't eat. Our habits were very different, and instead of talking about this issue, I would clam up. He assumed everything was okay. I had stopped all of my therapeutic rituals. I thought I had to do everything and be everything to everyone. I joined his church and immediately volunteered for a position that overwhelmed me.

Our relationship spiraled out of control. Neither of us was making sense anymore. I begged to go to the hospital. I wasn't actively suicidal, but I had thought about driving off the side of the road. I had stopped washing the dishes because I was afraid I would take one of those big kitchen knives to him or myself or the cat.

After four hours of arguing with the insurance company, I got them to agree to a seventy-two-hour hospital stay and then participation in a two-week outpatient program. My husband expected me to be completely better after I finished the outpatient program. I had no chance to have downtime, to heal. I continued to feel completely overwhelmed.

One night I separated all my jewelry, the antiques for my daughter, and told her to make sure my husband put it in a safe-deposit box. I began a long letter, locked the bathroom doors, and swallowed all the pills I could find. I came out and kept writing until I fainted and fell off the bed.

I remember nothing of the next three days. I didn't wake up until the third day and was groggy for one or two more. In the midst of all this, my thyroid tests showed conflicting results, so my family doctor suggested I switch from lithium to Depakote. Within four days, I was becoming manic. Within ten days, I was fully manic, and the psychiatrist put me back on the lithium as well as the Depakote. I had been at the private hospital for three weeks, and it was evident I was going to need to go to the state hospital. I needed long-term care until my body and behavior adjusted to the medication. My marriage, as far as I was concerned, had totally fallen apart. The psychiatrist and my family instructed my husband to move out when I came home, at least for a while, since my anxiety level skyrocketed when we argued.

I agreed but cried when I had to sign the papers to be committed to the state hospital. There are volumes I will write someday about that stay. Three months locked in with incurable schizophrenics, people who talked to the television like it was their therapist, men who manipulated the vulnerable young women for a feel or two, cockroaches on the dinner trays. Noise. Always so much noise. I was simply being housed until the mania came under control. There was not a whisper of any kind of cognitive or talk therapy. While I was there, a movie was filmed about a girl's stay in a private institution in the 1960's. They really had no clue as to what it was really like.

After three months, I was released to my father and allowed to go back to work part time. In the meantime, I granted custody of my daughter to my brother and his family. Upon leaving the state hospital, everyone, including my best friend (also bipolar) and my therapist, thought I was going to be as right as rain. I started back to work. I planned the date for my daughter to come home. My husband came to the house (we were separated by now), and I let him in. Two days later I attempted suicide again. I was just so tired, so numb, so sure my daughter and my whole family were much better off without me, so sure that if I could just sleep forever, I wouldn't have to feel the pain, wouldn't have to fake being okay.

This time I was sent to a private hospital with two psychiatrists and a well-educated, well-paid, caring staff. The atmosphere was bright, and I didn't feel locked in. There were no more than fifteen patients, and no one was chronically ill. For some reason, when the resident psychiatrist spoke with me, life looked so much better. He used the term "recovery" instead of "managing my illness." I had never had a remote thought of thinking about recovery before he said this. I began to paint for the first time in my life — just using a kid's watercolor paint set. I painted vases of flowers, sailboats next to a beach, flowers of all kinds, and copied as many of the paintings on the ward as I could. I wrote a contract for myself and my family that included plans to prevent another suicide attempt. It included my asking for help whenever I needed it. I set up a plan to have ladies from my church sleep at my house the first two weeks I was home. I set up a partial hospitalization program before going back to work. As much as it hurt, I asked my brother to keep my daughter through the next school year. I knew if I took her too soon, I could experience too much stress and end up in the hospital again or just not take care of her the way she needed. I decided I'd take an art class, and I did. I found a support group and went faithfully twice a month. I took a parenting class. I worked part time until I was bored at home and needed work to get me out of bed. I went to a lot of movies. I spent time with my best friend again. I helped my Dad around his house, cleaning, mostly. I asked to be moved to a more challenging position at work. I showed off my paintings at work and had two commissions. I entered my paintings in an art show. I brought my daughter home at the end of the school year.

Now there has been more time of wellness rather

than illness, but it's the bad times during the illness that stand out. I am in debt from all these medical expenses, but at least they don't charge interest. For the last year I have been stable and almost happy. I am exceedingly happy with my daughter being home. I am faithful to my medicine, my therapy, my sleep, and the other things I need to do to stay balanced and whole. I am now thirty-eight. I have many good years ahead of me, and I can see struggles without illness. I can see happiness without mania. I can see my daughter graduating from high school without experiencing her Mommy leaving her for the hospital again. I can see advancement and challenge at work. I can see friendships growing and new ones beginning. I can see a renewed relationship with my husband even if right now I can't live with him. But most of all, I CAN SEE who I am and that I am a worthwhile human being.

*"If one advances confidently
in the direction of his dreams,
and endeavors to live the life
which he has imagined,
he will meet with
a success unexpected
in common hours."*

HENRY DAVID THOREAU

My Journey with
Depression

By Janet Atkinson

I am an average woman. My life centered around
my boyfriend, kids, and friends. I worked in a group
home, did the grocery shopping, played with the kids,
went out with friends, but one day I felt different.

I was irritable. I couldn't sleep, or I'd have periods
of sleeping all the time. I had no energy or desire to
be with people, including friends and family. I just
wanted to crawl in a hole and live like a hermit. But,
No, there is nothing wrong, I told myself. People
around me started noticing my changes, though, and
started asking me all the time what was wrong.

I kept telling myself, *Jan, don't worry about it. It's
just early menopause or stress or lack of sex* — anything but the dreaded D word. I was driving my
boyfriend nuts with my mood swings and constant
nagging at him. All I did was listen to sad songs, and
I slowly withdrew from everything that meant any-

thing to me. *I DIDN'T HAVE A PROBLEM — THEY HAD THE PROBLEM* was what I told myself.

I ended up fighting with my boyfriend one night, and he basically told me that if I didn't go to the doctor to see what was wrong, we would have to consider breaking up, as he couldn't handle my denial that something was wrong with me.

Okay, okay, I know what you're thinking — will she listen to him, or will she say, "Excuse me, this is my life, and I'll live it any way I want." Well, I took the "I want a life, and I want to know what's wrong" route. I realized that there was something really wrong and that I wasn't myself, so with the help and support of my boyfriend and friends, I decided to see my doctor.

Finding out that I suffered from depression scared me but also gave me a chance to have something to strive to beat, or at least keep at bay for a while. I was happy that I knew what was wrong, but I was also frightened because I didn't know what was in store for me. I didn't want to be a grumpy mom or girlfriend anymore; I wanted my life back.

I went through a period right after I found out the diagnosis (I was also diagnosed with obsessive-compulsive disorder and anxiety) where I seemed to be floating out above myself, looking down on everyone. Right away, I read every article and checked out every Web site to find out more about depression. I even wanted to start a chat room for depressed people, which I still might do. I have a great doctor who is very supportive of me and everything that I want to do, but he also keeps me grounded.

I quit my job, as the depression was very severe, and sat at home, feeling like I let everyone down. But then I realized that this is something that EVERYONE suffers from at some time in his or her life. And I started to think about the positive things in life.

When I started taking my first medication, Serzone, it had really adverse effects on me, so my doctor took me off of it. Of course, I was worried about discontinuing it because I was afraid that I would get worse. But my doctor put me on Paxil, and it did the trick. The temporary side effects of taking Paxil were well worth it, as it seems to be working great. I experienced a period, though, where I was having a really hard time and ended up going into the hospital for a week. I had constant care and constant monitoring, and it helped. I realized that I can be okay and I can live with depression. Now, don't get me wrong, I still have days where I feel the world is ending and I'm in the center of it, and yes, I'll be honest: I have thought about suicide, but LIFE seemed more appealing even at the point when I felt the lowest.

I have a therapist whom I see every two weeks, and it has helped me a lot. I can go see him and say whatever I want, and he is there to listen, **NOT** judge, and he helps me think of positive things to do with my life when I'm feeling low. He was very honest with me right away in our first meeting and told me that things won't change overnight, and that I'll be on medication for a long time, but that I can't let it run my life.

I want to help people understand depression and know that common people, **EVERYDAY** people, suffer from it and that there are people out there to help.

I guess I should talk about when I told my family about the depression. I told my dad first. I called him up one day and said that I had something I wanted to discuss with him. He said, "Okay, shoot." I basically just told him that I have depression. He said, "Well, Hon, what do you expect me to do about it?" That left me speechless for a few minutes; then I thought, "Wait a minute. This is my dad. He's always been like this." Before you start thinking my dad is a mean man, let me tell you a little about him. He is the type of person who thinks that unless you're dying, it's not a big deal and you can handle it. I talked with him a bit more about it, and then I let him go. Just to let you all know, my dad is one hundred percent behind me and supports me no matter what happens.

My mom took it a little harder; she thought it was something she did. (I think that's a mom trait, as I do that with my kids.) I told her it was nothing she did, and I told her some sites to look up on the Web so she could understand depression more. Now she's okay with it, and she sees it as part of me. Speaking of that, I want people to know that depression **IS** a part of me, of who I am. It doesn't make me better or worse. I have an idea about people and the stigma of depression: **I THINK IT MAKES YOU STRONGER.** Depression isn't a burden that you have to carry around with you and let it drag you down; it is a path leading you to the top of the mountain that you want to climb.

I have lots of goals and hopes that I will achieve despite depression. This is my life, and a little thing like depression isn't gonna stop me! I hope that I can instill that into other people who suffer from it too. I want to help people understand it and help them to refuse to let it control them. There are always going to be times when I feel really down and like life is stomping on me, but I know deep inside that feeling will pass because I am strong enough to overcome anything that is thrown at me. Those days when I am down are evened out by the days I feel great. I will be on medication for a while, but I have great support to guide and help me. I still read everything new about depression because there is something always new coming out, and we should keep up to date. I try to keep upbeat about everything, and I like to joke about it sometimes. It upsets people sometimes when I joke about depression, but if you can't laugh about stuff in life, what can you do?

I have done a lot of soul-searching, read a lot of books, talked to a lot of people, but in the end I always remember that life is a challenge that is meant to be conquered, and I am one of those who is going to do it. I want to go to nursing school, and I want to become a doctor. I want to successfully grow tomatoes and actually grow some nails, and depression isn't going to stop me from doing that.

I hope that I have given you something to think about and maybe changed your view on depression.

*"Avoiding danger is
no safer in the long run
than outright exposure.
Life is either a
daring adventure
or nothing."*

Helen Keller

MENTAL HEALTH SANCTUARY

By Patricia Pheil

As a result of experiencing the better portion of my life as severely painful and chaotic on an emotional level, I have a tremendous passion for helping others find their way through this madness and have expressed this by building mental health Web sites on the Internet.

I am forty-three years old, and my diagnoses are bipolar disorder (BP), borderline personality disorder (BPD), generalized anxiety disorder, and panic disorder. These disabilities prevent me from working.

My childhood seemed fairly normal and uneventful. My family was considered to be upper class by some people. My father made good money from the telephone company, and my mother was a homemaker. I graduated a semester early from high school by going to summer school. I was in a hurry to get on my own and "fly."

Because I didn't want to be too close, I began study-ing at a state university at age seventeen. It was locat-ed a few hours away from home, and I lived in the dorm. This was the time in my life that I had the most fun. I attended many parties, became involved in a sorority, and still managed to keep my grades up. At this time, my disorders were manageable. I did, how-ever, have mood swings and sometimes didn't treat my boyfriend at that time very well.

I hadn't experienced any major stressors in my life until the following semester, after summer had ended. Within the first week of school, I received a call from my parents stating that my brother, who was a year and a half older than me, was killed in an automobile accident.

Of course, this affected me severely, and people have said that incident has changed me in a negative way. I do know that this was the first time I realized I was not immortal.

While in college, I took a semester off due to being abandoned in a relationship. I went down to Southern California and got a job as a receptionist while trying to heal. Of course, being a borderline, I called my for-mer boyfriend several times asking him to come back, making a fool out of myself. Relatives noticed that my response to being rejected was not normal and that I was unable to let go.

I returned to college and got my B.A. in philosophy. I really didn't think I needed a specific degree, as I knew that I would be getting married and would never have to worry about working. (Snicker.)

I married, in my senior year, a man eight years older than me. The marriage was short-lived, as we divorced five years later. We did, however, have a beautiful daughter together.

During the separation and divorce process, I realized I had to think seriously about what I wanted to do careerwise. I went to job agencies, and they informed me I might as well just have my high school diploma because my philosophy degree was worthless.

I decided that I did not want to be trapped forever in a job I didn't like. After much thinking, I decided I wanted to be a counselor/social worker. Since I was receiving child support and alimony for a short time, I decided to take this opportunity to return to school. I did receive my MSW and have been employed as a social worker for nearly ten years. During these years, I experienced what Janice Cauwels could not have put it better in her book *Imbroglio*. She says, "...the borderline appears always to function well, especially in professional or academic situations that are structured, supportive, or both. Meanwhile, she is binding her interior fragmentation with shoe-strings..."

I remember there were times I would yell and scream at my husband, and I thought this was normal. He was "bad" and deserved my outrage.

However, after my divorce, I became involved in many relationships that I now call the "relationships from hell." The men were usually substance abusers and could not make a commitment. This must have felt safe to me because after my divorce, I was scared to death of a commitment.

I was totally at the mercy of whatever man I was with at the time. That man kept me from being "invisible." He defined me completely. I did almost anything to keep from being abandoned, even if I didn't like or respect the man. I simply couldn't stand rejection and the feeling of not existing. It brought feelings of suicide and extreme emotional pain, and thoughts were very distorted. The longer I was away from this "mirror" of mine, the higher my stress level became; I was afraid of it and thus did anything to prevent abandonment.

When my rages and alcohol were mixed, I usually got into a lot of serious trouble. I have kicked in doors, smashed windows, and kicked a car. My last incident of this sort was about five years ago, when I was arrested, for the first and only time, for smashing into an old boyfriend's car. Your guess is correct — he was abandoning me. At that time, I was extremely disabled but had not received SSD yet and was being evicted from my home. I had bills piling up, and I was terribly afraid of being homeless. I knew I would be arrested before I left my home. I think I was seeking out assistance, and I wasn't receiving any from our county mental health system here in Oregon.

I was booked and released, and later the D.A. dropped the charges. The woman who released me stated that everyone who worked in the jail called me a hero. I certainly didn't feel like one.

In each and every relationship, I yelled and screamed at these men because, again, they deserved it, and I felt like I couldn't help but react this way. It was as if a very strong internal force that I could not control was driving me. Later I realized not only that these men verbally and emotionally abused me, but that I had verbally abused them also.

At the end of each relationship, I went to pieces. My

sensitivity to rejection was very strong, and I began to act in very sick ways. I would repetitively call these men or go by their houses — anything that would end my feelings of abandonment. I realized later that there were many times I really did not respect the man rejecting me, did not want him in my life, yet could not stand the feeling of being left. And my addiction to relationships was very strong. I experienced tremendous anxiety, only to be relieved by some small crumb from them. As I mentioned, I was afraid of this anxiety because its level rose very high and I did not know how high it could get. This was why I scrambled around, acting ill. I was trying to relieve this horrible feeling of anxiety. It was so bad that many times I just lived life feeling dead inside and tried to become numb on benzodiazepines.

Probably the majority of my adult life was spent living with some degree of depression. Counselors kept telling me I was depressed, but I was so used to living and feeling the way I felt, I really didn't know what it was like to feel normal.

At the age of thirty-three, in the initial stages of my social work career, I was voluntarily hospitalized due to "adjustment disorder." I was very depressed and was losing my coping skills. I was there for seven days, and it was during this stay that I was diagnosed with the borderline personality disorder. I was very angry and upset, as I knew the stigma that was associated with this disorder and was not yet ready to accept the depth of my "mental illness." I stayed in denial for many years. Unfortunately for me, my bipolar disorder was not diagnosed until much later. I understand this is not an uncommon experience. I had been seeing a counselor who was doing uncover work with me. We focused a lot on my childhood and the emotional pain in my life. This is dangerous stuff for a person with the borderline personality disorder. I spiraled down rapidly and had to take a leave from work.

It was during this time that I was unable to function on many levels. I was a single parent, and my daughter was eleven years old. I spent most of my time in my room, leaving my daughter alone much of the time. Many times I would give her money to go down to the market right next to us, where she would buy sandwiches, etc., for dinner, as I was unable to cook.

I was also unable to shower most of the time and lived and slept in the same clothes day after day. I was completely unaware of this. The drapes were drawn all the time, and it was very difficult to face the world outside of my home.

I realized it was not good for my daughter to be around this atmosphere, so I sent her to stay with her dad. Initially, this was very difficult for her, being away from me, and she would cry and cry, begging to come home. My heart sank so deep and so low that to this day, when I think about it, I feel emotional pain. All I could do was try to explain what I was experiencing and tell her I would be well soon. At her young age, she did not understand, and I believe she felt much rejection during this time.

After a brief period, my daughter not only adjusted to staying with her father but wanted to live with him permanently. I said no, that she was to live with me and that was that.

One weekend that her father had her, he called and

stated that he would not let her come home to me, that she had told him about buying food from the store and my not taking care of her very well. I became very afraid, and I phoned the police, as I had custody of my daughter.

I got her back that day, but my daughter was extremely angry with me. It was certainly clear that she did not want to live with me, and I believe she had lost respect for me. Not only was I unable to care for her properly because of the deep level of depression I was undergoing, but my boyfriend at the time was not a good influence. He was a drug user, and my daughter easily picked up that he was very strange, and she didn't want to be around him.

I never did street drugs, but I felt that I really didn't deserve better than the kind of men that I attracted. My self-esteem was extremely low, and my life and emotions were so bad, it was as if God was punishing me.

Finally, I told her that I don't keep hostages, and I let her live with her dad. For two weeks I couldn't get out of bed. My psyche was extremely fragile. I was very sensitive to noise or any external stimuli. I listened to tapes of Pavarotti and a thunderstorm tape. I would pretend that there was indeed a thunderstorm outside, and for some reason, that soothed me.

I felt suicidal every day, and I didn't know how long I would hold out. I always kept my old medications, thinking if I needed them again, it would circumvent a visit to the doctor. Many times I found myself staring at those pills.

I called my aunt every day and told her I was unable to leave the bedroom. I really think she helped

keep me alive. After the end of two weeks, we celebrated over the phone that I was able to go out into
the living room.

For a long time, I refused antidepressants. I was
afraid of them and didn't think they would do me any
good. Finally, out of desperation, I got on a tricyclic. It
was almost six weeks before I opened the drapes and
looked outside. It was as if I was seeing the world for
the first time. It seemed like a welcoming place at
last, and I felt good to be alive. I went to work not
much later.

It is difficult to really describe everything I felt during that time. I don't think the human language can
describe it. It was dark, black, and right next to death.
At times the emotional pain was simply unbearable,
and during those times, the only thoughts that entertained my mind was that I could kill myself to escape
it.

I wish I could say that this was the only time in my
life that I have experienced that deep a depression,
but there have been many more episodes since.

Even when I wasn't depressed, I was sick, which
was most of my life. It was like living in a tunnel, only
I didn't know I was living that way because I had
never been out of this tunnel. My friends and family
would talk their ears off, trying to help me. It was as
if they were explaining a whole different world or
universe to me, and as hard as I tried to understand
(believe me, I gave it my all), I simply could not fathom their view of it. Also, it is difficult to pay attention
when you live from crisis to crisis.

Later on, I began to notice something I had not
seen before. I would become extremely anxious and

"angry" (what or who at, I don't know), and I wasn't even in a relationship. There was no external reason for me to feel this way. I began to realize that the anxiety was not totally coming from being abandoned; it was physical. It was like it came from nowhere.

Many times I would experience an angry, irritable, restless feeling that felt very physical. For a long time, I thought something had triggered it. But later in life, I realized it came on for no reason. Later, when I met my present wonderful husband, he began to notice that there was a pattern or cycle to my "madness." He used to say that around 11:00 p.m., my "head would start to spin."

The patterns changed during some periods. Other times I noticed I was calm in the morning, and as each hour went by, I became more and more anxious. Actually, I may have been misusing the term "anxious." Many times it was pure rage — yelling, screaming, swearing, and sometimes kicking and hitting furniture. A few times I broke things.

As I learned more about the borderline personality disorder, I felt it was a BPD rage, pure and simple. So I began the long, long process of trying to find the right meds to make me feel normal.

I also began to notice other feelings that came for no reason. I would be having a good week, and overnight I would spend a whole day in severe clinical depression. I didn't know if I was coming or going. My moods were all out of control. When I felt anxious, I was also very tearful at times and would cry uncontrollably.

As time went by and no medication or combination of medications worked for me, my nurse practitioner began to question bipolar disorder. I was unable to see a psychiatrist, as no one wanted to accept me with my state health insurance.

My meds were switched to deal with the BP, and still I was out of control. I went through months of depression where again I slept in my clothes, wore them the next day, or for days went unshowered, etc. It was all I could do to just sit on the couch. I had many fantasies about what I would say in my suicide note to help my loved ones not blame themselves.

Once again I felt that utterly desperate level of depression where the emotional pain of it became so deep that it felt completely unbearable. I was unable to perform any tasks at all. I slept, ate, sat on the couch, and just survived physically. I felt dead inside.

Being this depressed does not allow one any energy to focus on anyone or anything else. A mild example would be having the flu. We are in pain, and we are only able to focus on ourselves. Depression is like this, but one hundredfold or more.

I went back to the hospital, as I was becoming very afraid of hurting myself. I really did not want to die. I wanted to live, but I could not stand the pain.

At this time I was considered "treatment resistant," as I had tried many drugs and nothing worked. I was becoming more and more afraid that I would never be well, and I could not fathom that kind of existence much longer.

I was finally able to see the county mental health psychiatrist, who evaluated my case. I sobbed through the whole session. He switched some of my meds and put me back on a low dose of a tricyclic that had worked for me in the past.

The next day it had most definitely put me into a manic episode. I was yelling and screaming at my poor husband and threw cups at him. In between the yelling, I would tell him how sorry I was, that I knew I was manic and he deserved better.

He placed a call to the mental health clinic, and they put me on Seroquel. Overnight and since then, I have been fine.

The suicide rate for both the bipolar disorder and the borderline personality disorder is very high. I believe what kept me alive was primarily my strong faith in God. I spent many years during my youth being angry with God because I was so miserable. However, as time went on, over and over again I witnessed miracles in my life. I finally reached a point where I have total faith in Him. It is amazing how I got from there to here — it is a miracle. This faith in God kept hope in me, and without hope, I really don't think I would have made it. I kept telling myself that one day I would not feel this way, that the correct drug cocktail would be found, and that is exactly what happened.

Besides dealing with depression, I dealt also with my borderline personality disorder. In the last few years, I quit living my life in crisis. I can almost mark the day I stopped. It was when I applied for Social Security Disability because I realized I simply couldn't work. I was actually disabled years before I fully gave up. A point came in my life where emotionally, physically, and spiritually I could no longer live in chaos. I was done, and it was not a conscious choice on my part. It is important to note that when this change happened in me, I still exhibited many physical symptoms of my disorders. I still raged at times and still had mood swings and depression. The physical symptoms didn't really go away until I got on the proper medication, and that didn't happen until about six months ago.

It was not long after I applied for SSD that I met my husband, a man I would never have dated in the past because he would not have been exciting enough. He is also the first man that I didn't verbally abuse. I really think this was the first time in my whole life that I was capable of real intimacy and the stability of a peaceful, quiet, and long-term relationship. I am more stable now than I have ever been in my entire life. No, I am not well or cured, just more stable. Also, I don't feel constant pain any longer. I am, however, very sensitive to any level of stress.

There is a big difference between experiencing life "in the tunnel" rather than "out of the tunnel." This is very hard for me to explain. I am much more in touch with which behaviors of mine are ill and which are normal. I view the world much more realistically, not through painful lenses that are terribly distorted. I am not in constant emotional pain like I was. It still feels very unusual to feel happy and contented — such a new experience for me. It feels strange to even write such a thing.

I never thought I would come this far in my recovery. It was an internal, unconscious feeling that I had been through enough, and it was this change that caused me to make different decisions in my life. I finally chose the things that were good for me. I finally decided to take care of myself. Our decision-making skills have a great deal to do with what our lives are like. Previously, I lived my life self-destructively. My decisions were self-defeating. I was reacting, not acting, because there was so much pain, and often my methods to get rid of the pain hurt me deeper.

As I look back and ask myself what I could have done differently in this tunnel I lived in, I would say I would have been much better off not being in a romantic relationship until I was well into recovery. I was much happier without one, even though I was lonely. I was simply too ill to handle a relationship, and when I got in one, I became VERY ill. I would rage at my partner and verbally abuse him, yet when he threatened to leave, I felt desperate.

I also would have taken a job that was much less stressful. As a social worker, I listened most of the day to other people's problems, and during most of my career, I was emotionally bankrupt myself. My cup was empty so much of the time, and the relationships I had with the men in my life only took more from me.

Had I known then what I know now, I would have visited the doctor and demanded the RIGHT medications. I wish I would have known before that what I was experiencing is a result of a brain disorder that cannot be controlled with therapy alone. This would have made a major difference not only in my life but in my daughter's life as well. It would have helped my mood swings, rages, and depression. Also, I would never have had a drop of alcohol.

This is the first time I have really had a stable existence, and I no longer meet the criteria for the borderline personality disorder. However, I have noted that many days I would eagerly wake up very early in the morning to work on my Web site, sometimes forgetting to eat and working for twelve to sixteen hours or so. My mind would race with new ideas, and I felt I couldn't put these ideas in motion fast enough. Some nights, I refused to go to sleep and would continue to work on the Web site though I was utterly exhausted. I just couldn't stop.

Some days, when I was able to tear myself away from the computer, I would go around the house and clean and clean, thinking, "I'm so glad I'm cured now. Life feels wonderful." I just couldn't find enough to do. I decided we should paint the house, and I had so much energy.

Then I would wake up one morning, and not only would this scenario all be gone, but I would feel utterly depressed. I couldn't get off the couch. Everything felt flat, and I couldn't do a thing — couldn't take a shower, etc. My thoughts were always full of surprise, and I thought, "I think the antidepressant just pooped out." I would stay depressed for a while, and then the meds were changed. I had to either wait until the meds brought me out of depression, or within twelve hours of taking or increasing the new antidepressant, I would feel really good once again, only to be dropped down into depression later.

I feel very comfortable discussing BPD, as I am well read on the subject and on the research. However, I am just now (10/99) beginning to learn about the bipolar disorder. I did read somewhere that it may indeed be common for people with bipolar disorder to wait years before their disorder is diagnosed.

The "symptoms" of BPD and BP are very similar, though mental health professionals who are very skilled can make an accurate diagnosis. From the letters I receive on my borderline site, it appears that many people with the BPD also have the BP. Some say they are not related; some say they are.

Another thing that is important to remember about both of these disorders is that it is uncommon to find them alone, without another disorder present. This is called the "affective spectrum," which you can read more about on the Web.

One thing I do know is that there is no cure for BP. We must take our medications the rest of our lives, or we will relapse. Many of us don't like the idea of taking medications. The way I look at it is not "When can I go off the meds?" or "I don't like taking meds," but "What do I need to do to feel and function better so that I can enjoy life and be the happiest person I can be?" I am a strong believer in taking medications because this is a very important aspect in taking care of me, and when I can do that, I can thus be there for others as well.

Presently I live in Oregon with my husband and our three cats that we call our "babies." BPD and BP are very emotionally painful disorders, and if you are like I was, they affect every area of life. For me, it was like a major earthquake crumbling not only my inner self but all aspects of my life.

It is not only okay, but it is essential that you begin to forgive yourself for your past behavior due to your illness. Having whatever brain disorder you have is not your fault. You didn't ask for it, and you didn't cause it. You and I deserve to be happy. It took me years to realize this. Mental illness is not widely understood, and for some it is scary. Others may insist that you are "bad" or "manipulative." You simply are not. I do not believe there are any bad people. No one could understand, for example, why I stayed in bad relationships. I am, in fact, a very bright person, which seems to be common with people who have the borderline personality disorder. However, my intelligence got me nowhere with this illness. I don't know why that is. I think BPD can be described as survival — surviving from pain, constant pain. The pain is so bad that we will do anything to make it stop.

Families, as well as sufferers, need support. They are deeply hurting, and their pain needs to be recognized. If you are at a time in your life where you can forgive your parents for whatever it is you hold against them, it will be a tremendous healing experience for you and for them. Not forgiving is a very heavy load to carry around. Reaching out to borderlines and bipolars was an important step for me. I felt less alone and cried and cried when I read stories that sounded just like mine. Much guilt was released also.

Chapter Six

SOMETHING TO BE THANKFUL FOR

By John McManamy

A Thanksgiving Tribute

It's like a cardiac arrest, only it happens in the brain — something responsible for holding the gray mass together abruptly shifts, there is a sickening feeling of something terrible about to happen, and next thing, your head is experiencing the awful sensation of being emptied out. From somewhere inside, the power goes down, and the body seems to collapse into itself like a marionette being folded into a box. You look for a way out, and what's left of your broken brain does its best to oblige with images of high bridges and frozen ponds and nooses dangling from balconies.

In January of 1999, when my family brought me to the emergency room at our local hospital, I could never imagine that, eleven months later, I'd be writing about anything I had to be thankful for, much less paying tribute to this beast inside that sent me there in the first place — the one that goes by two names, both of them woefully inadequate: manic depression and bipolar.

May as well call the thing Fred, as far as I'm concerned.

For most of my life, Fred has been my constant traveling companion, even as I denied his existence and tried so hard to pretend I was a master of my own fate. "I'm normal!" I kept insisting over and over, much to Fred's quiet amusement.

Twenty-one years ago, I was well on the way to proving it. After all those wasted years at the mercy of the very condition I denied having, I landed on my feet in New Zealand. I had successfully completed my second year of law school there, and I was married, with a beautiful three-month-old daughter. There had been some other Americans in our birthing classes, and we invited them over, together with another Kiwi-Yank couple we knew, to celebrate Thanksgiving. I recall lifting my glass to make a toast, but then words failed me.

We were seated on cushions on the floor, with the turkey and all the fixings on a low table. But the stars of the show were the new citizens of planet earth. I looked at the proud parents and their newborns, and all the baby paraphernalia they had brought, and simply choked out, "Thanks."

Life was beautiful.

Little did I realize in ten years I would find myself in another country, broke and alone and unemployable and in search of a convenient bridge to jump off. I couldn't blame it all on Fred. Besides, Fred has a way of convincing you he doesn't exist.

Boy, you showed them, Fred let me know less than a year later. *You're back on your feet again and working on your own terms, not theirs.* I had one book out and another on the way. And there was my daughter, now eleven, together with my parents in my apartment to celebrate Christmas. Like a considerate roommate, Fred made himself scarce.

When he showed up again, I was back in the States. Think of someone on a high hill, lobbing boulders at you — that was Fred. One large stone would hit me on the chest and send me into a crushing depression. Then the next one would come thudding down on me as I lay sprawled on the ground, compounding my despair with a depression on top of a depression.

But I made Fred work hard, damn hard. Several years and an untold number of boulders it took, but finally I went down and didn't get up. After all these years, I finally acknowledged Fred's dominion, not to mention his existence.

So now, at long last, I'm going to give Fred his due. After all, he made me what I am. Whatever our differences, he is responsible for me being me, so to hate Fred would be to hate me. Besides, having Fred around does have its advantages.

It is Fred who painted my brain with amazing visions and insights and filled my senses with the type of sensations few mortals experience. It is Fred who made it possible for me to find the sublime in even the most mundane, and it is Fred who cloaked me in a humanity and godliness that I would not exchange for a winning lottery ticket.

So yes, Fred, on this Thanksgiving, for the very first time, I will sing your praises and give you thanks. In a few months I will see my grown daughter, here from New Zealand, and I give thanks for that, too. I will give thanks to my family who were there for me and to a God who somehow has proved to me he does not and does exist.

And yes, Fred, I know one day again you'll be waiting for me in some dark alley. But for now, I invite you to pull up a chair while I lift my glass in a toast.

Alone Against the World

A blast from my past:

I was alone against the world. There was no other way to describe it. It was around ages eleven and twelve when I noticed that I was a lot shorter and skinnier than the kids my age. Then they all started sprouting hair in funny places and talking in deep voices in knowing ways, and the realization struck with biblical force: My God! I really was different!

It was like those dreams everyone seems to have of turning up in public in just your underwear. If only it were just that. If only the shame and embarrassment were for just one day. If only I could just go home and reach in the closet and slip into my leg and pubic hair, the way I could a pair of pants, and grow six inches and return to school and blend in and say things like "Eat it raw" like I really knew what I was talking about.

No, I was doomed to show up for school in the equivalent of my dream underwear every day for the next three years.

My inner immune system invented its own respite from the terror of school and the outside world. Just when I knew I could not ever possibly board that school bus one more time, my body would give out on me. My throat would constrict and flare up, my nose would heave up great gobs of green bloody snots, and I would cough the cough of the dead.

Then the healing would start. There in bed or on the couch, under a million blankets, shivering in a sweat-induced microclimate of Vicks VapoRub fumes, my strength would come back, slowly, over several days, a week, more. Then one day I would get out of bed and get dressed, too far behind in my schoolwork to ever really catch up but nevertheless ready to take what the day offered, one day at a time.

The only thing that I was ever good in, it turned out, was dodgeball. Prisoner's dodge, wall dodge, circle dodge — no one could get me out, not even the older kids. This was my true gift — the reflexes of a Jedi. Had dodgeball been a major sport, I would have been offered a full scholarship to Notre Dame and been a first-round draft pick in the World Dodgeball League.

Unfortunately, no one played dodgeball after sixth grade, and with all the other sports, I was always the last one picked. Nevertheless, when I hear the experts speak of a God-given talent, I know what they are talking about. I know what near-perfection is because, in one small, inconsequential realm of human activity, at age nine and ten, I had experienced it.

It seems, besides granting me Jedi reflexes, God also endowed me with a musician's soul, but one, oddly enough, not connected to my Jedi reflexes. I started on the trumpet in fourth grade and could have played it well into high school with no one really noticing or caring how bad I was, but then fate stepped in.

I switched to trombone in seventh grade, and by eighth grade I was the only one, more or less, left standing. Like a war of attrition. All the other trombones, it seems, had been taken out. It was just me. And this was the year the band director decided to form a Dixieland band.

To give you an idea of the company I now found myself in, one of the members of this little ensemble would go on to a career in music, and the others were good enough to give it a shot. Another would graduate from an Ivy League school, and the rest weren't far behind.

Then there was me.

The tenor sax in the group, the one who went on to the Ivy League, came over to me one day, grinning. "If you were my dog," he said to me, "I'd shave your ass and make you walk backward."

Later that year, we would be featured in the spring concert and win the school variety show hands down, no thanks to me, but the big surprise was just in store.

That summer we had an outdoor gig in the city park. We were part of a band concert, one of those Sousa-type bands, where the members had union cards. There must have been upwards of a thousand out on the park lawn, spread out on blankets or sitting in folding chairs, many with picnic dinners, all in a holiday mood. The Sousa band did their numbers, then it was our turn.

The clarinet player, who was the leader of the group, gave me the evil eye, as if to say, "You screw up here, and you're a dead man." I walked out onto the outdoor stage like I was going to the gallows, trombone in one hand, music stand in the other — four sheets of music clipped on with clothespins — praying to God we wouldn't have to do an encore because that fourth piece, to me, was as decipherable as the Rosetta stone.

The clarinet player counted off, and — bang! — we were into the first piece. It went off without a hitch, and by the second number, the crowd was getting into it. Then came the third number, which featured written solos from everyone in the group, me included. I reached way down low on the slide and hoped lightning wouldn't strike me dead.

Or maybe I wished it would; I can't remember.

We wrapped up the song, and the crowd was on its feet, cheering and stamping wildly. *My God!* I could only think, *there's going to be an encore!* And here I was with the Rosetta stone clipped to my music stand.

I'll just move my slide and pretend I'm playing, I thought. And that's sort of what I did. I tuned out the people on the lawn in front and the Sousa band behind and pointed my trombone down to the ground, hoping to turn invisible.

There was really only one note I had to hit, and that was when the piece changed key. My job was to reach out practically to the end of the slide and belt out a low C note. So up came the trombone, and out came the C note right on schedule. Back down to the ground I went.

Mercifully, it ended. I looked up, and the people out on the lawn were back on their feet. Then I looked back at the Sousa band, and THEY were on their feet. A standing ovation from the house band. Let me put this into perspective: More people have walked on the moon than have received a standing ovation from the house band.

Once off stage, my fellow tormentors actually congratulated me. Enthusiastically, at that. Then it sunk in: I had nailed my first three pieces. Not only that, my fake slide work on the fourth number had been mistaken for real jazz, not just kiddie-band Dixieland. This is why all those musicians with union cards behind us were on their feet applauding — it was because of me!

All four feet eleven and ninety pounds of me.

I had outplayed the others by a country mile, and the Ivy League tenor sax player and all the others were ecstatic. I had broken through. I was one of them. For one brief, shining moment, I was accepted.

But not for what I was. You see, after that, I went right back to not being able to play my trombone worth shit. Once more I was the butt of their jokes, the object of their gossip, the source of their malicious amusement. I was right back to where I had been before — me alone against the world.

Not long after, I entered a high school from which I would fail to graduate. The constant daily round of humiliations and put-downs had begun to take their toll. The fun-loving child in me no longer existed. In his place was a thirteen-year-old, going on fourteen, rendered numb by the constant grind of being too little to face too much.

No longer could the world and all its trials hurt me. I had entered a dark but comfortable realm beyond sense and feeling. President Kennedy would get assassinated, and I wouldn't shed a tear. Winter would descend with bitter terror, and I wouldn't feel the cold. The Beatles would prove to be the biggest thing since the Coming of Elvis, and I would barely notice.

I was the nearest thing on earth to a shade; a shadow soul, bound to a netherworld existence somewhere beyond the River Styx. Someday, I allowed myself to think, things would be different. Someday, I would be great. Someday, I would be famous. But first, as my school performance deteriorated and took a dive, things would get worse.

I was fated to go through tenth grade twice, once in the public school and once in a Catholic school, both times in my sleep. But oddly enough, in blanking out my outer world, I began to pick up a certain profound inner sensibility, one that, I would later discover, was very highly tuned.

I had acquired a mystical third eye of sorts; it turned out it was real Jedi power — my reward, it seems, for all those lonely years of darkness. Mostly I used it to tune in to some different plane, where I lived a kind of rich inner existence, but when I returned to earth, the greens would be greener and the reds redder than other people experienced them.

I could never go back to being like everyone else, even if I tried. But now I no longer cared. I wasn't like everyone else. I now had something the rest of them didn't. Somehow, in some way, I knew I was going to make it.

To Madness and Back

Allow me to describe my journey to the edge:

Few of you have ever had the experience of waking up from a drunken stupor in a strange city in a strange country, jobless and friendless and nearly penniless. You don't really want to be sober, for aside from the unwelcome intrusion of reality, you also find your psyche playing host to the type of cold fusion nuclear reaction that demands instant release.

"Rage, Goddess, sing the Rage" — a line from Homer. The shrinks have no adequate description for it: agitated depression, dysphoric mania, a mixed state, mania and depression fused into an explosive kinetic ball of emotional kilotonnage, one that makes the very act of living totally unbearable. It was simply a matter of following through.

Meanwhile, as I lay sprawled on the floor of an apartment that I could ill afford to pay the rent on, it was a beautiful summer day in Melbourne, Australia. Outside my window, the eucalyptus trees that lined my street created the impression of an urbanized Eden, while the kookaburras' shrill laughter in the distance sounded forth a Midsummer Night's Dreamscape of fairyland gaiety.

But the rumbling of the tramways around the corner represented my one-way ticket out of this life, out of my private little hell. I only had to change trams maybe once or twice to put me within walking distance of the suspension bridge that spanned the harbor.

Only seven months before, I had been on a plane to Melbourne, bound for a bright new life. I had sent out my resume to the major Australian newspapers and business magazines, and four editors had made me an offer. Oddly enough, I snapped at the one that offered the least money, lured by the idea of making my mark on a paper going through the kind of changes I reveled in.

This had been my modus operandi in New Zealand, taking over stodgy publications and giving them the old razzmatazz. I had done this on a law journal, an accountant's journal, a finance journal, and the business pages of a national Sunday newspaper. My average tenure lasted about a year. My longest stay was three years. On my last job, they integrated the Sunday paper into the daily one, and I had been left out in the cold. Looking back, my downsizing only served to delay my ultimate crash and burn.

Oh, the motor had been running hard back in New Zealand. The new Labor Government there had surprised everyone by becoming more right-wing than the right-wingers had ever been, and a whole new Wild West economy had been born, dominated by capitalist cowboys with paper fortunes who had Parliament at their beck and call. Suddenly, instead of operating on the fringes of journalism, we business/finance journalists were front stage center, smugly looking down our noses at our less knowing brethren in the parliamentary gallery.

Fifteen-hour days were par for the course, and twenty-hour days were not uncommon. In the meantime, my dress had become slightly eccentric, featuring brightly colored socks and ties and a collection of broad-brimmed Humphrey Bogart fedoras. The thing I am most proud of during all that time was that, unlike many of my colleagues, I never glorified any of these capitalist cowboys. It would have been easy to fill up space with material put out by their PR flaks, but I resisted pressure from a lot of quarters and put my readers first.

It took me a little while to find my rhythm in

Australia, but by September my old habits were returning. Then came the stock market crash of October, 1987, and thanks to all those paper fortunes going up in smoke, nowhere in the world did it hit harder than in Australia and New Zealand. By then, I had found my niche as the paper's cowboy capitalist reporter, and I covered the spectacle of their downfall across the entire continent plus New Zealand. I treated the airline as my bus service — up to Sydney and back again the same day, perhaps Brisbane, over to Perth for a longer stay, not to mention New Zealand — always on short notice, usually not knowing for sure when I would return.

Often I literally composed the stories in my head, dictating them over the phone to someone at the other end in hopes of making it into the next edition. On one occasion, I actually found myself reviewing a Frank Sinatra concert, which got major play on the paper's entertainment pages, together with about three or four pieces of mine that appeared on the business pages that same day. An acquaintance from New Zealand then living in Melbourne called me up and commented on my output, for which I had a ready answer: "Yeah, well, it was my turn to write the paper that day."

Oh, I had the one-liners coming. I was floating on air. On a return visit to New Zealand, I was even nice to my ex-wife and her boyfriend. Somewhere, I found the time to fit in a brief fling with someone who had just left her husband.

But the high was beginning to turn on me. Sometimes I found myself snapping at people, which was very uncharacteristic of me. Once, on the tram on my way to work in the early morning, I found myself on the brink of physically attacking some wiseassed teenager. I actually got up out of my seat and went for his neck before I caught myself. And then there was the issue of my six-month salary review.

Based on my performance, I was certainly entitled to a substantial raise. No, it was not delusional. The delusional part came in thinking I couldn't be replaced. When the editor failed to make me a decent offer, I quit in a huff, bitterly resentful over his treatment of me. Furious, in fact, in a blind rage. I told my colleagues what had happened, and they looked at me like I was crazy. Didn't anyone understand?

Hell with them, I thought. *I'll just apply for another job.* But this time there were no takers. No one would touch me with a ten-foot pole. I happened to encounter one of the paper's big-name journalists in a nearby pub, and he literally turned his back on me, pointedly refusing to acknowledge my existence.

I was nothing, a nonperson, a pariah.

Meanwhile, I would walk for hours, occasionally breaking out into a run, feeling the cold fusion inside my psyche pulsing and surging and desperately seeking a fast way out. Going to sleep was like the Fourth of July. All I had to do was close my eyes to experience the fireworks flashing onto my retinal screen. I would open my eyes only to find shadows and objects merging in the dark into an ominous new hellscape. I was on the brink of breaking out into full-scale hallucinations, and I knew that fairly soon I would be going mad.

I'M NORMAL! I wanted to shout. I've always been

normal. This was just stress — that was it. New location, crazy working hours. I just needed to slow down, that was all.

But no, that wasn't it, I decided in a Damascus Road flash of insight. I needed a religious experience, a spiritual transformation, a Zen moment, a cosmic turbocharge. Then everything would be fine. Better than fine, in fact — perfect. I could walk the earth as an enlightened being. I'm ready! I let God know. Plug me in.

I found myself prowling the bookshops, spending my dwindling supply of funds on books about Tibet and Eastern religions and white magic. I tried to float out of my body and talk to spirits and will my hair to grow in and move objects by thought, knowing the only thing holding me back was my lack of ability to change my vibrations and concentrate my mind.

But it was only a matter of time.

But now there was the small matter of me on the floor, emerging from a drunken stupor in a strange new country with no job, no friends, almost no money, and no hope of finding work. But just when the idea of jumping off a bridge seemed my only alternative, another option presented itself.

I'll write a book, I thought. *On the stock market crash.* The idea had actually crossed my mind much earlier, while still at work, but now there was a certain desperate quality to the proposition. That day, instead of throwing myself off a bridge, I grabbed hold of a typewriter and began pounding on the keys. "A stock market crash has no setting," I wrote. "It occurs in people's minds, a collective will that determines what is valuable and what is worthless from day to day, minute to minute. To understand finance has nothing to do with economics or accounting. Instead, it is a philosophical discipline of the mind determining reality, the natural territory of Kant and Plato and the rest."

In nothing flat I filled up a page, then another and another, all rushing out in a frothy stream requiring very little rewriting. Paradoxically, this new state of productive mania pulled me away from my more destructive old state. As the days went on, I began to enjoy my new life working from my apartment. I would pour a glass of wine or make myself a cup of tea, put on Duke Ellington or Beethoven or any number of composers in between, and settle in for a pleasant round at the keyboard. Later I would go out for a walk in my urbanized Eden.

The creative afterburners were running white hot by the time I put sheet number two hundred in my typewriter. "One would never know there'd been a crash," I banged out. "It was a different sort of disaster in a new world of intangibles far more subtle than a nuclear bomb, one that could practically be willed away in a Berkeleian-Kantian outburst of subjective idealism — or was it the other way around?"

I finished my book in five weeks, and very soon after, I found an agent and a publisher. Lest I be seen to be giving my manic phase all the credit, let me make it clear that I did not write that book so much as retrieve it. The book was actually the product of six years of immersion in the world of business and finance, several years before that in law, many more years working at my craft as a writer, plus a whole lifetime of reading and learning. By the time I came to sit down at the keyboard, my brain knew exactly what to do. Mania may have been a part of the process, but only as an accessory to the deed.

Once I had a publisher lined up, the inevitable letdown occurred. I literally didn't get out of my bed for weeks. Meanwhile, my depression was punctuated by the kind of rages that could very easily be mistaken for mania. In fact, mania may have intruded into my depression. These "mixed" states, by the way, continue to perplex the psychiatric profession, who can't seem to agree amongst themselves.

Over time my depression eased, and I took on another major writing assignment. As for my Damascus Road experiences, there was no turning back. I now began to explore my innate spirituality in a far less delusional fashion and experienced several immediate benefits. The meditation and yoga I began practicing brought me back from the edge and gave me a sense of hope. I also found that, after years in the single-minded world of business and finance, my thinking became far more three-dimensional.

But my miraculous "recovery" prevented me from seeking real help. My minor successes only served to fuel grandiose ideas, and my resurrection back into the real world gave way to the intoxication of mild mania. In time I would be felled by a cascading series of killer depressions. It was only when I had an irresistible vision of myself swinging from the balcony of my bedroom that I finally called out.

Healing

By now I was back in the United States. I had survived my worst round of depressions yet and was still in a state of shell shock from the experience. One of the first things I did, when I crawled out from under the covers, was get to the computer. I was new to the Internet, and I was new to finally acknowledging depression, and I was also coming to grips with my diagnosis as a manic-depressive, something I had somehow known all my life but, up till now, had steadfastly refused to accept.

I bounced from Web site to Web site, reading about what devastating illnesses both depression and manic depression were, but I also found that both were treatable and that I had a major role in my recovery. Then I discovered various mental health bulletin boards and even started replying to messages, once I worked up the courage. Over the next few weeks, I found myself gravitating to one particular board that was frequented by bipolars.

Someone there had posted ten reasons you know you're bipolar. Reason number ten, as I recall, was you know you're bipolar if you think Robin Williams should stop being so laid-back.

Somehow I knew I had found a home of sorts.

A few weeks later came a cryptic posting calling for writers. I was a writer. I replied. It turned out the person who ran the board, Colleen Sullivan, was the mental health editor for an Internet community, Suite101.com. Colleen was looking for someone to write on depression.

So I sat down at the keyboard and typed: "Depression isn't the word for it," I wrote. "We're talking about a condition that can take over your mind, rob you of your dignity, deprive you of all the joyful offerings of life, and leave you nose down in two inches of water, feeling totally abandoned by man and God."

Next thing I know, I was the Suite's depression editor.

I would write as I learned, I decided, one article at a time. It would all be tied into my recovery. In the space of one week, I banged out three articles, then another three in another week, all backed up and waiting to go. There was no question in my mind now I would have plenty to write about.

In nothing flat, I was also publishing my own newsletter, "McMan's Depression and Bipolar Weekly."

Writing is what helped bring me back from the dead. For me, it is a healing activity. If I were a basketball player, I'd be shooting hoops; if I were a gardener, I would be out with the petunias. Healing is about finding something that makes you feel alive and doing it. When I'm in full flight, there is no time and space. The sun takes its leave, booming music falls mute, and the steaming hot cup of tea by my side is stone cold when I pick it up a minute later.

After untold months in the land of the living dead, I was writing again, and really writing. I was still writing in the shadow of depression, but I was writing. I was reclaiming my life, one article at a time, one reader at a time. I was healed. I was healing. I was on my way.

Postscript

At a recent National Depressive and Manic-

Depressive Conference, Dr. Charles Nemeroff, a prominent psychiatrist, reminded us, "You can't do this alone. You can't take on responsibility for your illness all by yourself."

After years of denial and trying to fight this thing on my own, I finally have the good sense to take advantage of the help that is available to me. First, I work closely with a psychiatrist, who prescribes me a mood stabilizer, Depakote, and an antidepressant, Remeron. I know these drugs work for me (everyone is different) because once I was hospitalized with a severe digestive disorder and was unable to hold anything down, including my medications. After two nights, I found myself starting to hallucinate.

But don't mistake your medications for little happy pills or think they will get the job done all by themselves. Depression and manic depression are seldom so obliging.

I also worked with a therapist who helped me attack some of my destructive thought patterns with a technique known as cognitive therapy. In addition, I go to a weekly support group.

Good diet and exercise are as important to winning the battle as medications and therapy. I make sure I practice both as well as maintain a regular sleep schedule. Finally, you need to find a reason for getting up and facing whatever the day may bring. My writing is doing the trick for me. The joy of spending the morning with your friends may be all it takes for you.

*"The intellect has little to do
on the road to discovery.
There comes a leap in
consciousness, call it intuition
or what you will,
and the solution comes to you
and you don't know
how or why."*

ALBERT EINSTEIN

A BIPOLAR LIFETIME

By Colleen Sullivan

My mother had Bipolar Affective Disorder (manic-depressive illness was the diagnosis at that time). Strangely, her manifestation of the illness began with a severe postpartum depression at my birth. I have often wondered if that had anything to do with the fact that, of her three children, I would be the one to go on to develop the disorder myself. She was twenty-nine years old when it began, and in an ironic parallel, twenty-nine years later, I was diagnosed.

Of course, I have no memory of those early years and must rely on what I have been told. In 1950 there was no specific treatment for the illness, and she was subjected to many electroshock (ECT) treatments and heavy antipsychotic medications. She was institutionalized for the first six months of my life, and I lived with my paternal grandmother. Did this also help set the stage for my future lapse into bipolar disorder?

I have read so much about genetics, trying to figure

out the how and why of my diagnosis. Why me, and not my brother or sister? We were raised in the same environment, and her illness would surely have the same effect on them as it did on me. Or would it? "Why me?" is a common question asked by bipolars.

My mom died in 1974 and never knew that I would be afflicted with the disorder. How often I have wished she were here to answer my questions and support and guide me. I know that, more than anyone, she would have understood.

I have vague memories of my early years when things were not quite right — memories of a quiet and subdued mother who would lock herself away for days on end, refusing to participate or even have a meal with her family. But I remember at other times having an excited, elated mom who was truly "supermom" and could take on the world.

I remember more specific details and events that happened as I grew older, and it is with regret and shame I recall my reactions. I thought Mom was lazy, a hypochondriac and procrastinator who would avoid anything resembling work or responsibility. As my sister and I, at an early age, took on more and more of the household tasks, she retreated further. Much of the care of my brother, born nine years after me, became our responsibility as well. *Mom, I am so sorry. If only I had been able to see clearly with the eyes that I have now.*

Being psychotic is certainly not funny, but I remember one episode that had its humorous side. Mom had been sick for a while, and the doctor had finally talked her into going to the hospital. Being the clean, meticulous person she was, she refused to go without first bathing and putting on clean clothing.

Dad agreed and filled the tub for her. She went in the bathroom and locked the door. After a few minutes, she came back out and, in a bewildered voice, said, "I can't have a bath; there is no room in the tub for me." My dad went in, and sure enough, there wasn't. She had taken EVERYTHING that wasn't nailed down in the bathroom and thrown it in the tub — towels, shampoo, boxes of powder, you name it! Dad phoned for an ambulance, and she was taken to the hospital. Later that night he found her wedding ring in the trash. Such a sad story, but a true one.

Soon after my first son was born (he was about four months old), Mom had another severe depressive and psychotic episode. She had locked herself in her bedroom for days and days and was certain, absolutely convinced, that someone had killed my baby. When Dad phoned and asked me to bring my son there so that she could see he was truly alive, I agreed. When I got there, Mom came out, took the baby from me, went into her bedroom, and locked the door again. I was truly frightened. "She won't hurt him?" I asked my dad. He reassured me, and I talked to her through the locked door. After about forty-five minutes, she unlocked the door and returned the baby to me unharmed, without comment.

When I had my first neurotic episode and was subsequently diagnosed with bipolar disorder, I had a whole book of bad memories to browse through. I was scared; there is no other word to describe it. I was also lucky to have a wonderful psychiatrist, who had also treated my mother and knew her case history well. At my very first appointment, he told me that, if this had been twenty years ago, I would have likely spent the remainder of my life in an institution. With the discovery of lithium and other medications pertinent to bipolar disorder, I was very lucky and would most likely spend my life at home.

Time has proved him correct. I have had multiple hospitalizations, but between the severe episodes, I have maintained a reasonably stable and content lifestyle.

Note to Mom: I now realize how lucky I was to have you, Mom, and the odds that were stacked against you. If only you had received the same modern medications and treatments that are available today, things would have been so different for you, and for us. It is too late now to express my love, understanding, compassion, and absolute empathy. I promise you, though, that I have become a better person through the sharing of this illness with you.

If you have a Mom, cherish her!

Doomed for Life at Twenty-Nine

Mood swings have been with me all my life, at least as far back as I can remember. I remember the happy, hyper, excited times when I would stay up night after night, working on "the most important project of my life." And my face pinks still when I recall the times, as a teen, that I would ride down the main drag of town with my upper body out the window, singing along with the radio at the top of my lungs.

Even more, I recall the times when I became morose and depressed, withdrawing from friends and family, spending hours in my room simply "thinking" thoughts that had no beginning or end but circled like a panther closing in on its prey. At these times, tears were always close to the surface, and a comment, whether of support or censure, would have them streaming down my cheeks in torrents. Yet I had no explanation for why it happened.

These periods were mostly short-lived, a week or less in duration, and not so severe as to cause undue concern. Teenage hormones were the cause most cited by my parents. Manic depression was never considered even though my mom had it. My small episodes were nothing compared to the major ones she experienced.

I was twenty-three when my second son was born. His birth was followed by depression more deep than I had ever experienced, but he had been born with a heart problem (now corrected), and the depression was easily explained. After a couple of weeks I was able to bring him home, and my mood gradually improved.

It was autumn, 1979. The beauty of the sunshine and splendor of the gorgeous leaves in hues of gold, red, rust, and orange had passed its peak. Dead leaves were falling everywhere, to crackle and disintegrate beneath my feet as I walked. The scurry of the chipmunks and squirrels gathering their winter supply of food had all but ceased. Looking around me, I saw death and destruction and cried at the loss of precious life.

Each day was a struggle, first to open my eyes, then to move my body. It was as if a solid weight had settled on me, and it took superhuman effort to move beneath it. I had a good job and a mission to support my young family, so every morning I made that effort and amazingly survived the days. The depression worsened daily, and I would cry all the way to work and all the way home but was able to carefully mask it while there. A few weeks later, the day came when it could no longer be hidden.

I had not eaten or slept for some days. My face was haggard and gray, and I cried copiously all the time. I could barely force myself to walk, so leaden were my feet. I had been seeing a clinical psychologist whom my husband had been involved with, and he made a referral to a psychiatrist. By this time I was severely depressed and needed only to be relieved of the inner pain and torment. I would have sought that help any-where, if it were available. Secretly, I prayed that a psychiatrist was not what I needed (the flashbacks from my mom's suffering were ever present), but log-ically, I was already putting two and two together.

The appointment was a week away; I did not make it that long. My husband took me to my family doctor, where I sat for a full hour, crying and trying to choke out answers to questions. He prescribed some medi-cine, and I went home with a tiny ray of hope that it would fix everything. It didn't. By the time I saw the psychiatrist (the same one who had treated my moth-er), even speech was next to impossible. Still, I was not expecting his words, "You must be admitted to the hospital immediately." I stared blankly at him through the bleak, black holes in my face, thinking, *You have just verified my most frightening suspicions. You are saying I am like my mother.* I crumpled in my chair, defeated.

My memory of being in the hospital is not clear. I have flashes of memory — of remaining in bed, total-ly mute, curled in the fetal position, not recognizing even my husband and children. I remember a special nurse, Rose, who sat on the bed next to me, hugged me to her, and told me again and again I would get better. I still was not able to eat and, over the eight weeks in the hospital, lost fifty pounds.

Gradually, I did improve. Eventually I returned home, and two weeks later I returned to work. Pressures of finance would not allow me the time for total recovery. I continued to see the psychiatrist regularly and to take my medication but never truly achieved the state of normalcy I had enjoyed before the depression started. All was well though; I was able to carry on with my life.

It was autumn, 1980. Depression once again lowered its boom. This time, though, I knew what it was, and my doctor was aware. Changes in medication followed but to no avail. My mood moved inexorably down at an even quicker pace than the last time. One year almost to the day after my first admission to the hospital, I was admitted again, severely depressed and hopeless. I could not live my life this way. I despaired completely of any expectation of improvement. I was doomed for life, and at that time I made a vow to myself that if this was the quality of life I could expect, I would not live it.

Although I had not exhibited signs of mania at this point, my psychiatrist decided, on the basis of my mom's history, to start me on lithium, a mood stabilizer specifically for manic-depressives. One morning a week or ten days later, when he came to my room, I smiled a genuine smile, and he grabbed me and hugged me. I think that was the first time he had ever seen me smile.

My diagnosis at this point was manic depression. In later times, the hypomania would make its presence known in countless ways. Once started on the appropriate treatment, I improved, though it took some time. For two years I had spent Christmas in the hospital, leaving two small boys at home without their mommy. My guilt and regret over this alone has never left me.

I will never forget Dr. Johann Schwarzl. He was a wonderful man who was claimed by ALS some years after he began treating me. His kind ways and answers to my questions always left me feeling that he truly understood and cared. One day, bothered by problems with my memory, I asked him, "Doctor, why is it that I cannot remember things the way I used to?"

I have never forgotten his reply: "When you are depressed, your mind is like a camera without any film. At the time you see and are aware of everything that happens. Nothing is recorded, though, because you have no film."

I understood.

This is not to say I never had a problem again; far from it, in fact. For the next eight years, though, I remained relatively stable (still with minor up- and downswings, but easily controlled with medication and without hospitalization). I was able to work regularly, laugh and joke with customers, do my job with none of my previous difficulties with comprehension, concentration, or poor judgment, and enjoy it. Every day brought new joys with my children. I continued to keep regular appointments with my psychiatrist and take medication faithfully. I thought I had it beat. I truly did! I was one of the lucky ones!

In 1989 my luck changed. Severe episodes, multiple hospitalizations, and serious results marred the years that followed. I honestly don't remember how many times I was hospitalized over the following eight years, although I have a record of the most serious ones. From 1990 on, it seemed I did not recover from one episode before finding myself in the midst of the next. Medications were changed often, but my moods continued to be unstable, moving from mania to hypomania and severe depression to mixed episodes, and rapid cycling.

Early in 1993, I was sent to a hospital five hundred miles from home for ECT (shock) therapy. Several months later, I made a serious attempt at suicide and was in the hospital for over three months. This was the one that put an end to my being employed. I was declared permanently disabled and started on a pension. In 1994 I lost a very close friend to suicide. Other hospitalizations were interspersed with the main ones, but it was clear that my most difficult time was the fall of the year. I did not recover this time, and other local hospitalizations followed until September, 1995, when I was sent to a provincial psychiatric hospital three hundred miles from home. The treatment I received at this hospital was the turning point to recovery once again. It was to be a long and rocky road, to be sure, but progress was once again being made.

I was twenty-nine when I was diagnosed with manic depression. At the age of twenty-nine, I was doomed for life to carry the label and the illness. Was it really such a bad thing?

Picking up the Pieces

I would be hard-pressed to tell you which was the most difficult part of picking up the pieces and going on. It may have been the acceptance of having a chronic mental disorder and coping with it. It may have been dealing with the shame so rampant of being labeled mentally ill, or it may have been recovering my self and sense of self-esteem.

When I was in the hospital the first time, my best friend Mary gave birth to her third child, a baby girl, and after two boys, there was much rejoicing. I missed her baby shower and the birth but had already crocheted a beautiful white layette, just waiting for the pink or blue ribbons, and bought several "tiny" gifts for the new baby. Soon after my release from the hospital, I completed the gift and wrapped it. Mary lived just a few doors away, and I went, gift in hand, eager to see both her and the baby. She came to the door and held it open about a foot, accepted the gift and, to my surprise and dismay, did not invite me in. I could see the fear in her eyes and turned and walked away. I never went back, nor did I hear from her again. I had had my first experience with discrimination. (It was far from being the last.)

Stigma approaches from many quarters, not just personal ones like I have described here. Every day, every newspaper across the country has at least one article relating to the mentally ill and their instability or criminal behavior. Television, billboards, and magazines point fingers at the mentally ill for everything from driving health care costs up to murder. One never sees a news story about a person who has made a positive achievement captioned, "So and so is a normal person," but often one sees captions reading, "So and so found insane" or "So and so suffers from mental illness." No one stops to think that this is the minority of the millions of people with mental disorders or that there is indeed a certain percentage of so-called "normals" doing the same deeds and committing the same crimes.

My own personal shame that I had learned growing up was possibly even more difficult to understand.

Great strides have been made by mental health advocacy groups and individuals to educate the public and their peers about the true nature of mental illness — of the fact that in many instances it can be treated and that, even though they carry the label, many people being treated for mental illness lead perfectly normal lives. Unfortunately, the press is able to reach far more individuals, and their prejudice is quoted and believed by many. Each of us must do our part to seek understanding and acceptance for those with mental illness.

But first we must accept ourselves, and I believe it is not an acceptance that comes quickly or easily. It is not like having a doctor tell you that you have developed an illness that will be cured in two weeks with medication and bed rest.

Some years ago, Dr. Elisabeth Kubler-Ross authored a book titled *On Death and Dying* that went on to become a world-famous best-seller and then a classic. Her book outlines her theory of the five stages a dying person goes through on being told he has a terminal illness.

I have looked at these stages in the terms of my bipolar disorder, and the similarities are revealing. The first stage is DENIAL. "NO, they must be wrong. Something else is the problem. I will not take this medicine they prescribe. I will see a different doctor, or a hundred different doctors, till one tells me I don't have this terrible disorder. Me mentally ill? Not a chance!!" In this stage we fool no one but ourselves! Many people diagnosed with bipolar disorder remain at this stage for a long time, self-medicate, try every new product they hear of, and continue to suffer.

I remember well my own reactions in the next stage, ANGER!! I was furious that I should be the one chosen of three siblings to have this disorder. "WHY ME?" I cried in anguish. "Why not them?" I was angry with my mother, who had died six years earlier, for having the genes she passed on to me. I was angry with my doctors for having the nerve to label me with such a permanent diagnosis. I was angry with myself and guilty for not having the strength to overcome it. I was just plain angry, with everyone and everything. God got His share of my anger as well, and it was at this stage that I lost much of my faith.

Pictures of my mother's suffering were fresh in my mind, and I begged my doctor to reassess my condition. Perhaps there was too much stress in my life? Could that be it? I could reduce the stress! I pleaded with God to take this awful affliction from me, and I would do anything He asked of me. I was in the third stage, the stage of BARGAINING.

DEPRESSION followed closely on its heels as I realized that no amount of denial, anger, or bargaining would change the facts. I had Bipolar Affective Disorder, and not a darn thing would change that fact. I thought seriously about running away to a place no one would know of my shameful secret. I thought about suicide.

But eventually I reached the final stage of ACCEPTANCE. Partly through my own recovery, partly through my doctor's assurances that treatment was available, and partly through the support of friends and family, I gradually accepted the disorder and made efforts to learn all I could learn about it and how to cope with it.

Twenty Years Later ~ Looking Back, Looking Ahead

It was Brian Kiley who wrote:

"I went to a bookstore today; I asked the woman behind the counter where the self-help section was.

"She said, 'If I told you, that would defeat the whole purpose.'"

My experience with Bipolar Affective Disorder has been much like that for the past twenty years as I have struggled to learn and understand the illness. The lady in the bookstore represents the many brick walls I have run up against in my search not only for knowledge but also for understanding, empathy, and compassion.

My doctor gave me a bare-bones description of the disorder and a vague prognosis all those years ago. He did say that I was lucky that it was 1980 — that even twenty years earlier, before the advent of effective medications, I would have been institutionalized, probably for the rest of my adult life. He did not, could not, answer my questions about what the future would bring. Fortunately for me, there was no crystal ball to predict the events that would follow. If there had been, I would have given up in defeat, never attempting to fight the fight or win the battle.

Reading was a consummate passion from the time I was able to put "Dick, Jane, and Spot" together at the age of four. I looked to books for everything and well remember the visits to the local library every Saturday morning to choose five (the limit) books to read during the following week. By Wednesday or Thursday I normally had nothing left to read and was climbing the walls in anticipation. Quite naturally I turned to books for more education about bipolar illness. From medical encyclopedias, personal accounts, scientific journals, the *Physicians' Desk Reference*, and anything I could find, I gradually learned more about it. Remember, though, it was 1980. Bipolar disorder was still a shameful and hidden mental illness. It had not had its coming out, and literature was scanty.

Today, books are readily available, from the easiest to read to the most scientific reports. With the advent of the Internet, up-to-date information has become accessible almost instantly. The Internet offers not only information about the disorder, but support in the way of bulletin boards, chat rooms, and even on-line psychiatrists! Oh, how I wish it had been available to me all those years ago!

In 1997 I got my first computer. Several months later, barely accustomed to the computer, I decided I had a message about bipolar illness I wanted to share. I had no knowledge of HTML language at that time (what was that?), but step by step I learned and am proud of *Bipolar World* and my contribution to the bipolar community on-line.

Looking back, I can see that it was not until I became involved with support groups, both on-line and at the local group, that I found my forte. Meeting and talking with others who shared the same disorder, understanding their pain, feeling the words they were unable to speak, and sharing my experiences with them gave me a sense of acceptance and contentment I had not experienced in a long while. I must admit that support became, and continues to be, a selfish thing, as it is me who grows with each experience.

Yes, I have been through hell and back at the mercy of bipolar disorder. Could it have been worse? My response is an unqualified, "YES!" I have been most fortunate to have the love and support of family throughout. My dad [poor Dad, who has lived with the effects of bipolar disorder for fifty (that's 50!) years between my mom and me] has remained my strength, a staunch and loving support throughout. My husband of nearly thirty-one years has stood beside me through thick and thin, and my children, firmly supportive, treat me like a normal mom. Thank God for these blessings. I have made friends, mostly bipolar, who have given me hope and the will to go on. I am fortunate indeed.

I have no idea what the future holds in store for me. I no longer worry about it, nor do I want to know. I have reached the point in my life and in the illness where I live each day as it comes, rarely looking back despondently at the past and rarely wasting time trying to predict the future. What will be, will be, and I do not have the power of control.

I do my part, taking medications; keeping doctor appointments; cooperating with treatment plans; eating, sleeping, and exercising to keep my body well; and reducing harmful stress in my life as much as possible.

I watch with great interest news of new medications being discovered and new and effective treatment plans being made operational. I read news of the genetic search for the cause of bipolar illness and pray for the scientists and researchers carrying out the research. My vision of a cure for the illness at times dances vividly in my mind as I think of all the individuals who might be spared the agony many of us have been through. It may be too late to be of benefit to me, but generations to come may never have their lives disrupted by bipolar illness as mine has been.

I think of my grandson, eleven years old, who has been diagnosed with the disorder, and hope that wonderful discoveries and great strides will be made in time to help him live a normal life. I think of all the other children and adolescents, currently at the mercy of mood swings, being magically cured by an injection like a smallpox vaccination or a simple drug taken once daily. And my heart soars! It can happen!

I look forward to the day when bipolar disorder is no longer a source of shame and stigma. The day when people realize we are valid and valuable individuals with an illness, not an illness attached to a body. The day when, for every source of discrimination, there are five of support! The day to rejoice.

In reality, though, I know nothing of what the future holds for any of us. Minds much greater than mine are unable to predict the effects Y2K might bring, and that is only months away!

Peace can be achieved by living only for the present. That has become my motto.

As Robert Louis Stevenson wrote:

"Anyone can carry his burden, however heavy, until nightfall. Anyone can do his work, however hard, for one day. Anyone can live sweetly, patiently, purely, until the sun goes down. And that is all life really means."

Some of us were unable to carry our burden.

My Friend Jeff

It was 1992 when Jeff attended his first bipolar affective disorder support group meeting...a charming young man with dark, crinkly hair and fathomless, dark eyes. At this first meeting, he revealed little of himself other than to say he had been diagnosed with bipolar disorder many years before and had had many hospitalizations. He also revealed that for many years he had self-medicated with alcohol. Mostly he listened throughout the evening, and it was difficult to tell if he was shy, bored, or perhaps depressed.

At the end of the meeting, he approached me and asked if I had time to go somewhere for "a quick coffee," as he had some questions he wished to ask. I agreed and met him at a coffee shop not far from our meeting place. We talked and shared over endless cups of coffee. The pot was bottomless, and neither of us even noted the waitress refilling our cups, so intense was our conversation. The closing of the coffee shop in the wee hours of the morning sent us home, both of us feeling we had met someone very special who truly understood! We had exchanged phone numbers, but I really was not expecting him to call, just hoped that he would be at the next meeting in two weeks.

To my surprise he phoned the following day, and we chatted for an hour on the telephone and made arrangements to meet again the following evening for coffee. This was the beginning of a developing pattern. From that time on, there was rarely a day gone by that we did not meet or talk to each other on the telephone. Some days we would go somewhere and walk and talk, other times a coffee shop was our meeting place, and still other times (rarely) I would go with him to a bar. I didn't drink and urged him not to, because of the medication he was taking, but did not resist when he really wanted to go.

One day, early in our friendship, he told me that his mother had committed suicide when he was three years old. He remembered it! He told me he was outside playing and his baby brother was sleeping in the carriage in the yard when he heard the shot. His dad, a teacher, was at work. He ran into the house and found his mother in the basement, then ran to a neighbor for help. Though his dad later remarried and had two more sons, Jeff never truly felt he belonged. He had never seen his mother's grave, and we went out to the cemetery to look for it. When we finally located it, his eyes filled with tears. I opened my arms, and we embraced, holding each other tightly, as I tried to transfer some of my strength and deep sympathy to him. That hug was the beginning of many and a changing point in our friendship.

Jeff had married young, at the age of eighteen, to his high school sweetheart, and went to work at the city's main industry. He was a hard worker and successful at his job. He loved his wife and simply adored his two little girls. He would tell me how he had loved to spend special time with them after dinner, bathing them, getting them into their pj's for the night, and then reading to them before bed. His voice grew husky as he described it, and I could hear the tears in his voice.

They were together for ten years before the stress of his illness and drinking led to a marital breakdown. His wife took the children and moved over a thousand miles away. Jeff was crushed. His bipolar episodes came closer together and were severe.

Following the divorce, he was involved in three short-term and ill-advised relationships. In our conversations he talked about them. As a matter of fact, we talked about everything; our deepest thoughts and feelings were bared. No person had ever known the inner me as he did, and I had never been attuned to another's feelings as I was to his.

When I was in the hospital, Jeff visited regularly, often twice a day. When he was in the hospital, I did the same. I remember one time when he was manic and had gone on a rage the night before. He had been asked to leave an establishment and had kicked in the plate glass door as he left. Before the police arrived, he had broken several doors and windows as he made his way up the street. He was taken to the psychiatric unit and was in isolation, with nothing more than a mattress on the floor. I kneeled down beside him and asked what I could do to help. He had not eaten, and his mouth was so dry from medication, he could barely speak. He said that he needed a cigarette, and I got the attention of one of the nurses and pleaded with her to bring an ashtray and allow me to give him one. I also asked for a glass of ice water. I promised to remain and watch him while he smoked, and finally, permission was granted. Once again I kneeled beside him, and I helped him to a sitting position and held the ice water to his lips. At first he turned his head away; then, as the cold sweetness touched his lips, he drank deeply and greedily. I gave him a cigarette, then another, and watched as he slowly quieted.

These scenes or similar ones were repeated many times. The blind leading the blind, some might say — first him supporting me, then me supporting him, as the occasion warranted. Sometimes we clung to each other like rats sinking in a sea of misery.

In the fall of 1993, Jeff sunk into a severe depression. We were in constant communication, and having attempted suicide myself just a year earlier, I recognized the signs. I listened, and I tried to encourage him, but in early winter I received a phone call from the girl he was living with, telling me he had jumped in the partially frozen river but was home; what should she do? The zipper on his jacket was frozen closed, and icicles had formed in his hair and on his lashes. I told her to get him into a warm bath and, as soon as he was warm and dry, to take him to a hospital. I spoke also with him and told him it was best he go and that I would meet him there. He was there just a few days and convinced the doctor he had learned his lesson, had found God, and was fine. He was released.

Less than a month later, he called again in crises. I picked him up and delivered him, psychotically depressed, to the hospital. After forty-eight hours, he was released.

At this point he had been phoning me every morning, and I had been seeing him every evening. One night he told me in a sad voice that he could not fight anymore, that he had made a decision to end his suffering. I did not argue with him. I simply said that, if that was his decision, there was nothing more I could say or do but that I understood, from the bottom of my heart, how he was feeling. Our evening ended with a long, fierce hug.

The following morning, there was no phone call. As Jeff sometimes slept in, I did not become overly concerned until about one in the afternoon. Then I contacted the girl he lived with and asked for him. "Jeff's not here," was her response. "He has gone to play pool with Don, but he is picking up my daughter from school and will be here by three at the latest. I'll have him call you."

Instantly, the hairs on the back of my neck were on alert, but not wanting to alarm her, I thanked her and hung up. Jeff had not played pool with Don for months. In fact, he had not been anywhere in months.

Within ten minutes, I called her back and asked her to check with Don and let her know how concerned I was. Within minutes, she called me back. Jeff was not with Don. In fact, it had been weeks since Don had heard from him. "Call the police," I urged her.

"I can't do that. Jeff is driving without a license and will be furious if he is stopped by the police. He has never failed to pick up my daughter when he has promised. Let's wait until three."

When the phone rang shortly before three, I knew, deep in my gut, that it would not be good news. Her daughter had phoned, and Jeff had not shown up. Still she did not want to call the police but had no way to look for him, so I picked her up. "Go to the river," she said, referring to the spot where Jeff had jumped in before. Instead, recalling the clues Jeff had given me, I unerringly drove to the city dock. It was a horrible, snowy, windy day, and as I pulled to the end of the dock, I saw the van with the driver's door open and engine running. I breathed a silent sigh of relief. We were in time.

As soon as the car stopped, we were out, calling for him. Then I noticed one set of footprints in the snow going to the edge of the dock. That was enough for me. I ran to a nearby dive shop and asked the man to call the police. We were suddenly surrounded by emergency vehicles of every kind, and curiosity seekers began to gather. As we saw two divers jump into the water and an ambulance back up to the edge of the dock, we were placed in a police cruiser and moved to where we could not see the events taking place. Then the ambulance left, siren screaming. We clung together in the car, hoping that the siren meant he was alive.

It was February 28, 1994. Jeff was dead at the age of thirty-six.

I was numb. The next days I lived in a cocoon of silent misery; his funeral, a vague and blurry memory. I didn't cry. I couldn't. I was frozen solid, all my emotions encased in a block of solid ice. People rallied around me, knowing the closeness of our relationship, but I was barely aware of their presence.

The nightmares started. Every night I woke in a fever of tortured pain. And during the day, I minutely examined everything I could remember about our relationship. When the block of ice melted, it left behind a searing pain and guilt. Though I buried it within me, I lived with it for many years. What more could I have done? Did he think I was giving him "permission" and my blessing the night before he died? I questioned myself constantly, certain that I was in some way responsible.

For two and a half years I held it all inside of me, unable to release it, unable to trust another to see so deeply into my soul. With time I recovered on the surface, took up my regular duties, and went on. Time truly is a wonderful healer. The poison deep inside of me remained. I would take it out and examine it and promptly bury it again. The nightmares receded in time, though even now they return to haunt my sleep occasionally.

I met a bipolar on-line in 1998 who was to have great influence in allowing me to release and express my grief. Without ever pushing me, he let me know he was interested in hearing my story and that he cared. I don't think I would ever have been able to do it in a one-to-one "in person" conversation, but gradually I opened up to him.

As I came to know him better and trust him, deeply buried thoughts came to the surface. My own suicide attempt and my feelings about it, the years of agony I had gone through, and my present feelings were all discussed. He knew, and so did I, that there was still a huge blockage to overcome, and until it was out in the open, I would never heal. I tried several times to tell him and couldn't do it. Finally, one day he suggested that I write about this obstacle, that there would be catharsis and healing in just getting it out and no longer internalizing it.

This suggestion made a lot of sense to me. Journalizing and getting things on paper had stood me in good stead and helped me before. So I wrote a brief, unemotional, one-page summary of what was a very large and very special part of my life. When I finished, I mailed a copy to him.

Our on-line meetings continued, and over time he was able to pull out the emotions, the anger, the rage, the sadness, and the grief. I ranted, raged, and at times spewed venom at him. And I cried, rivers of tears, and the tears cleansed me. I gradually accepted his words that I did not have the power to make another person's choices, that I had done the best I could, and that no one could ask for or expect more.

Through our sharing we became very close friends, and there will always be a special spot in my heart for him.

I still don't like to talk about Jeff's death — or think about it, for that matter. It was an experience that totally devastated me for a long time. Now, though, I feel freer to talk with people going through the same thing, offering loving support from one who has been there and understands.

I have become a better person for having gone through it, survived it, and learned from it. When, in my darkest moments, my own thoughts turn again to suicide, I no longer look at it from a purely selfish view — *(I cannot stand the pain! I need to end it now!)*; I also think of the everlasting effect it will have on my loved ones. This thought has stopped me more than once from acting.

Have I coped with suicide? I think so, at least as well as anyone can cope with the loss of a loved one. The years I lost between the event and my acceptance of it were very, very difficult. My wish is that no individual will ever have to experience the things I went through, but sadly, I know it will happen over and over again.

Bipolar disorder is a serious mental illness, but today it can be treated quite successfully, and many with this diagnosis lead productive lives in their chosen fields. I often liken it to diabetes. Both illnesses are incurable at the present time, but proper medications and treatments often lead to stability and the ability to make great strides in life. Our goal is to first accept it, then do all we can to promote our own well-being. By supporting each other, sharing experiences, and learning, we will overcome the symptoms.

At the same time, we pray for new knowledge...a cause and definitive cure!

See my Bipolar World Web site at:

http://bipolar.virtualave.net

"It takes one a long time
to become young."

PABLO PICASSO

THE TWILIGHT YEARS

By Susan Carolyn French

Living with the Anguish of Mental Illness

I grew up in a nice middle-class neighborhood in North Toronto. I attended a rather academic high school, and even though I had just been an average student, I managed to keep up with the eggheads in my class. I was pretty, popular, and always stylishly dressed. I had lots of girlfriends and, by grade nine, was starting to date.

In grade ten, at age fifteen, two of the most important things in my life happened. First, I met a boy and fell madly in love. We became inseparable and talked of marriage, children, and what our home would be like, when we weren't billing and cooing like two lovesick turtledoves.

The second thing that happened to me was much more nightmarish than reality and was to change the course of my life. I had some sort of anxiety attack right there in the classroom where I was striving to be a better-than-average student.

It started with insomnia, which gradually built into a total absence of sleep for many nights in a row. I became agitated, talking incessantly and laughing inappropriately. I was such a disruptive element in class that I had to be removed and sent for assessment by the school guidance counselor. He referred me to a psychiatric clinic, where a psychologist and a psychiatrist interviewed me at length to gain some insight into the reasons for my sudden and emotional outbursts.

My parents were beside themselves and had yet to learn ways of coping with my erratic behavior. They both seemed guilt ridden, as if they had done something to cause the aberrant behavior.

After many interviews and psychological testing, the doctors were able to tell me that I had manic depression. But I wasn't depressed at all. In fact, I was euphoric. The world seemed rosy, and I was omnipotent. There wasn't a task I couldn't perform, any problem I couldn't solve.

It was explained to me that there is a manic side to this affective disorder. (That was the new way they liked to refer to mental illness.) Someone who only exhibits the manic side of the illness is said to have unipolar disease and is referred to as a pure manic. Perhaps only three percent of all manic-depressives are pure manic. About ten percent of the general populace suffers from the disease.

Another generally depressing fact about the disorder is there is no cure. It may be transmitted genetically from one generation to the next. It is a recurrent disorder and does not seem to be triggered off by any one cause, such as stress or diet. So what can be done about it, and how effective is treatment?

In 1963 the treatment of choice was to administer orally very high doses of a major tranquilizer called chlorpromazine. Chlorpromazine is just one of the members of a larger family of major tranquilizers called phenothiazines. This drug was so potent that a patient receiving it often required hospitalization, if only to have constant surveillance for untoward effects.

My parents refused to have me hospitalized, and so, under very careful observation, I was given the drug at home. My parents kept watch over me day and night. For the first eight hours, I slept so heavily that, when I finally awoke, it seemed I had been asleep for seventy-two hours.

My eyes were narrow slits as I tried to focus on my room and the harshness of the daylight streaming in through an opening in the drapes. I tried to lift my head off the pillow — it was like a giant sledgehammer knocked me on the forehead, forcing me back to the horizontal position. My mouth was so dry and my lips so parched that, when I attempted to speak, my words were thick and slow and so slurred that no one could understand me. My thought processes seemed to come lightening fast, but I could no longer formulate them into verbalizations. The light hurt my eyes, and I had a dull headache. In total, I felt as though I was in another body, one with stiff and deadened limbs that were incapable of acting on the messages my brain was sending. I do not know of a more tumultuous assault on the human body; it could be likened to a stroke.

Gradually, I became coherent. The high feeling I had experienced earlier had now been replaced with a terrible deadness caused by the drugs. Whenever I began to revive from the deadness, I would be given another dose of chlorpromazine, and the vicious cycle would begin again.

It was about three weeks — three weeks of living hell — until I responded favorably enough to be weaned off the drugs.

I had to go back to school among lies and whispers that I had suffered a nervous breakdown. People avoided me like the plague. My boyfriend David stuck by me and was perhaps the only bright spot in my life.

Throughout high school I continued to have these manic relapses, as many as three per year. When I failed grade eleven twice, I was ready to quit school immediately. My older sister, who herself dropped out in grade eleven, gave me the courage to go on.

Whenever I got manic, I was cloistered at home. My parents tried to protect me, as best they could, from harming or embarrassing myself with others outside the family. For this reason, I was often kept within the confines of my own room, being allowed to join the family at mealtimes and during supervised activities. It seemed a cruel punishment, and I was often consumed with the feeling that four walls could not contain me. On one such occasion, I escaped unnoticed into the brisk winter air of a February evening. I was free at last. Thinking very quickly that I had to get away from the house as fast as I could, I decided to go to my sister's house. She lived about two and one-half miles away as the crow flies, and that is exactly how I plotted to get there. I tramped through a series of yards and gardens, leaping fences with ease, facilitated by the deep snow. I reached her home, at once out of breath and perplexed as to the reason for my coming. My sister and her boyfriend took me inside and tried to calm me down and reason with me. Something they said made me angry, and I left abruptly.

I made my way to a busy intersection. I felt alone and abandoned. I went into a restaurant to get warm, discovering I hadn't brought any money with me. I sat down at the counter and began to cry. The restaurant owner offered me a glass of water and asked me what was wrong.

I just kept saying, "I don't know. I'm all alone." I asked for a dime to make a phone call, and he gave it to me. I thought of phoning my parents. Probably they were frantic by now. Instead I called the police and asked them to come and get me and take me home.

Within minutes a squad car arrived, and two uniformed policemen ushered me into the safety of the awaiting car. I told them my address and that I didn't have subway fare to get home. They listened with feigned interest and began driving across town.

After what seemed like an eternity, we arrived at a great set of iron gates that marked the entrance to a massive brick edifice encircled by crumbling stone walls.

"Where are we?" I asked. No reply.

I was led into a dark corridor, and after a short exchange with a night clerk, a uniformed matron came and took me away. She directed me into a large tub room and instructed me to strip off my clothes and climb into the swirling tub. I told her that I had bathed that morning.

"It's hospital policy," she said curtly.

"What hospital is this, then?"

"999 Queen Street," she said matter-of-factly.

Oh, no, I thought. *This is the nuthouse! I'm not staying here,* I thought to myself. I was at once paralyzed with fear.

There was much heartache. My sixteenth birthday was celebrated in a drug-induced fog. When I blew the candles out on my cake, I wished for death rather than having to endure another bout with the disease and those oh-so-dreaded drugs.

When my older sister married, I was in the hospital and so far out of control that I couldn't even attend her wedding.

The world seemed to pass me by as I stood marking time with the chalky taste of medicine on my tongue, a dazed look in my eye, and a sinking feeling in my heart.

In the summer of my eighteenth year, my doctor suggested putting me in the hospital for the entire summer vacation. It had been determined that my system was very sensitive to medication, and it had been difficult to stabilize me on some of the different drugs I had been given. The doctor thought they could try a whole range of different types of drugs, over the eight-week period, and find the one that would work best for me and have the fewest side effects.

And so the experiment began, with me as a sort of

human guinea pig. It was a nightmare from start to finish. I tripped out on each and every drug I was given. I didn't know who I was or where I was or even why I was. It was much like the trips that teenagers took on LSD in the '60s. To this day I'll never understand how people can put harmful chemicals into perfectly healthy bodies and eventually destroy part of their minds.

It was near the end of the experiment, and I just wasn't responding favorably to any of the drugs. There was a young senior resident named Dr. Michael King, whom I shall never forget. He had been working closely with my own psychiatrist, Dr. Dayton Forman. Dr. King suggested trying a new drug called lithium carbonate. At that point it was still an experimental drug in Canada. They had found some success in treating manic-depressives with lithium in Sweden. They were able to get the go-ahead from the government to use the drug experimentally on me.

In a matter of weeks, I began to respond positively. My mood swings adjusted to within normal limits. I felt well. There were no more untoward effects from the drug. It was just like taking a vitamin pill.

My blood levels were monitored daily for the first two weeks of lithium therapy. There is a danger that just a little too much of it can be very toxic to the body. Lithium is a common salt that exists in minute quantities in the brain's chemical makeup. There is a theory that patients with manic depression have a slight deficiency of this chemical in their brains.

When lithium levels were stabilized, I was given a supply of those pale green oval-shaped tablets with instructions to take one three times a day for the rest of my life. I was also advised to have my serum lithium level checked every month and, of course, to report any new symptoms promptly to the doctor.

I couldn't leave the ward without saying good-bye and a heartfelt thank-you to a beaming Dr. King. He had virtually saved my life, one that had been full of worthlessness, agony, and despair. As I expressed my gratitude for offering me a new life of hope and happiness, he said to me, "Susan, I think we have found the wonder drug!"

The impact of those words changed my life. I did finally graduate from high school. I went on to attain my diploma in nursing.

Today I am rewarded with a wonderful husband, a lovely home, and a gratifying career as a Registered Nurse.

Yes, I still have manic depression, but the relapses are less frequent, shorter in duration, and decidedly less severe than those anxiety-ridden days of old. I was able to beat the odds of this disease through the continual support of family, friends, and two dedicated doctors who really cared. My own raw courage helped me through the hardest moves, but after all, "Through this life, you go but once."

Chapter Seven

THE WINGS OF MADNESS

By Deborah Gray

LET me tell you right away that I am uncomfortable recounting my experience with depression. Not because it's painful to talk about (though it is), but because I created my Web page about depression to help other people, not to go on and on about myself. However, I can't forget how illuminating William Styron's account of his depression in *Darkness Visible* was to me before I was diagnosed and treated. It really was the book that made me recognize my illness and therefore led me to seek professional help. Since Styron is so much more eloquent than I could ever be, I urge you to read his book. If nothing else, it will help you explain your illness to other people, or help you to understand a loved one's pain if you are close to someone who suffers from the "black dog," as Churchill called it. If you are interested in my story, read on. You may recognize yourself or someone else in it.

My parents divorced when I was two, and I essentially lost my father. My mother and my sister and I moved across the country to live with my grandparents, and I only saw my father every few years when I was growing up. My mom remarried, when I was almost four, to the wonderful man I consider my real father, who has been there for us one hundred percent ever since. However, the loss of my biological father had profound effects on my personality. Many people who suffer depression lose a parent early in life, either to death, divorce, or abandonment. I don't know if I would have suffered from depression without that early loss. Perhaps my depression is wholly chemical. I do know that the only picture of me as a child that shows me laughing was taken before my father left. Every picture taken afterward shows a solemn child who smiles only diffidently.

I was a painfully shy child. I had very few friends, was terrified of talking to strangers or a group of people, and was careful never to draw attention to myself. I was afraid that, if I was the center of attention, I would look stupid or do something wrong. It's likely that, as a child, I thought my father's leaving was due to my behaving badly or doing something wrong, so I was always afraid of doing that again and making my mother leave. I sought refuge in reading, confident that in books I could never say or do the wrong thing. That served to cut me off even more from the rest of the world.

As a teenager, I was moody and self-absorbed. Of course, that's common for teenagers, so my behavior was written off as normal. Unfortunately, I also had no interest in school, sports, clubs, etc. Part of it was the fog that was beginning to descend over my mind from time to time, and part of it was a fear of failing in anything new. The only time I felt good about myself was when a boy was chasing after me. Of course, the flip side of that was that a rejection from a boy I was interested in sent me into a black mood, unable to do anything but cry. Occasionally I thought of going to a psychiatrist and saying, "Help me," but in that scenario I also saw rejection. I pictured the doctor saying, "There's nothing wrong with you; why are you wasting my time when I could be seeing people who really have problems?"

My college years, for the most part, were relatively free of depression. I was much more social, and with the exception of being expelled for one semester due to a lack of interest in my classes, I was more motivated academically until what I think of as the "black hole time," what was probably my first major depression. I was in my last semester of school, worrying about finding a job in time so that I could stay in Boston with my boyfriend and panicking over the prospect of being entirely on my own. The semester before, I had been raped by a male friend, and this may have been a trigger. My moodiness got worse and worse, and I was constantly fighting with my boyfriend, through no fault of his. In my mind, I vividly saw myself teetering on the edge of a bottomless black hole. I felt that if I fell in, I would never stop falling.

In desperation I went to the walk-in clinic of a local hospital and told the doctor that I thought I had very bad PMS. I described my symptoms, and he told me to keep a record of my moods. I promised to do so, but I was in no shape to follow through. I could barely get my schoolwork done and certainly didn't have the energy to keep a log on top of that. I found out years later that he had made a notation concerning possible depression in my file and that he would follow up with me. He didn't get in touch with me again, probably because I graduated a few weeks later.

The next few years I went in and out of major and minor depressions, although I didn't recognize either for what they were. I remember a few periods of doing nothing but dragging myself to work and, in my free time, reading romance novels. My roommates would try to coax me into going out and barhopping (which I normally loved), but I just didn't feel like it. In the summer of 1990, as I've said, I read Styron's *Darkness Visible.* As I read it, I kept saying to myself: *This is me; I've been feeling all of this.* However, I still hesitated to see a psychiatrist. Not that I wasn't seeing a doctor — I was overwhelming my family doctor with visit after visit, sure that I had this disease or that ailment. I think I was in his office every two weeks, on average, that year.

My hypochondria wasn't the only problem, though. My memory and concentration, which had always been excellent, were completely shot. I couldn't retain anything I read. I lay in bed every morning, trying to think of a reason to get up and go to work. When I wasn't at work, the only thing I had the energy to do was watch TV. I had been dating a man for a year who not only was depressed himself but also was an alcoholic. I had been pressuring him to make some sort of commitment to me without understanding why it was so important to me.

Finally, the morning after a particularly nasty argument, as I lay in bed, the sound of his car driving off made me crack. I started screaming and couldn't stop until I was hoarse. Shaken, I called my family doctor and asked for the name of a good psychiatrist. I saw the head of psychiatry at the local hospital a few days later. I remember sitting in his office, twisting my hands together in my lap as he asked me about my family history and my symptoms. At the end of the hour, he told me he thought they could help me (the most beautiful words I could remember ever hearing) and that he would set me up with a therapist and a psychiatrist at the hospital's mental health clinic. He also mentioned that they might want me to go on medication, an idea that I negated immediately. I had hated taking medication since I was put on tranquilizers for migraines when I was a teenager.

The next few weeks, which were at Christmastime, were horrendous. I went to a dear friend's wedding but was only able to endure half an hour of the reception before escaping, crying on the drive home. I kept hold of myself all Christmas Day but started crying hysterically as soon as I left my parents' house and cried all the way home. Things got slightly better after the holidays, and I was going to therapy once a week. I was gaining insight into what made me tick, which was helping me to a great extent in my relationships. However, it was not alleviating what was steadily growing into a shrieking storm inside my head.

In early spring I sat in my bedroom and decided that if this was the kind of pain I was going to live with for the next fifty years, then life would hold absolutely no appeal for me. Strictly speaking, I wasn't thinking of suicide, but I'm sure it would only have been a matter of time before I sought that relief. I told my psychiatrist that I was ready to try whatever medication they wanted to give me. He put me on Norpramin, which is a type of antidepressant. The side effects (dry mouth, shaking hands, dizziness in the morning) were unpleasant, but I was determined to stick it out for the six weeks they told me it would take for the medicine to take effect. This was my only chance at having my life back.

Not only did I get my life back, I got a new life. At first I noticed only that the noise in my head was fading and I was beginning to take an interest in things going on around me again. But as the weeks went on, a whole new personality emerged. Instead of the classic clothes in smoky colors I had always worn, I now was gravitating toward flashy clothes in bright colors. Now I *wanted* to draw attention to myself — I loved it! I, who had always been so shy, was now smiling at strangers and eagerly entering into conversation with them. I was suddenly interested in everything — food, clothes, science, sports, history, etc. Not only did I have a thirst for knowledge, but I also had the energy to follow through on it. I read voraciously, but for the first time, I wasn't trying to escape into a make-believe world; the one I inhabited fascinated me.

I felt that, for the first time in my life, my "real" personality had emerged. Going on the medication did so much more than I expected. The only thing that marred this rebirth was the thought that I had wasted so many years living in the fog of depression. I mourn all the years lost, all the opportunities missed, and all the friends that I had alienated. If I had understood more about this illness, if there weren't so many misconceptions about it, I probably would have gone to a doctor years before.

Now, ten years later, the only time my depression has come back has been when I've gone off my medication or the level of medication in my blood has become too low. I have high and low moods like everyone else, but the low moods are always of short duration, a day or so, and always in reaction to something negative or stressful happening in my life. In other words, my moods are normal.

I'm begging you, if you think you have depression, get help. Although it's true that not every case is as successful as mine is, around eighty percent of people who have depression can be helped, and that number is rising all the time as new medications and combinations of medications are used. I'm not advocating medication for everyone. I have a friend whose outlook on life has been changed by psychotherapy as much as mine has been changed by the combination of medication and psychotherapy. Every case is different. Your best bet is to educate yourself as much as possible about this illness, in addition to seeking professional help. Depression is a terrible, soul-stealing illness. I don't know if we will ever be able to eradicate it, but from my own experience, I know that the tools to defeat it are there. You owe it to yourself to give those tools the chance to rescue you from the pain and emptiness of depression.

*"A foolish consistency
is the hobgoblin of
little minds."*

RALPH WALDO EMERSON

THE COLOURING TO EVENTS: THE DEATH OF MERIWETHER LEWIS

By Kay Redfield Jamison, Ph.D.

We were now about to penetrate a country at least two
thousand miles in width, on which the foot of civilized man
had never trodden; the good or evil it had in store for us
was for experiment yet to determine... .
However, as the state of mind in which we are,
generally gives the colouring to events... .
I could but esteem this moment of my
departure as among the most happy of my life.

—MERIWETHER LEWIS,
April 7, 1805

*T*HE young red-haired Virginian had thought hard and well about the provisions his men should take with them, but the planning cannot have been easy. A few dozen men were about to set out on an eight-thousand-mile journey across the unmapped American wilderness. There was little they could draw upon to predict the quick variability of the land or to grasp its vastness. The expedition would be far afield from usual calculation and experience, but because of this it would in the end be unmatched for what it discovered about the country, its inhabitants, and its resources.

The trip would be dangerous, it would be arduous, and it would take more than two years to complete, but the expedition's leader was anything but bowed or intimidated. He had the confidence of the president who had chosen him, as well as a firm, well-placed belief in his own ability to command men and to carry out the scientific work at the heart of the expedition's mission. He had prepared for the trip with care and intelligence, and he was exhilarated to have the chance to explore and chart the unknown lands.

His country had just, overnight, doubled in size. On July 4th, 1803, the U.S. Congress had purchased the Louisiana Territory from Napoleon. For three cents an acre, the government had acquired the vast, murkily bordered lands stretching from the Mississippi River to the Rocky Mountains. It was clear to some that it was only a matter of time until America pushed past the western mountain ranges and took the nation's expanding borders to the Pacific Ocean. In the meantime, the country needed knowing.

Captain Meriwether Lewis, the young Virginian who had drawn up the plans for the westward expedition, was a U.S. Army officer who had lived in the wilderness frontier and was well acquainted with Indian cultures. He was six feet tall, restless, intrepid, and profoundly and wide-rangingly curious; he knew life not only from the frontier but, more recently, from the inside of the president's house as well. Thomas Jefferson, two weeks before taking office in February 1801, had written to Lewis asking that he help with the "private concerns of the household" and, more intriguingly, "to contribute to the mass of information which it is interesting for the administration to acquire." Lewis's "knowledge of the Western country, of the army and of all of it's interests & relations has rendered it desirable" that he join Jefferson as the president's private secretary.

Meriwether Lewis accepted the position with speed and delight, and for two years the fellow Virginians, separated in age by nearly thirty years, shared meals, confidences, and several hours of most days together. Both men were singularly inquisitive by nature, and both were passionate for the exploration of the country's vast lands — the young officer for the exploration itself, the president for what could be learned from it. In 1802, Jefferson decided that Lewis should command an expedition to the Pacific Ocean; he then set out for the young officer a remarkable course of tutelage in subjects ranging from geography and natural history to medicine, botany, and astronomy.

Jefferson had high expectations for the westward journey, and he had a thousand questions and requests: "The object of your mission," the president wrote Lewis in June 1803, "is to explore the Missouri river, & such principal stream of it, as, by it's course & communication with the waters of the Pacific Ocean, may offer the most direct and practicable water communication across this continent, for the purposes of commerce." Lewis was to "take observations of latitude & longitude...with great pains and accuracy," and he was to make several copies of all notes and observations — one to be written "on the paper of the birch, as less liable to injury from damp than common paper" — in order to guard against damage or loss. Lewis was to determine the names of the Indian nations, "& their numbers; the extent & limits of their possessions...their language, traditions, monuments; their ordinary occupations in agriculture, fishing, hunting, war, arts...the diseases prevalent among them, & the remedies they use... peculiarities in their laws, customs and dispositions."

Lewis and his men were also to record the "soil and face of the country, it's growth & vegetable productions...the animals of the country generally...the mineral productions of every kind...Volcanic appearances." Climate was to be carefully noted "by the proportion of rainy, cloudy & clear days, by lightening, hail, snow, ice, by the access & recess of frost, by the winds prevailing at different seasons, the dates at which particular plants put forth or lose their flowers, or leaf, times of appearance of particular birds, reptiles or insects."

Jefferson's instructions to Lewis could not have been written by anyone else. As Donald Jackson, the editor of the correspondence and documents of the Lewis and Clark expedition, has put it: "They embrace years of study and wonder, the collected wisdom of his government colleagues and Philadelphia friends; they barely conceal his excitement at realizing that at last he would have facts, not vague guesses, about the Stony Mountains, the river courses, the wild Indian tribes, the flora and fauna of untrodden places."

The president had no doubt that if anyone could be trusted to carry out his requests, it would be Meriwether Lewis. "Capt. Lewis is brave, prudent, habituated to the woods, & familiar with Indian manners & character," Jefferson wrote to Benjamin Rush, the eminent Philadelphia physician from whom Lewis was to learn medicine in order to look after his men on the expedition. "He is not regularly educated, but he possesses a great mass of accurate observation on all the subjects of nature which present themselves here, & will therefore readily select those only in his new route which shall be new." After Lewis died, Jefferson elaborated further upon his friend's temperament and character: "No season or circumstance could obstruct his purpose," Jefferson wrote. He possessed a passion for "dazzling pursuits"; had "enterprise, boldness, and discretion," "courage undaunted," and a "firmness and perseverance of purpose which no thing but impossibilities could divert from its direction." His fidelity to truth was "scrupulous."

In the final paragraph of the president's extraordinary and detailed instructions to Lewis, Jefferson requested that he designate a second in command who could take over Lewis's responsibilities should he die on the expedition. Lewis decided to appoint a co-leader instead and chose for the position William Clark, an officer he greatly admired and liked and under whom he had previously served.

By the late summer of 1803 the expedition was under way. The leaders and their men set out with fishing hooks and tents; mosquito netting, whiskey, and salt pork; Pennsylvania rifles and axes; sextants and telescopes; lamps and kettles and saws. They left with provisions for most imaginable contingencies, and they took, as well, items of exchange for the Indians they would encounter: boxes of fabrics and bright things — 500 brooches, 72 rings, 12 dozen looking glasses, 3 pounds of beads — tomahawks and knives; striped silk ribbons and calico shirts; and 130 rolls of tobacco. There were, for the inevitable fevers and injuries along the way, tourniquets, lancets, and medicinal teas. Laudanum, an ease for almost any ailment, was boxed up as well, as were cloves and nutmegs to disguise the acrid taste of improvised brews and tonics. Peruvian bark, containing quinine, was included to fight malaria.

With what they had and knew, the men could cross rivers and plains, build boats, and survive in the mountains. They could barter for goods, and they could defend themselves. But two of the men, Lewis and Clark, could also measure, describe, and write down what they had observed and where their journey had taken them. They had provisions for history — 100 quills, 1 pound of sealing wax, 6 papers of ink powder, and 6 brass inkstands — and with their quills and ink they filled red morocco-bound journals and an elk-skin field book with precise and captivating scientific records of their twenty-eight-month journey across the American continent.

The Corps of Discovery — Lewis and Clark and their small contingent of soldiers, hunters, woodsmen, blacksmith, cook, and carpenters — went into the country's unmapped territories and mapped them; explored its rivers and mountains; dug canoes out of cottonwood trees; did commerce with the

Indians; and at times stayed among them. They caught fish and shot game. They walked forever, took the measure of the lands and rivers they crossed, and then, after extracting from the stars what they needed for their bearings, the leaders of the expedition would start to write. They filled their journals with detailed descriptions of the plants and trees they had discovered, new animals encountered, the flowings of waters and the structure of the mountains, and the medicines or the discipline they had doled out to their men.

The journals of Lewis and Clark are vivid and immediate; they pull the reader into the unexplored continent and wildlife of wilderness America. Here, for example, is Lewis writing about weather, the taste of a beaver tail, and the gait of porcupines. It is May 1805, and the expedition is making its way upstream on the Missouri River:

Thursday May 2nd, 1805
The wind continued violent all night nor did it abate much of it's violence this morning, when at daylight it was attended with snow which continued to fall untill about 10 A.M. *being about one inch deep, it formed a singular contrast with the vegitation which was considerably advanced, some flowers had put forth in the plains, and the leaves of the cottonwood were as large as a dollar, sent out some hunters who killed 2 deer 3 Elk and several buffaloe; on our way this evening we also shot three beaver along the shore; these anamals in consequence of not being hunted are extreemly gentle, where they are hunted they never leave their lodges in the day, the flesh of the beaver is esteemed a delecacy among us; I think the tale a*

most delicious morsal, when boiled it resembles in flavor the fresh tongues and sounds of the cod-fish, and is usually sufficiently large to afford a plentifull meal for two men.

Friday, May 3rd, 1805
We saw vast quantities of Buffaloe, Elk, deer principally of the long tale kind. Antelope or goats, beaver, geese, ducks, brant and some swan. near the entrance of the river mentioned in the 10th. course of this day, we saw an unusual number of Porcupines from which we determined to call the river after that anamal, and accordingly denominated it Porcupine river....
I walked out a little distance and met with 2 porcupines which were feeding on the young willow which grow in great abundance on all the sandbars; this anamal is exceedingly clumsy and not very watchfull I approached so near one of them before it percieved me that I touched it with my espontoon. — found the nest of a wild goose among some drift-wood in the river from which we took three eggs. this is the only nest we have met with on driftwood, the usual position is the top of a broken tree, sometimes in the forks of a large tree but almost invariably, from 15 to 20 feet or upwards high.

Neither Lewis nor Clark was a professional naturalist or geographer, but they were fastidious in their measurements and descriptions of the places they had been and the wildlife they had seen. Along the way, they sent back to Jefferson and scientists in Philadelphia the moon rocks of their time: nearly two hundred different specimens of trees and plants — grasses from the plains, currants, wildflowers, sage-brush, flax, Mariposa lilies, spruce, and maples — most of which had been, until that time, unknown to leading botanists. They shipped crates full of roots, seeds, and bulbs, as well as the skins and skeletons of weasels, coyotes, squirrels, badgers, birds, antelopes, mountain rams, and scores of other animals. "Few explorers have undertaken a larger task or achieved greater success in carrying it out," observed one writer. "Their survey notes were meticulously recorded, and their maps of the areas explored were the best available for fifty years."

In September 1806 the Corps of Discovery completed its journey. Jefferson's initial hope of finding a Northwest Passage that linked the Atlantic with the Pacific was not realized, but the exploration was otherwise a success beyond the imaginations of imaginative men. When Lewis and Clark and the rest of their expedition arrived in St. Louis, they stepped from their boat into a swirl of acclaim, society balls, and national celebration. "Never," declared Thomas Jefferson, "did a similar event excite more joy in the United States." Meriwether Lewis, however, only thirty-two years old, began the descent into the last three, deeply unsettled years of his life.

It is nearly two hundred years since Meriwether Lewis died of gunshot wounds in a cabin seventy miles from Nashville. The circumstances of his death remain charged with controversy and rancor, although suicide seems by far to be the most likely explanation for his death. But suicide is at odds with a country's notion of what a hero should be. Thomas

Jefferson, who for two years had lived intimately with Lewis and who had treated him like a son; William Clark, who had shared leadership, adversity, and triumphs with him for at least as long; and those who were with Lewis during the last hours and days of his life had no doubt that his wounds were self-inflicted. Yet the possibility that Lewis might have killed himself proved unthinkable to many who had never even met him. Derangement, as several who observed his mental state toward the end of his life described it, seemed, for some, inconsistent with courage, honor, and accomplishment of the first rank. Conspiracy theories and speculation about murder cropped up to "protect" the blackened reputation of the explorer. But what was the evidence of suicide? Who could imagine that Lewis's reputation needed defending? And why should suicide be seen as a dishonorable rather than just dreadfully tragic act?

Contemporary accounts of the weeks leading up to Lewis's death make a compelling case for a deeply distraught and troubled man who was drinking heavily, spending and investing money irrationally, and acting in a way that caused others to be concerned for his safety and well-being. His position as governor of the Louisiana Territories, taken up after his return from the West, was marred by conflict and questionable judgment, and he was hopelessly behind in preparing the journals of the expedition. Jefferson was clearly exasperated: "I am very often applied to know when our work will appear," he wrote to Lewis. "I have so long promised copies to my literary correspondents in France that I am almost bankrupt in their eyes. I shall be very happy to receive from yourself information of your expectations on this subject." The inordinate delay in forwarding the highly awaited information about the journey was not the first time there had been gaps in Lewis's writing. Most of them, interestingly, showed a similar seasonal pattern, occurring during August and/or September; some extended through late fall or early winter, as well (Lewis died in early October 1809). In that same time of the year, in August 1809, Lewis also wrote the only introspective and rather melancholic entry into his journal:

This day I completed my thirty first year, and conceived that I had in all human probability now existed about half the period which I am to remain in this Sublunary world. I reflected that I had as yet done but little, very little indeed, to further the hapiness of the human race, or to advance the information of the succeeding generation. I viewed with regret the many hours I have spent in indolence, and now soarly feel the want of that information which those hours would have given me had they been judiciously expended, but since they are past and cannot be recalled, I dash from me the gloomy thought, and resolved in future, to redouble my exertions and at least indeavour to promote those two primary objects of human existence, by giving them the aid of that portion of talents which nature and fortune have bestoed on me; or in future, to live for mankind, *as I have heretofore lived* for myself.

In early September 1809, the month before he died, Lewis set off for Washington and Philadelphia to straighten out his financial affairs and to work on the publication of his expedition journals. William Clark, who had tried to help Lewis sort out his expense accounts, was clearly concerned about the state of Lewis's mind: "Several of his Bills [to the government] have been protested, and his Creditors all flocking in near the time of his Setting out distressed him much, which he expressed to me in Such terms as to Cause a Cempothy which is not yet off — I do not believe there was ever a honester man in Louisiana nor one who had pureor motives than Govr. Lewis. if his mind had been at ease I Should have parted Cherefuly." A week after leaving St. Louis, Lewis drew up a will, and a few days later he arrived at Fort Pickering (Memphis). The commanding officer of the fort, Captain Gilbert Russell, heard from the crew on Lewis's boat that Lewis had twice attempted to kill himself. Russell himself observed that Lewis had been drinking heavily and was, at the time he arrived at the fort, "mentally deranged." The commander, afraid that Lewis would take his own life, unloaded Lewis's boat so that he could not escape and kept him under constant surveillance for several days:

> In this condition he continued without any material change for about five days, during which time the most proper and efficatious means that could be devised to restore him was administered, and on the sixth or seventh day all symptoms of derangement disappeared and he was completely in his senses and thus continued for ten or twelve days.... In three or four days he was again affected with the same mental disease. He had no person with him who could manage

or controul him in his propensities and he daily grew worse untill he arrived at the house of a Mr. Grinder...where in the apprehension of being destroyed by enemies which had no existence but in his wild imagination, he destroyed himself in the most cool desperate and Barbarian-like manner, having been left in the house intirely to himself.

The U.S. agent to the Chickasaw Nation, James Neelly, who was with Lewis for the last three weeks of his life, wrote to President Jefferson shortly after Lewis's death: "It is with extreme pain I have to inform you of the death of His Excellency Meriwether Lewis, Governor of Upper Louisiana who died on the morning of the 11th instant and I am Sorry to Say by Suicide." He reported, as Russell had, that Lewis had been mentally "deranged" off and on for some period of time. The details of Lewis's suicide were later recorded in detail by his friend, the eminent ornithologist Alexander Wilson. He wrote his account after interviewing the woman at whose inn Lewis had died:

Governor Lewis, she said, came hither about sunset, alone, and inquired if he could stay for the night; and alighting, brought his saddle into the house. He was dressed in a loose gown, white, striped with blue. On being asked if he came alone, he replied that there were two servants behind, who would soon be up. He called for some spirits, and drank a very little. When the servants arrived...he inquired for his powder.... [He] walked backwards and forwards before the door, talking to himself.

Sometimes, she said, he would seem as if he were walking up to her; and would suddenly wheel round, and walk back as fast as he could. Supper being ready he sat down, but had eaten only a few mouthfuls when he started up, speaking to himself in a violent manner.... He smoked for some time, but quitted his seat and traversed the yard as before. He again sat down to his pipe, seemed again composed, and casting his eyes wistfully towards the west, observed what a sweet evening it was. Mrs. Grinder was preparing a bed for him, but he said he would sleep on the floor, and desired the servant to bring the bear skins and buffalo robe, which were immediately spread out for him; and, it now being dusk, the woman went off to the kitchen and the two men to the barn which stands about two hundred yards off.

The kitchen is only a few paces from the room where Lewis was, and the woman being considerably alarmed by the behavior of the guest could not sleep, but listened to him walking backwards and forwards, she thinks, for several hours, and talking aloud, as she said, "like a lawyer." She then heard the report of a pistol, and something fall heavily to the floor, and the words "0 Lord!" Immediately afterwards she heard another pistol, and in a few minutes she heard him at her door calling out, "0 madam! give me some water and heal my wounds!"

The logs being open, and unplastered, she saw him stagger back and fall against a stump that stands between the kitchen and the room. He crawled for some distance, and raised himself by the side of a tree, where he sat about a minute. He once more got to the room; afterwards he came to the kitchen door, but did not speak; she then heard him scraping in the bucket with a gourd for water; but it appears that this cooling element was denied the dying man.

As soon as the day broke, and not before, the terror of the woman having permitted him to remain for two hours in this most deplorable situation, she sent two of her children to the barn, her husband not being home, to bring the servants; and on going in they found him lying on the bed. He uncovered his side, and showed them where the bullet had entered; a piece of his forehead was blown off, and had exposed the brains, without having bled much.

He begged they would take his rifle and blow out his brains, and he would give them all the money in his trunk. He often said, "I am no coward; but I am so strong, so hard to die." He begged the servant not to be afraid of him, for that he would not hurt him. He expired in about two hours, or just as the sun rose above the trees.

Captain Russell's account of Lewis's last hours was even more dreadful. After twice shooting himself with his pistol, Russell reports, Lewis "got his razors from a port folio which happened to contain them and siting up in his bed was found about day light, by one of the servants, busily engaged in cuting himself from head to foot."

William Clark was stricken at the news of his friend's death, but he was not entirely surprised by the accounts that Lewis had killed himself: "I fear 0! I fear the weight of his mind has overcome him," he wrote to his brother two weeks after Lewis died. And Thomas Jefferson, in a short memoir about Meriwether Lewis, wrote:

> Governor Lewis had, from early life, been subject to hypochondriac [depressive] affections. It was a constitutional disposition in all the nearer branches of the family of his name, and was more immediately inherited by him from his father. They had not, however, been so strong as to give uneasiness to his family. While he lived with me in Washington I observed at times sensible depressions of mind: but knowing their constitutional source, I estimated their course by what I had seen in the family. During his western expedition, the constant exertion which that required of all the faculties of body and mind, suspended these distressing affections; but after his establishment at St. Louis in sedentary occupations, they returned upon him with redoubled vigour, and began seriously to alarm his friends. He was in a paroxysm of one of these, when his affairs rendered it necessary for him to go to Washington....
>
> About three o'clock in the night he did the deed which plunged his friends into affliction, and deprived his country of one of her most valued citizens.... It lost too to the nation the benefit of receiving from his own hand the narrative...of his sufferings and successes, in endeavoring to extend for them the boundaries of science, and to present to their knowledge that vast and fertile

country, which their sons are destined to fill with arts, with science, with freedom and happiness.

Jefferson's account of his friend's death would seem to many, myself included, a thoughtful and compassionate portrayal of the death of a courageous man. But others have felt differently. Some simply cannot reconcile the outward realities of Lewis's life with his desire to leave it. Olin Dunbar Wheeler, historian and editor, was one of these. "It seems impossible," he wrote, "that a young man of 35, the Governor of the vast Territory of Louisiana, then on his way from his capital to that of the nation, where he knew he would be received with all the distinction and consideration due his office and reputation, should take his own life." Biographer Flora Seymour, writing in 1937, thought suicide totally out of character: "Many believed that Governor Lewis, ill, dejected, despairing of justice, had died by his own hand.... But those who had been with the brave young captain on the long journey West felt that this could not be the solution. The Meriwether Lewis they knew did not lose his courage nor his head in times of trial."

A more recent biographer, Richard Dillon, takes Seymour's argument further, determined to clear Lewis's name of the "crime" of suicide:

> Is it likely that the cause of Lewis's death was self-murder? Not at all. If there is such a person as the antisuicide type, it was Meriwether Lewis. By temperament, he was a fighter, not a quitter.... Sensitive he was; neurotic he was not. Lewis was one of the most positive personalities in American history.

Not enough has been made of the factors weighing against his taking his own life. His courage; his enthusiasm; his youth (thirty-five); his plans — to return to St. Louis, after seeing his mother and setting things straight in Washington; to engage in the fur trade with his brother, Reuben, and his best friend, Will Clark....

In a democracy such as ours — to which Meriwether Lewis was so strongly dedicated — it is held in the courts of justice that a man is presumed innocent of a crime until proved guilty. Meriwether Lewis has not been proven guilty of self-destruction at Grinder's Stand in the early hours of October 11, 1809. Therefore let him be found NOT GUILTY of the charge — the crime of suicide.

Yet others have stated that Lewis's death was somehow "beclouded" or "tainted by dishonor"; some, believing that Lewis was murdered, have impugned Jefferson's integrity for concluding that Lewis's death was self-inflicted: "It seems to me that Jefferson's ready acceptance of Lewis's death by suicide was a disgraceful way to treat a man," wrote physician and historian E. G. Chuinard a few years ago. David Leon Chandler, a Pulitzer Prize-winning journalist, put Jefferson in the center of a convoluted conspiracy (the title of his book is *The Jefferson Conspiracies: A President's Role in the Assassination of Meriwether Lewis*) and states, among other things, that "Thomas Jefferson's complicity is a substantial one and includes his endorsement of the suicide theory.... He accepted the stigma of suicide because he feared a greater scandal." Less darkly, William Clark's son, Meriwether Lewis Clark, said simply that he wished no stigma "upon the fair name I have the honor to bear."

Underlying the suicide-murder controversy run several streams of thought: it is a disgrace to die by suicide; that Lewis was too young or too successful to kill himself (neither of which, of course, protects against suicide); or that committing suicide is intrinsically a cowardly act and therefore a great and courageous man could not have done such a thing. Others have argued that Jefferson would not have appointed Lewis to command the westward expedition had he actually known of any mental instability in Lewis or his family line. This argument has been further buttressed by repeated assertions that, in any event, Jefferson could have had no way of knowing of any mental illness in Lewis's family, despite the fact that Jefferson and Lewis had lived together for two years and presumably had had many intimate discussions which neither of them committed to paper. There is, in fact, no way of knowing what confidences about family and self they shared. It is difficult, short of weaving an elaborate conspiracy net, to imagine why Jefferson would write what he did about Lewis and his father's family unless he believed it to be true. (Interestingly, there may have been instability on both sides of the family. Lewis's half brother, Dr. John Marks, his mother's son by her second marriage, at one point had to be confined because of "mental problems"; there was also a great deal of intermarriage, nearly a dozen marriages, between the Meriwether and Lewis families.)

Jefferson's conjecture that Lewis's melancholic tendencies were put on ice as long as he was actively and physically engaged but emerged later during slower, more sedentary times is perceptive, telling, and completely consistent with what is known about restless, energetic, and impetuous temperaments that have an obverse inclination to despair. Stephen Ambrose, in his excellent biography of Meriwether Lewis, *Undaunted Courage,* discusses at some length Meriwether Lewis's occasional quickness of temper: "He had, however, four times lost his temper and twice threatened to kill. His behavior was erratic and threatening to the future of the expedition.... He had a short temper and too often acted on it.... [He] could not keep his 'boisterous' passion in check."

Lewis, then, had a family and personal history of depression, a quick temper and a restless disposition, and a tendency to drink heavily and, toward the end of his life, to be financially reckless and rather unaccountable in his professional obligations. He twice attempted suicide and was placed on a close suicide watch by a fellow officer. His closest friends, William Clark and Thomas Jefferson, believed the eyewitness accounts of his last days and hours, all of which had concluded that he had killed himself.

Why, then, the convoluted theories of conspiracy, of malaria, or of syphilis, all of which have been offered as "explanations" for his death? There is little credible evidence for the "Jefferson conspiracy"; improbable speculation only for the theory of murder (much of it based on the magnification of inevitable inconsistencies in the accounts of witnesses); and next to no evidence at all for syphilis, although it is possible he had it. He may well have suffered from malaria, which was endemic along the frontier; this has been suggested by some as the explanation for his "derangement." Cerebral malaria, which occasionally results in impulsive and self-destructive acts, is very uncommon. (Of the malaria cases reported in the nineteenth century, as well as the tens of thousands detailed in World Wars I and II and the Vietnam War, fewer than 2 percent were cerebral malaria; of those that were, suicide was a rare outcome.) A medical cause for irrational behavior may be more palatable to some historians, but it is not more plausible.

Douglass Adair and Dawson Phelps of the Oregon Historical Society raise, I think, the critical question: "Apparently," they write, "most of Lewis's contemporaries who knew him well...were either not surprised to learn that he had killed himself, or had extremely persuasive evidence that his death was suicide. Does the murder theory reflect the unwillingness of American scholars (the frontier specialists in particular) to admit that a man as great as Lewis had shown himself to be...could become so spiritually desolated or mentally ill that he could kill himself?"

I think the answer is yes, that scholars and laypeople alike find it hard to hold in their minds the thought that a great man could have been deranged or that a courageous man could have killed himself. But such men do. And the same bold, restless temperament that Jefferson saw in the young Meriwether Lewis can lie uneasily just this side of a restless, deadly despair. It is to the great credit of Jefferson that he was able to understand this complexity of human nature and to Lewis's credit that he chose as his co-leader and explorer William Clark, a man of a complementary, more even disposition.

In recent years, there has been a rumbling to disinter the remains of Meriwether Lewis. It is argued that doing so would settle the truth of his death once and for all, and perhaps it would. One reader of the *Washington Post*, for example wrote, that if it could be proved that Meriwether Lewis had been murdered, "then a blot is removed from the name of the explorer." I wrote a letter to the *Post* in response. I thought it was extraordinary that suicide should be seen as a "blot"; that there was a compelling case that Lewis had suffered from manic-depression and had killed himself; and that however Lewis had died, he had lived a life of remarkable courage, accomplishment, and vision. Suicide is not a blot on anyone's name; it is a tragedy. I believe, as do many others, that he should be allowed to keep such undisinterred peace as he might have. He has earned his rest. And, in the end, for all of us, it is his life that remains. Lewis was, as Ambrose writes, an explorer first, last, and always:

> He was a man of high energy and was at times impetuous, but this was tempered by his great self-discipline. He could drive himself to the point of exhaustion, then take an hour to write about the events of the day, and another to make his celestial observations.
>
> His talents and skills ran wider than they did deep. He knew how to do many things, from designing and building a boat to all the necessary wilderness skills. He knew a little about many of the various parts of the natural sciences. He could describe an animal, classify a plant, name

the stars, manage the sextant and other instruments, dream of empire. But at none of these things was he an expert, or uniquely gifted.

Where he was unique, truly gifted, and truly great was as an explorer, where all his talents were necessary. The most important was his ability as a leader of men. He was born to leadership, and reared for it, studied it in his army career, then exercised it on the expedition.

MERIWETHER LEWIS was a great man and the circumstances of his death unbearably sad. Shakespeare, in writing of the suicide of Mark Antony, said it best: "The breaking of so great a thing should make / A greater crack: the round world / Should have shook lions into civil streets, / And citizens to their dens."

> *"It is difficult to make a man miserable while he feels worthy of himself and claims kindred to the great God who made him."*
>
> ABRAHAM LINCOLN

HONESTLY

By John F. Brown

ALTHOUGH the journey has been long and arduous, there is light at the end of the tunnel.

I am sitting on my couch with a shotgun under my throat. My world, as I know it, is hell on earth. The only respite I get is when I'm sleeping, so I try to sleep as much as possible, sometimes up to twenty hours a day. It is early April in Central New Jersey, where I live, around six-thirty in the morning. It's going to be one of those very bright and warm spring days, made even brighter because the leaves on the trees have yet to bloom. It's the kind of day I believe most people look forward to after spending the past few months bundled up from winter's grip. So why am I sitting here contemplating suicide?

I had just been released from my first sleepover at a psychiatric hospital. This occurred after months of feeling hopeless, useless, and worthless. I didn't want to do anything that normally interested me, and I certainly didn't feel like eating. My energy level was at an all-time low. How was this possible? Why did this always seem to occur at the same time of year? How was I going to get out of this nightmare? I had a little glimmer of hope when I agreed to voluntarily sign in to the psychiatric ward. But now I wasn't sure. That experience left me with mixed feelings.

The day of my admission to the hospital was probably one of the worst days of my life. I was at work and driving in the rush hour traffic on the Garden State Parkway. I was smoking cigarettes, one after the other, and having the most painful time in all my life. I decided that when I reached the Edison Bridge, I would stop and jump off. I sort of felt guilty for the traffic jam I would cause and the anguish my family and friends might feel from this outrageous act, but damn it, this is too much pain for anybody to walk around with. A good friend had killed himself in December of 1990, so I knew firsthand what my family and friends were about to go through. This really didn't matter to me. I had to end this constant seven-day-a-week, twenty-four-hour-a-day pain. Month after month, year after year, always the same, but now it was becoming unbearable. Something had to change. I wished I didn't have to pee, but I had to stop. As I approached the bridge, traffic became quite heavy, so I decided to stop at the rest area before the bridge. *I might as well call my wife and at least tell her good-bye,* I reasoned in this highly delusional state.

After relieving myself, I dialed her at work. It was hard for me to talk, and I started to cry. I'd been doing a lot of crying lately. When I explained my reason for calling, she asked where I was and assured me that she would get me some help if I would just hang on.

What did I have to lose? This just seemed like post-poning the inevitable, but I agreed to meet her at her place of work. It even amazes me today, as I write this, that I was able to complete that drive because not only was I in the most desperate shape I had ever been in, but my wife immediately notified the New Jersey State Police of this predicament. I am very grateful that I was not spotted and pulled over because I might have begged that poor soul to just shoot me and put me out of my misery. Police are trained for many things, but I don't think any compensation is enough for having to deal with anyone in this most desperate of states. I was not capable of coherent thoughts. Thank God I made it there without any problems.

We went home to figure out what to do. I felt a bit of relief knowing we were going home. Home is a safe place, the place where I had been isolating for the past few months. Once we got there, all I could do was cry. I felt embarrassed, guilty, weak, ashamed, and any other adjective that describes a loser. Why was this happening? What was happening? How did I get here? Who do you call? What do you do? Where do you go? Which direction do you head in? CAN ANY-ONE HELP ME? I'M DYING HERE!

Unfortunately, in today's health care system your choices are narrowed by the very people you need to rely on to obtain help — the type of insurance you have determines the type of treatment you receive. After some calls made by my wife, we were headed to a nearby hospital's crisis center. A doctor and a nurse led us to a room, where he asked many questions about how I was feeling — will I kill myself; did I have a plan — questions like that, what I imagine to be a routine questionnaire for those in crisis. His bedside manner left me to believe that we were holding him back from something, but the nurse appeared compassionate and more understanding, as evidenced by her looks of sympathy and deep sighs as I tried my best to explain why I wanted to kill myself. Once the question-and-answer part of this appointment was over, the doctor announced that I would be fine in a matter of weeks and gave me a prescription for Prozac. He then instructed me to come back and see him in two weeks. All was going to be fine. I thought my wife would blow a gasket. She was livid, absolutely beside herself. Didn't this jerk understand I wanted to kill myself today? He's got to be kidding.

"Take some Prozac and come back and see me in two weeks."

"Buddy, I didn't think I would make it through another day, let alone two weeks."

Thank God for Bonnie. Next stop was Hampton Hospital for the behaviorally challenged, mentally ill, that is. A swimming pool but no movie stars.

Checking into a psychiatric hospital is something I believe everyone might find educational. I had been in hospitals before, but this was entirely different. There wasn't any hustle and bustle like most hospitals I'd been to. It was quiet, with only a few people visible at any one time. We were led to a waiting room adjoining the front desk. Here my wife filled out forms, filling in information that I could not possibly decipher if I had to do them myself. I was feeling ashamed, embarrassed, guilty, hopeless, and completely alone. Bonnie assured me repeatedly that everything was going to be all right. It didn't help. I tried not to cry, but it hurt so much that I just couldn't help myself. Tears of remorse, inferiority, and hopelessness.

After filling out the forms and saying our good-byes, I was led to the wing I would call my home for the next ten days. Though the doctors needed time and patience to make an accurate diagnosis, my insurance company knew that they would figure it out in ten days. Thank you, managed health care. How did we get along without them for so long? As we passed through doors that were unlocked through an intercom system, I began to feel more like a prisoner than a patient. I was given a room without a roommate and, at the time, was grateful to be alone. My room came equipped with tamperproof screws on anything that used one to hold it in place. I had seen these before on a construction job at a new jail. A mirror made of metal was in the bathroom. I remember having a hard time shaving in front of this and wondering if I was leaving the bathroom with my face half done. People might really suspect I was crazy then. After all, you do want to look your best even when you're feeling your worst.

The first night sleeping in a foreign place, with plastic under the sheets and people checking on you every fifteen minutes, was difficult. Your door is left open. I was tempted, after hours of trying to fall asleep, to lock the door so the person checking would freak out the next time he came around. I knew then that I had not lost my entire sense of humor, but I didn't have the energy to get up and do it. Oh well, it's still funny to think of it.

The day starts at six with vital signs taken at the main nurse's station. This is the time of day people with depression fear the most. "Please, no, it can't be morning already." For a split second every morning, I would dream that this had all been a nightmare, only to realize that this was really happening and my entire existence was a horrible dream only those with depression know. Your absolute worst nightmare come true. "How am I going to possibly make it through another day? God, PLEASE HELP ME!" This had been my morning mantra for more years than I care to remember. Since I wasn't home and there were rules to follow and people who could take my off-the-floor dining privileges away, I reluctantly got ready for the day.

The days were quite structured during the week: Breakfast, followed by morning meds. Meds, followed by morning meetings till lunch, where you or some of your lucky wardmates would get to talk about how they were feeling. Lunch, followed by maybe music therapy, psychodrama, or art classes. Music therapy was my favorite because it usually involved some time with my eyes closed. As long as you didn't start snoring, you could get away with a little rest without being caught and losing your dining room privileges. In psychodrama, the patients acted out parts about things that were troubling in their lives. Put a positive slant on them, I suppose. Art classes consisted of painting things. I remember painting a ceramic pig and a turtle. The eleventh commandment in art class was not to leave any of your artwork behind when you went home for good, or you were destined to return to the ward in the future. I thought this was a bunch of bull, so I left my turtle behind when my sentence was up. I returned eight months later for stay number two. You're damn right I made sure I left with my artwork that time. I now have a pink pig and a green turtle.

I believe that mealtime was my favorite time on my psychiatric vacation. As you can imagine, the food was — well, let's just say that they meant well. One thing I wished we were allowed was caffeine drinks. I don't know anybody who drinks coffee for the taste, and I believe a little caffeine boost would have helped us make it through the day. Fortunately, they did have ice cream. It really was pretty good during certain mealtimes. I even ate there for lunch during my outpatient sessions. Although, come to think of it, I did get some rather odd looks from the staff during those dining experiences. Oh well.

There is an interesting phenomenon that occurs at the end of the day. Patients become more relaxed, and even the deeply depressed appear livelier as bedtime arrives. I only know for myself that the security of the night brings a sense of relief, as I know I'll be unconscious soon. My heart goes out to those who have depressive episodes and cannot sleep. New patients arrived sometimes in the evening, and you would be introduced to them in a more relaxed atmosphere than at other times of the day. When patients on a psychiatric ward — as, I would imagine, in most hospitals, for that matter — introduce themselves, they tell you their name and their diagnosis, if they have been given one.

I remember this one guest who introduced himself and said, "Hi, I'm Martin, and I'm here for arson." At that point everything became very quiet until he added, "and depression."

I felt like Arlo Guthrie in "Alice's Restaurant" when the murderers and father rapers all moved away from him when he told them he was in jail for littering. Then they all moved back when he added, "and disturbing the peace." Even in a room full of mentally ill, prejudice exists. What a concept. Well, enough about the hospital stays; let's talk about what happens when you leave.

The first time I left, my folks and my oldest sister came to take me home, as my wife needed to be at work. As we were driving past the front door, my dad says with comfort, "Well, at least you won't have to go back there." I tried to explain to him that if I needed to, I was glad there was a place to go. I didn't understand this attitude of his, but it made me feel uncomfortable. There were many more of these attitudes to come. I felt as if my own family didn't know how to treat me.

One of my best friends called, about a half hour after I got home, to tell me that his older brother had died from complications and infection from a brain aneurysm. My younger brother answered the phone, and he checked with my mother to see if it was all right to tell me. He was worried that something like this might set me off. Fortunately, I took the call and agreed to meet my friend the next day. He asked if I would accompany him and his dad to the funeral home to make the arrangements because they were emotionally drained and they wanted me to come along to help with the proceedings. Hey, they didn't know I had just spent the last ten days in a psychiatric ward. Would I be of some assistance? Absolutely.

It was really wonderful to be asked to do something responsible, as everyone else seemed to be walking on eggshells around me. No one knew what to say, and we were all having an awkward time. It's comical to think back, and I know my friend's brother was getting a good laugh in heaven because, for most of his life, he had had bouts with severe episodes of depression. At the funeral parlor, the funeral director would ask a question. My friend and his dad, both in a state of emotional strain, just couldn't think clearly. They would turn to me and ask, "What do you think?" And I would point out why I thought this way. They all listened attentively as I spoke, and we would come to a conclusion and make a decision. This went on throughout the meeting. I told my friend, at the gathering after the funeral, that I had just gotten out of a mental hospital, and he couldn't believe it. How could I have been that much assistance the day before if I couldn't think straight myself? How could I think clearly while taking an antidepressant medication? Why hadn't anyone even told him I was in the hospital?

Another wonderful form of responsibility came from my neighbor. This kind and gentle man, whom I had always loved to talk with, called and asked if I would watch his three horses and his dog while he went away for the weekend. He had never asked me to watch his animals before because he felt it was a dangerous undertaking for someone who was not familiar with horses. But he had recently met a wonderful woman whom he would marry a year later. She thought it would be great for me to give it a try, and besides, she wanted to get away for the weekend. What was the big deal?

The time came for me to learn what to do, so we went down to the corral to go over the procedure. My neighbor was adamant about not getting too close to the horses. If you had to, give them a gentle nudge to keep them away. If that didn't work, haul off and give them a good whack, but by no means allow them to get in a position where you would be between them and the stall walls. He explained that you could easily be crushed or stepped on.

I was ready. Didn't this guy know I just got out of a mental hospital? I can handle this.

It went very well, and I was even asked to do it again. I really loved those animals. I remember his sister visiting, and I stopped over to find them giving one of her children a ride on the gentle mare. The older horse, Braun, started to run towards me when I entered the corral. His ears were back as I walked towards him to grab him by the head and have a talk.

Afterward my neighbor's sister asked me, "Do you know what that means when a horse has his ears back?"

"I thought he was happy to see me," I replied.

"Just the opposite," she laughed. "You must be crazy!"

"Sort of," I laughed. She didn't know where I had been, and there was no point in telling her.

Alcohol and drugs became a mainstay during my late teens, up to the time I stopped using at the age of twenty-six. I realized that having two DUI's by the time I was twenty-two wasn't normal, so I decided to give all of this up on my own. I certainly would not recommend this to anyone because so much has been learned and there are many good Twelve-Step programs out there today. My advice would be to ask for help. I didn't, and it shows. I've been to three different colleges, had two different majors and accumulated a total of one hundred forty credits. I stopped going to school with nine credits left for a degree in accounting. Commuting to school by train at night became a real pain in the ass, not to mention the fact that I really couldn't comprehend what I was doing anyway. College became a place to fall back on because I really didn't know what direction to go.

I blamed this period of confusion on the drugs and alcohol, but really, in looking back, it was the undiagnosed depression I lived with year in and year out. The alcohol and drugs masked the real problem; it was easier to point at them. People talked about those kinds of things. They don't talk about mental illness. I thought that everyone had thoughts of suicide; they were just too embarrassed to talk about it. Maybe I could find some other thing in my life that needed fixing.

I thought that if I had a good job, maybe got married and built a new house, my life would get better. I had the good job working for very nice people, but that didn't help. I built a new house for my new bride, but that didn't help. I tried health foods, spiritual books, exercise, and anything I could get my hands on, but that didn't help. My life was chaotic for six months out of twelve, and it all appeared to be hopeless. I couldn't go on like this anymore.

Which brings us back to the point of the beginning of this story. I am sitting on the couch with the shotgun propped up under my throat, crying uncontrollably. My mind is all over the place. My body is full of all the anxieties and fears that have ever been created. I am ready to literally come apart at the seams. I am shaking, crying, ranting, and pacing, about to totally lose it. I need to think, think, think and figure out what to do. I'm nervous, anxious, and this all feels so utterly hopeless. *I can't do this here. No one will want to buy the house when Bonnie will be forced to sell it after I'm gone. Maybe I could drive somewhere, get out, and do it in the woods. But what about the person or persons who find me with my head blown off? That certainly won't be fair to them. And what if there really is an afterlife, and when you commit suicide, you are doomed to spend the rest of eternity in this state of mental horror? I can't take that chance.*

I felt like Prometheus, of Greek mythology. Prometheus did not tell Zeus the prophecy that one of Zeus's sons would overthrow him. In punishment, Zeus commanded that Prometheus be chained for eternity in the Caucasus. There, an eagle (or, according to other sources, a vulture) would eat his liver, and each day the liver would be renewed. So the punishment was endless, until Hercules finally killed the bird. The only difference in my story is that there is no Hercules, and now I'm chained to living a life of endless pain and mental torture and totally afraid to commit suicide because of this giant fear about the possible endless torture in the afterlife.

You talk about a rock and a hard place. I can't bear living, and I can't bear dying. What the HELL am I supposed to do?

"PLEASE, GOD, HELP ME!" I cried out in desperation.

My first episode of depression accompanied by thoughts of suicide started when I was in the seventh grade and I was thirteen years old. I know this because school became difficult for me, whereas before this period, the work was a breeze to the point of being easy. Now it didn't matter how much I studied; I couldn't comprehend what had normally come crystal clear for me. My life started to become miserable. I remember thinking that it just wasn't worth living. As I went through my teens, I started to experiment with alcohol and drugs. It was good to not feel the depression, so I used more and more. I didn't realize I was only making matters worse for myself.

People didn't talk about their emotional state. But even if they tried, I certainly, from all outward appearances, could fool anyone. I was one of those good-looking kids with blond hair and blue eyes. The girls in grammar school nicknamed me Maybelline because my eyelashes were so long. The orthodontist gave me the best weapon a person with chronic depression could ever want: When someone would ask me how I was doing, I could flash those pearly whites and appear absolutely calm from the outside while on the inside, I was coming apart at the seams. At times I felt like two separate people — one looking good; the other, a pile of shit and a total fraud.

So I did the only thing I had left: I cried out to God for help. And not three seconds later, the telephone rang. It was my wife, and for the first time in my life, I felt compelled to be totally honest. This was my spiritual awakening. I vowed from that point on to ask for help and to live a life of honesty. It has not been easy and actually has become a nightmare at times. But I always have hope.

As I've said, I spent two periods in the hospital. I've seen seven different doctors over a period of four years. I've been diagnosed as clinically depressed, manic-depressed, temporal lobe epileptic, and currently as clinically depressed with dysthemia. I've taken Prozac, Paxil, Zoloft, Depakote, and Tegretol and am currently having great success with Effexor XR. I have worked with three therapists during this period who have been invaluable in helping me to understand the people and situations that trigger my depressive episodes. This is an ongoing process, and it takes much hard work and pain, but the rewards far outweigh the dedication. There is so much to be learned about the last great frontier, the brain. It is imperative that I work with and receive help from as many people as possible. Some of the work has been rather startling.

My very first session with my very first therapist started with her telling me that I must know someone because she was not taking new patients. Not exactly a confidence booster by any means, although she did help me once we got over that comment.

One of the doctors in the hospital, while sitting in a chair, asked if I had any thoughts of suicide. When I responded to the affirmative, he immediately sat up in his chair. Oh, sure, I'm going to trust this guy. I didn't go to medical school, but I certainly knew, from my brief education into depression, that suicide thoughts are a symptom of depression, just as coughing is a symptom of a cold.

Another doctor I went to would throw a stuffed toy turkey at me from behind his desk when I questioned his authority. He would bring up the fact that he had a one hundred sixty-seven IQ and **HE** was the doctor. I know you're reading this, Doc, and I just want you to know that comment always made me think of the saying about people who ask the price of something. If they need to ask, they can't afford it in the first place.

I called up the hospital on a weekend because I was

having a very difficult time and wanted to speak with someone on call. The attendant told me that since it was a nice day, go for a walk or maybe try some fishing. I couldn't even get out of bed, so how would I go for a walk?

My first week in outpatient therapy, the therapist showed a Winnie-the-Pooh cartoon. I still laugh when I remember the looks on the faces of the staff members and her new boss when they walked by the room while the cartoon was playing.

But the best of all of those has to be the doctor with the giant IQ convincing me that my condition could be arrested if I would move, as eighteen of his former patients had. His theory was that the conditions of temporal lobe epilepsy would subside by simply moving anywhere around the world as long as you stay between the thirtieth parallel north and the thirtieth parallel south. The closer you got to the equator, the better. A wavelength of light existed there that, taken through the pupil, would trigger the brain to stop having petit mal seizures. He believed this to be the problem and cause of my depression. Since this wavelength did not exist in New Jersey during the winter months, a move might help.

My episodes of depression usually start sometime in December and last till late April or early May. The peak is usually February and March, and at these times I have, for the past four years, been confined to the home and usually spent my time in bed. I had had enough by the spring of 1997 and announced to my wife that I would be making the move to either Costa Rica or Hawaii. To say she wasn't exactly thrilled would be an understatement. It wasn't until two weeks before I was scheduled to leave that my wife decided to accompany me.

We decided to go to the island of Kauai, because neither one of us speaks Spanish. I had some friends who had been to Kauai to go surfing, so on May 11, 1998, we arrived in our new environment. In about eight weeks I weaned myself off the Tegratol and started to work off the thirty or so pounds I had put on from a combination of medication and a sedentary lifestyle brought on by the depression. Life was looking up.

You can imagine my utter disappointment when, walking to the beach one day our first December here, the suicidal thoughts started. I knew exactly what was coming next, and for most of December and January, I fought the inevitable as best I could. By February I was bedridden. I had met a good friend who saw me walking late one day (I was literally dragging myself out at the end of the days and forcing myself to walk). We talked, and since he's a retired doctor and someone who intimately knows about depression, he suggested I go and see his doctor. I agreed, and he told me he would make the arrangements. This was at 6:30 p.m. on Saturday, February 16, 1999. I received a call from Jon Nakamura, M.D., an hour later that same evening. He asked the usual questions, and we agreed to meet first thing Monday morning. Had he not made this simple yet profound act of concern and kindness, I don't believe I would have kept that appointment. For the first time I felt trusting of my doctor. It's amazing what a telephone call and a little compassion will do.

We agreed to try a different class of antidepressants since I had not responded well to all the others. It took nearly three weeks before I felt well enough to leave the house. Because the good doctor allowed me to increase the dosage at the minimum recommended time intervals, we reached the level he was hoping would work for me in twelve days. I requested that we do this because I wanted to find out as quickly as possible if this was going to be the drug that worked for me. If it wasn't, I was quite familiar with the drill and knew it would be some time before I was weaned off this medication to try another. Bonnie would leave for work in the morning, and when she returned, I would be in one of three places: I would be lying in bed, lying on the couch, or lying on the floor.

I really don't understand how she maintained her sanity. The people who live, love, and care for those of us who carry this gift of mental illness are by far the most compassionate, understanding individuals on this planet. I'm not sure that "thank you" and "I love you" are adequate. This group is indeed very special, and I really can't express in words how uncommon, exceptional, extraordinary, and remarkable they are.

Once the physical adjustment my body and brain made to the Effexor XR occurred, my life began to make a dramatic change. I started out walking a little each day. I began to read. My interest in life and those things that I'm attracted to when I'm not depressed began to return. I started to go surfing, running, biking, and talking with all the people I'd needed to isolate from while depressed. My coherency and comprehension have returned to a level that I experienced before all this started. I have returned to a place I haven't been in twenty-seven years. I have started my life all over again. I certainly am not implying that this has occurred solely because of the medication, however.

When I met Dr. Nakamura the very first time, he stressed the point that the medication would relieve the physical effects of the depression; I needed to also work very hard with a therapist if I expected to find any long-term relief. Also, he pointed out that keeping in good physical shape helps the brain produce endorphins that help you feel good. It was a three-part plan that needed all three parts in order to work effectively. With the doctor and medication in place, I started to do the hardest emotional work of my life.

I met my therapist over the phone. Many believe, as I do, that there are no coincidences in life. I called Janet Oliver about three weeks before I went to see Jon Nakamura. I called her because she was listed as a Unity Minister for the Unity Church that sends me a daily meditation. As I stated earlier, I am not a religious person, but I was at my wits' end and needed to speak with someone, so I called. To make a short story of it, Janet has been counseling people with depression for thirty years and lives about a mile away from me. With her guidance I was able to identify the people and situations that trigger my depression. She has been invaluable to the success of my recovery, and I look forward to working with her. I trust her implicitly. This has not been an easy road, but I believe you need to work for all the really good things in life.

What am I doing now? This is a common question from friends, relatives, and the general public. I'm finally doing something that I have always enjoyed doing. The difference is that today I'm doing what I'm doing because I believe I can, with the help of many,

many others, change the negative stigma that is so prevalent in society regarding mental illness. I believe that this discrimination was born out of fear of the unknown. Mental illness is no different than having a problem with any other part of your body. The problem is that it occurs in the head, and it forces people to act in ways that are contrary to their normal way of living. I know it's very difficult for someone to try to understand, and when you couple that with a belief that we're always supposed to be healthy, you can begin to appreciate what we, the afflicted, are up against. We certainly did not choose to be like this, and if it were possible to snap out of it, we damn sure would. It's not possible for many without medication, hospitalizations, therapists, doctors, and so much more. But the most important element, if any of this will work, is the love and support of those around us.

When I was told for the first time that I had a mental illness, it was hard for me to accept because of the way people treat you.

"You're not really sick; you're lazy."

"You need medication to help you think; therefore, you really aren't capable of your own thoughts."

"You're a drug addict," I heard at many Twelve-Step meetings.

"If you are taking antidepressants, you'll become addicted."

"What about the side effects?"

"Aren't you worried about the long-term effects?"

"You need to be more responsible."

"Get a grip on life."

The underlying premise is that I had a choice in whether my depression affected me — if I used more willpower, exercised more, changed the way I ate, prayed more often, and a number of other well-meaning suggestions. The bottom line is clear to me today: It didn't matter what I did. If I didn't have the correct medication, the physical symptoms would stay on their course. And I cannot stress enough the guilt I have felt in the past because I believed it must be me. I must be doing everything wrong. I must not be trying hard enough. These shame-based feelings only do one thing: They compound the problem for the depressed individual. Many of these feelings come from the people we are relying on to help us. If you or someone you care for is depressed and you want to help, educate yourself! There is more information out there today than ever before. If you're afraid of mental illness and what it's going to do to you, educate yourself! It's really quite easy.

I'm happier today than any other time of my life. I've started a nonprofit foundation *THE FUN FOUNDATION*. Our mission is to end the stigma associated with mental illness, through education, and financially assist those individuals who cannot afford to live up to life's responsibilities while starting a medication process for depression.

I'm in good physical shape, and most importantly, I can think clearly, comprehend, and make plans. I don't have any doubt that this series will help change the public perception of mental illness and help millions to discover the life we all truly deserve — one filled with happiness, joy, and hope. Remember, life's too short to take seriously. Be well, and thank you for reading this book.

RESOURCES

The organizations listed below can provide useful information, products, and services for people who have depression.

Agency for Healthcare Research and Quality
2101 E. Jefferson St., Ste. 501
Rockville, MD 20852
Phone: (800) 358-9295
E-mail: info@ahrq.gov
Web site: http://ahcpr.gov

The AHRQ (formerly known as AHCPR) is a government agency charged with supporting research designed to improve the quality of health care, reduce its cost, and broaden access to essential services. The agency has developed a number of clinical practice guidelines, including one on the treatment of depression. Versions for both professionals and consumers are available online and in print.

American Academy of Child and Adolescent Psychiatry
3615 Wisconsin Avenue NW
Washington, DC 20016-3007
Phone: (800) 333-7636
Web site: http://www.aacap.org

This professional association provides free information and referrals to psychiatrists specializing in children and adolescents.

American Association of Suicidology
4201 Connecticut Avenue NW, Ste. 408
Washington, DC 20008
Phone: (202) 237-2280
E-mail: berm101@ix.netcom.com
Web site: http://www.suicidology.org

This nonprofit organization provides free information and referrals to crisis centers and support groups.

American Psychiatric Association
1400 K Street NW
Washington, DC 20005
Phone: (888) 357-7924
E-mail: apa@psych.org
Web site: http://ww.psych.org

This professional association provides free information on mental disorder issues and referrals to state psychiatric societies, which can make referrals to local practitioners.

American Psychological Association
750 First Street NE
Washington, DC 20002-4242
Phone: (202) 336-5500
Web site: http://www.apa.org

This professional association provides free material on mental disorders and referrals.

AMI-Quebec
5253 Decarie Blvd., Ste. 150
Montreal, Quebec
Canada H3W 3C3
Phone: (514) 486-1448
E-mail: amique@dsuper.net
Web site:
http://www.dsuper.net/~amique

AMI-Quebec is a grass-roots support and advocacy organization for families and friends of people with mental illnesses. Located in Montreal, it offers a variety of self-help groups, seminars, education programs, and other resources, primarily for the English-speaking population.

Canadian Medical Association
1867 Alta Vista Drive
Ottawa, Ontario
Canada K1G 3Y6
Phone: (613) 731-9331
Web site: http://www.cma.ca

The Canadian Medical Association is a valuable source of medical information and resources, geared mainly toward the professional. The group's Web site contains a search engine that will help you locate links to specific medical topics, including depression.

Center for Cognitive Therapy
3600 Market Street, 8th Floor
Philadelphia, PA 19104-2649
Phone: (215) 898-4100
Web site:
http://www.health.upenn.edu/psycct

This organization, which is part of the University of Pennsylvania, provides referrals to cognitive therapists worldwide.

Clarke Institute of Psychiatry
A Division of the Centre for Addiction and Mental Health
250 College Street
Toronto, Ontario
Canada M5T 1R8
Phone: (416) 979-4747
Web site:
http://www.camh.net/CLARKEPages

The Clarke Institute of Psychiatry, affiliated with the University of Toronto, is a research center for mental health issues. The center offers treatment programs, continuing education seminars, and free informational literature.

Depression and Related Affective Disorders Association (DRADA)
Meyer 3-181
600 N. Wolfe St.
Baltimore, MD 21287-7381
Phone: (410) 955-4647 (Baltimore)
(202) 995-5800 (Washington, DC)
E-mail: drada@jhmi.edu
Web site: http://med.jhu.edu/drada

This nonprofit organization provides free information on mood disorders and

sponsors workshops and support groups, mainly in the Baltimore and District of Columbia areas.

Federation of Families for Children's Mental Health
1021 Prince St.
Alexandria, VA 22314-2971
Phone: (703) 684-7710
E-mail: ffcmh@ffcmh.org
Web site: http://www.ffcmh.org

This national parent-run, nonprofit organization focuses on the needs of children and youth with emotional, behavioral, or mental disorders and provides free information to their families.

Health Canada
A.L. 0904A
Ottawa, Ontario
Canada K1A 0K9
Phone: (613) 957-2991
E-mail: info@www.hc-sc.gc.ca
Web site: http://www.hc-sc.gc.ca

Health Canada is the federal department responsible for helping Canadians maintain their health. The department promotes disease prevention and healthy living. You can search Health Canada's medical database for information on specific health-related topics, including depression.

National Alliance for the Mentally Ill (NAMI)
Colonial Place Three
2107 Wilson Blvd., Ste. 300
Arlington, VA 22201-3042
Phone: (800) 950-6264
TDD: (703) 516-7991
Web site: http://www.nami.org

This nonprofit association is the umbrella organization for more than 1,000 local support and advocacy groups for families and individuals affected by serious mental disorders. It provides support to families and free information and mental disorders.

National Depressive and Manic-Depressive Association
730 N. Franklin St., Ste. 501
Chicago, IL 60610-3526
Phone: (800) 826-3632
E-mail: arobinson@ndmda.org
Web site: http://www.ndmda.org

This nonprofit organization provides referrals to support groups and free information on depression and manic-depressive illness.

National Foundation for Depressive Illness, Inc.
P.O. Box 2257
New York, NY 10116
Phone: (800) 239-1265
Web site: http://www.depression.org

This nonprofit organization supplies recorded information on the symptoms of depressive illness and how to get help; it also provides referrals.

National Institute of Mental Health
NIMH Public Inquiries
6001 Executive Blvd., Rm. 8184
MSC 9663
Bethesda, MD 20892-9663
Phone: (301) 443-4513
(800) 421-4211 for free brochures
E-mail: nimhinfo@nih.gov
Web site: http://www.nimh.nih.gov

This federal research organization provides free information on depression and other mental disorders through a number of programs as well as its Web site.

National Mental Health Association
1021 Prince Street
Alexandria, VA 22314-2971
Phone: (800) 969-6642
Web site: http://www.nmha.org

This nonprofit organization provides information on mental health topics, referrals to mental health providers, a network directory of national and local mental health associations, and more.

Center for Mental Health Services
Knowledge Exchange Network (KEN)
P.O. Box 42490
Washington, DC 20015
Phone: (800) 789-2647
TDD: (301) 443-9006
E-mail: ken@mentalhealth.org
Web site: http://www.mentalhealth.org

This agency — which is run by the Center for Mental Health Services, part of the U.S. Department of Health and Human Services (USDHHS) — provides the *Mental Health Directory*, a state-by-state listing of mental health facilities, and other free information.

National Organization for Seasonal Affective Disorder (NOSAD)
P.O. Box 40190
Washington, DC 20016
Web site: www.nosad.org

This nonprofit organization provides free information on seasonal affective disorder (SAD).

SHARE YOUR STORY

Continued from page 1

This will give you a general idea of the structure of the stories for the series, borrowing the concept from the *Big Book of Alcoholics Anonymous* that has worked tremendously for so many millions of people, i.e., sharing our experience, strength, and hope.

I. Experience
    a) The experience of living with depression before you sought help
    b) Why and how you sought help
    c) How you felt about the diagnosis

II. Strength
    a) Support
    b) Inner experience
    c) Therapy

III. Hope
    a) Medications
    b) Therapy
    c) Education
    d) Future

This outline is meant as a guide if you have questions. It is not meant to replace the creative genius that lies in all of us. I know from experience it is very difficult to read during a depressive episode, and I want to make this as enjoyable as possible. Thank you for your time and consideration.

Sincerely,
John F. Brown
THE FUN FOUNDATION
2721 Poipu Road, Suite 533
Koloa, HI 96756
Phone: 808-742-2353

E-mail: jfb@hawaiian.net
Web site: www.findfun.org